SUEZ AND AFTER

SUEZ AND AFTER
Year of Crisis

by Michael Adams

with cartoons by Low

Beacon Press   Beacon Hill   Boston

To my father with gratitude.

Contents

SUEZ AND AFTER

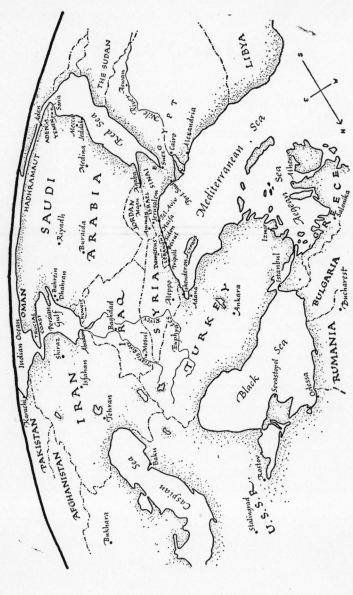

The Middle East Shown From the Northwest

Foreword

I came out to the Middle East early in 1956, as correspondent for the *Manchester Guardian*, with a little previous experience of the area, but none of post-revolutionary Egypt. Fortunately a few quiet months gave me a chance to find my feet, before the events described in this book claimed the attention of the world.

No one could report events in the Middle East for long without becoming to some extent involved in them. Where principles are in conflict, and prejudices heartfelt, only a saint or a cynic could retain his detachment, and I am neither. In preparing these dispatches for publication, I have left them substantially as they were, altering nothing and eliminating only what was irrelevant to my theme (though on that point opinions will differ), because it seemed to me unfair, where my judgment had been proved false by succeeding events, to try to disguise the fact. As a result, the story has emerged, accurately I hope, but with imperfections in the telling, for which I can apologise, but which I cannot disown.

My grateful acknowledgements are due to the Editor of the *Manchester Guardian*, for permission to reprint these dispatches, which are here published in book form for the first time; to the librarian, Mr. George Whatmore, for his energetic help in collecting them for me; and to Mr. John Rae, Middle East representative of the B.B.C., for reading my manuscript and suggesting countless improvements. I should also like to thank Mr. William Polk, of the Middle Eastern Studies Center at Harvard University, who first gave me the idea of writing this book, for his help and encouragement at every stage of its production.

MICHAEL ADAMS

Beirut

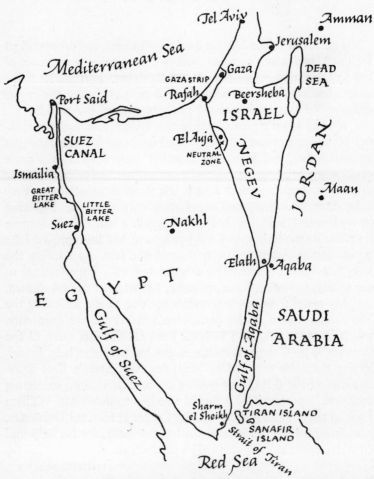

The Area of the Suez Controversy

PART 1   Nasser Defies the West

On July 26, 1956, I drove from Cairo to Alexandria to hear a speech by Gamal Abdul Nasser, president of the Egyptian republic. It was the fourth anniversary of the day when King Farouk left Egypt for ever, ousted by the revolutionary group of whom Nasser was the moving spirit.

But it was clear that this would be no routine celebration of Egypt's day of deliverance. A week earlier, President Nasser had returned from a meeting with Mr. Nehru and President Tito at Brioni, to learn that the American government had withdrawn its offer of assistance in the building of a high dam at Aswan. This was the project on which Nasser's government had founded its plans for the economic future of Egypt; it had been approved by experts on behalf of the World Bank, which had then agreed to advance $200 millions towards the cost of the dam, making its offer conditional on American and British participation. Thus America's refusal of the promised aid ruled the project out for the time being, since the World Bank's offer was at once withdrawn, and the British government too announced that it was following the American lead.

These refusals—which were accompanied by critical commentaries on the state of the Egyptian economy —were taken in Cairo as a political rebuff. President Nasser had made an angry speech on July 24, ridiculing the idea that the American decision had been taken for any but political reasons, and promising "to go into these questions at greater length" in his speech at Alexandria two days later.

There were probably only three people in Cairo who knew what was in the president's mind. To the rest of us the most likely guess seemed to be that

1

*Nasser would announce that the Russians had agreed
to finance the dam (rumours to this effect had been
current in Cairo since the visit in June of Mr. Shepilov,
then Soviet Foreign Minister). This did not fit in with
what I held to be Nasser's central purpose at that time,
of playing off East against West, in order to gain an
alliance with the West on his own terms. But apart
from a pact with Moscow, what was there that he could
pull out of the bag that would restore his prestige and
rescue him from a difficult situation? I did not know* ✓
*and neither did anyone else, so that the announcement
of the nationalisation of the Suez Canal Company took
us all by surprise.*

ALEXANDRIA, JULY 27

President Nasser's bombshell exploded with great effect here
last night, though it is worth recording that apart from the
thousands who formed the president's audience in Liberation
Square, Alexandria preserved its normal air of political detachment. Streets and coffee houses were full, an occasional radio
was relaying the speech, but few stopped to listen, and when all
was over and thousands of words were streaming to the far corners
of the world, Alexandria strolled and danced and drowsed as easily
as before.

It had been clear for several days that something unusual was
afoot, and this was confirmed last night when, with the crowd in
place in the square, under flags flapping in a fresh sea breeze, and
with distinguished visitors seated on the balcony of the stock exchange, the full array of Egyptian ministers took their places flank-
ing the president's empty chair.

A roar of motor-cycles heralded his arrival and the crowd rose
expectantly below. There was a pause while the president
mounted the stairs and then a murmur of surprise when he
appeared followed by Gamal Salem, who was recently removed
from the post of deputy premier, his brother Salah Salem, who
lately emerged from political disfavour to edit the newspaper
El Shaab, and Khalid Mohieddin, who left Egypt three years ago
to avoid trial as a Communist and turned up again recently.

This was the first indication that Mohieddin had returned to favour and the fact that he and the Salem brothers found places among the ministers was an intimation to those who still doubted it that last week's decision in Washington and London had put an end to the recent, short-lived experiment in friendly relations between Egypt and the West.

President Nasser opened his speech quietly. He appeared nervous at first and made more use than usual of notes. As he went on he quickly regained confidence and the speech as a whole, for all its momentous content, was unusually lighthearted in tone, even at times—as when he described his meeting with the State Department's envoy Mr. George Allen—frivolous.

The president followed, as usual, an orderly pattern of ideas, starting with the part played by the West in the creation of Israel, going on to speak of his hopes for Arab unity (with a favourable mention for the new plan for federal union between Egypt and Syria), and claiming wide success for the recent Brioni conference. He spoke of the West's refusal to give him arms after the Palestine debacle and so came to the arms deal which, he asserted, had involved no commitment on Egypt's part, but which had given her a strength soon reflected in the more respectful attitude of the outside world to Egyptian policies.

Turning to the High Dam he declared that the West's offer of financial assistance was accompanied by impossible conditions, involving the independence of Egypt. Here the president allowed himself two pieces of misrepresentation without which his arguments on the financing of the High Dam would have been greatly weakened. The World Bank's intention all along, he asserted, had been to trick Egypt into subjection by promising the money and then, when the dam was under construction, refusing payment. And discussing Britain's insistence on getting Sudanese agreement to the High Dam project he alleged that Britain had "tried in every way to make the Sudanese hate us."

From the president's account of the later stages of the negotiations with the West it was hard to understand why the Egyptian ambassador in Washington was finally instructed to apply for the American loan. Summing up this part of his speech, the president declared, "The reason why America and Britain

denied the loan is not our economic position, but the fact that
we have decided to equip our army and follow an independent
policy. We don't want our freedom to be tied to any other
nation."

And then, after a brief account of the history of the Suez
Canal, came the bombshell which brought the crowd to its feet
to cheer in wild abandon. The argument was simple: "The Suez
Canal was built by Egyptians: it belongs to Egypt." The president
declared, without any apparent justification, that the decision to
nationalise the canal had "been approved by the public" and said
Egypt would take $100 millions from its revenues for the building
of the high dam.

History repeats itself, said President Nasser. But he probably
was not thinking of Mossadegh.

> *Mossadegh's fate was in all our minds during those*
> *first twenty-four hours. Surely Nasser had overreached*
> *himself in seizing control of something so vital to so*
> *many nations as the Suez Canal? Surely he had broken*
> *an international treaty (but what treaty?) which safe-*
> *guarded the international status of the canal? In any*
> *case, how could he withstand the counter-measures*
> *which Britain, in particular, was bound to take against*
> *him?*
>
> *Very quickly, doubts began to intrude. There was*
> *no treaty involved, only that tiresomely contradictory*
> *document, the Constantinople Convention of 1888,*
> *over which we correspondents, along with the diplo-*
> *mats, now began to puzzle. And if there was no treaty,*
> *could there be any justification for retaliatory measures*
> *against Egypt? And again, if such measures were taken,*
> *would not the West be in danger of suffering worse*
> *injury by the destruction of oil wells and pipelines in*
> *the vast Middle Eastern oilfields?*
>
> *Already the rift was beginning to appear in public*
> *opinion in Britain, which in the end was to divide the*
> *country as nothing else had done since the abdication*
> *of King Edward VIII, between those who favoured the*

use of force to bring Nasser to his senses, and those
who felt that whatever else could or could not be done,
armed intervention would be morally wrong and prac-
tically ineffective.
Meanwhile the Egyptians faced no such dilemma.

CAIRO, JULY 29

President Nasser received a tumultuous welcome yesterday on his return from Alexandria, where he had startled the world with his announcement of the nationalisation of the Suez Canal Company. It would be going too far to describe this as a spontaneous welcome, since organised parties were on the move all over Cairo early in the morning, complete with banners, cheerleaders, and sometimes loud-speaker vans, converging on the centre of the city and the route the president was to follow from the station.

But if little had been left to chance there was still no doubt of the general reaction to Nasser's surprise move. With the exception of a very few wiser heads, the Egyptians were delighted by a step that appealed at once to their nationalistic feelings, their growing confidence in Nasser as the man with an answer for everything, and, not unimportantly, to their strong sense of humour. The kind of joke that appeals most to Egyptians is the one where pride is seen clearly to go before a fall, and Nasser's riposte to what were considered here the insulting communiqués of the American and British governments, together with the light-hearted tone of much of the Alexandria speech, gave them just this satisfaction.

The strong police detachments which yesterday guarded the British and American embassies had an idle day, for the mood of the crowds was anything but belligerent. It was rather that of a man who has had a good day at the races and finds himself temporarily relieved of everyday cares. The danger lies in the fact that Egyptians, who are never difficult to lead, are now like the children of Hamelin to Nasser's Pied Piper. They know and care nothing about the technicalities of the Suez Canal dispute: they see only that Nasser has once again turned the diplomatic tables on Western statesmen. And in facing any counter-moves of these statesmen, Nasser will be able to count on firmer support at home than ever before.

As with any Middle Eastern problem, consideration of this one brings us back to Israel. Resentment at the existence of Israel and the sense of national humiliation at the way it was achieved still smoulder deep in Egypt's consciousness. This resentment and humiliation are felt personally by President Nasser and his closest associates. They are the unescapable reminder of the one thorn in Egypt's flesh which has not yet been removed but for whose removal there is a deeper and more general longing than for any other objective of internal or external policy.

Imperialism and exploitation are widely recognised as editorial bogies by people who have known the benefits as well as the frustrations of foreign rule. But Israel is the albatross about the neck of a people which finds itself to-day in a mood of ebullient and unquestioning self-confidence. The pressure for decisive action against Israel, always strong at moments of crisis, is bound to grow if Nasser's Suez Canal gamble comes off—especially since his speech at Alexandria contained one of his most bitter attacks on Israel for many months.

For this situation, with all its attendant dangers for the Middle East and the Western powers, the statesmen in London and Washington must bear a heavy share of responsibility. Their brusque rejection of the High Dam scheme coming on top of their earlier anxiety to forestall the Russians in financing the dam, the terms in which that rejection was couched, and, in particular, its timing invited a violent reaction from Egypt.

The result has been to strengthen Nasser's position inside Egypt and in the neighbouring Arab countries, which, with the exception of Iraq, have already expressed their solidarity with Egypt. It has left the West with the alternatives of protesting ineffectually or employing military or material sanctions whose justification whould be doubtful.

Of course, Nasser's gamble may not come off. He may find that by stepping voluntarily outside the ring of accepted political morality to demonstrate his independence and achieve his High Dam—the objectives come in that order—he has sacrificed too much. But, even so, the West will be the loser because of the ill-considered and ill-timed action of the State Department, with Downing Street and the World Bank in its train.

The High Dam may not be built and Nasser may be humbled, though it looks very unlikely. But unless the Western powers are prepared to take a firm step back into history and reoccupy the Canal zone, they must reconcile themselves to uncertainty about their oil supplies and communications in the Middle East, and to the probability that Egypt will drag the Arab world with her into the Eastern camp, from whose threshold she was turning back ten days ago.

At first the reaction in Britain had been almost unanimous. The leader of the opposition had backed Sir Anthony Eden's condemnation of Nasser, Egypt's sterling balances had been frozen, and while the international lawyers settled down to arguing the legal points involved in the nationalisation edict, French and American representatives had been invited to London to concert a common Western policy towards Egypt.

The vigour with which the West reacted seemed to take the Egyptian government by surprise—illustrating the political immaturity of Egypt's small governing junta. But they soon gained encouragement from the obvious differences which began to develop between the attitude of Washington, on the one hand, and that of London and Paris on the other.

While the politicians wrangled over policies, ship owners throughout the world (and importers and insurance agents and all the other groups whose interests were involved) were thinking about the canal itself. Was it still safe, would shipping have to be rerouted to avoid it, and especially, to whom should the dues be paid by ships which continued to use the canal— to the old, dispossessed Suez Canal Company, with its offices in Paris and London, or to President Nasser's newly constituted Suez Canal Authority?

Up to yesterday 149 ships had passed through the Suez Canal since the announcement of its nationalisation on Thursday. Of these 23 were British, and it is reported that these were allowed to pay their dues in the normal way, that is by cheques payable in Paris or London.

For the moment all eyes are on the London talks between the British, French, and American representatives, and the question asked is whether the three countries will agree on measures to be adopted. It is being suggested here that the American government, whose precipitate action ten days ago started the present crisis, now favours a more complaisant policy than Paris or London.

There has been no public recognition here of the fact that the figures given by Nasser in his speech at Alexandria—an income of $100 millions a year—were misleading. However, it is unlikely that publication of realistic figures would make much difference, for the High Dam has long since been submerged by a tidal wave of popular enthusiasm for Nasser's move—enthusiasm which takes no account of its potential results and makes no attempt to understand them.

The angry words of the politicians were not reflected in any hostile gestures towards foreigners in Egypt. All the same, an ugly situation was building up, for both sides to the dispute had adopted positions which seemed to allow no room for manoeuvre—and as far as Egypt was concerned, popular support for President Nasser was growing, while there was no attempt to explain to the Egyptian man in the street what was at stake, or why the world took so serious a view of Egypt's action over the canal.

If the Western powers urge the formation of an international body to supervise the running of the Suez Canal, it is most unlikely that the Egyptian government will agree, except under the strongest pressure. President Nasser's speech at Alexandria yesterday showed no sign of any wish to compromise. Indeed, phrases like "Arab nationalism from the Persian Gulf to the Atlantic Ocean is now aflame" indicate his apparent determination to fan the flames he himself has done most to kindle.

As far as Egypt is concerned there is no doubt that President Nasser is supported now with more enthusiasm than before last week's turning point. There is no inclination here to examine the questions raised by the nationalisation of the canal, such as Egypt's ability to run it or the nature and extent of the threat to which Egyptian control would subject the shipping of other nations. No one stops to ask what profit Egypt will gain from the canal if she maintains it properly—the question is approached only on the demagogic level on which President Nasser placed it and on which his speeches do their best to keep it, with a subservient press following his example.

This is not to suggest that international tension over the canal dispute has brought about a correspondingly tense situation inside Egypt. There is no molestation of foreigners, and the attitude of the man in the street remains courteous and friendly. But if political deadlock should lead to military action and President Nasser called on the Egyptians to follow him, they would—in ignorance of what is really at stake and placing perhaps too much reliance on assurances from the Arab world that "We shall be at your side."

The same day I paid the first of many visits to the canal itself, driving down to Suez to talk to shipping agents, and then following the canal north to Ismailia, where Egyptian officials had taken over the work of the old Suez Canal Company. Both agents and officials took a suspicious view of journalists at this moment (the British, French and American representatives were still thrashing out a plan for a London conference on the future of the canal), and there was little to be learned either at Suez or Ismailia.

Talking to shipping agents in Suez, one could only confirm that traffic in the canal was normal, averaging about forty-five ships every twenty-four hours and that before long a crisis must come over the question of how dues are to be paid. Until last

week's nationalisation edict, this was done through agents who
had credit with the Suez Canal Company's offices in Paris or
London and drew on this for each ship they passed through.

A circular issued by the Egyptian government on July 27 said
dues must be paid to the order of banks in London, Paris, or
Cairo for the account of the Suez Canal Authority. So far as
anyone knows here this order has not yet taken effect—and will
not until the existing credits with the old company are exhausted.
Then the question will have to be faced—and it is a vital one,
since lawyers might dispute endlessly the question of who is in-
terrupting free navigation of the canal: the agent who refuses
payment to the new authority, or the authority which then bars
the ship from using the canal.

The Egyptian authorities are evidently most anxious not to
precipitate this question, and an earlier order to the effect that
payment might be made as usual until the end of this week was
later rescinded. No time limit now exists, and the question will
present itself when agents' credits are exhausted and further payments become necessary. The sums involved are considerable,
with forty or fifty ships passing through every day. A liner like
the "Himalaya," for instance, pays about £7,000 for her twelve-
hour passage.

The "Himalaya" was one of a northbound convoy which
left Suez at 8:30 A.M. yesterday. The convoy also included the
small Italian liner "Surriento," a Portuguese freighter, and tankers
from Holland, Liberia, Yugoslavia, Norway, Greece, and the
Soviet Union—a fair commentary on the importance of Suez to
all seagoing nations. This convoy met a southbound one at the
bypass north of Ismailia, near the half-way mark in the canal.

The southbound convoy consisted of four freighters, from
Egypt, Greece, Britain, and Holland, and five tankers, three of
them flying the Norwegian flag, one French, one Liberian. (Since
the nationalisation a week ago 22 Liberian ships have passed
through out of a total of 280, as against 91 British, 33 Norwegian,
and 25 French.) While these waited in the bypass to let the
northbound convoy through, two Egyptian feluccas, with graceful
sails bellying, took advantage of a breeze from the north to sweep
past them, keeping outside the buoys which mark the central

channel of the canal, which can take ships with a draught of up to thirty-five feet.

Both at Suez and at Ismailia, the town which owes its existence to the canal and which has been the company's headquarters for most of a century, it was clear that representatives of the new authority, who have been grafted on to the working body of the old company, had firm and narrow instructions for dealing with any inquiries.

The canal was functioning normally—this was repeated so often and with such unction that, looking out of the window at the canal itself, one almost expected the sides to fall in—and beyond this there was "really nothing to say," though of course if one had specific questions to ask they would be answered. But not here, not now.

It was at Ismailia yesterday that the Egyptian minister of commerce, Mr. Abu Nosseir, lunched with members of the newly constituted Suez Canal Authority and afterwards presided at the first meeting of the authority in the board room of the Canal Company. The bust of De Lesseps looked on unmoved at journalists sprawling on the trim lawn outside the conference room. But when the doors opened and the new administrators of the Suez Canal came out into the sunshine, it was noticeable that the board room and every adjacent office had been embellished with at least one—usually two—of the ubiquitous photographs of President Nasser, which smile down from office walls all over Egypt to-day.

The minister's aides who earlier had promised that a press conference would follow the board meeting, now stated that plans had been changed and that the minister had nothing to say. This did not surprise the journalists, who in Egypt never expect anything to go according to plan. Nor did it deter them from clustering about Colonel Mahmud Yunis, managing director of the new Suez Canal Authority and an engineer, who, as director of the government refinery at Suez, has gained a reputation as an administrator.

Colonel Yunis parried questions with an engaging smile. It was for the minister to make a statement if there were anything to say, and if the minister wouldn't, why then, there was nothing

to say. The most he would let fall was that the authority's first
decision had been to send a message of congratulation to President
Nasser, who at that moment was speaking in Alexandria, telling
his audience that Egypt was "determined to defend our rights."

The next day Egypt was invited, along with
twenty-three others countries, to send a representative
to the London conference convened by the British,
French and American governments.

There followed an uncomfortable week, during
which we waited for President's Nasser's reply and kept
an uneasy eye on Egyptian public opinion. But how-
ever intransigent they might be in their speeches and
notes, the Egyptian leaders were careful to avoid pro-
voking any outbursts of feeling against foreigners in
Egypt. We went about our daily life in a somewhat
unreal atmosphere of official hostility, which did noth-
ing to affect the courtesy with which we were treated
as individuals.

The evacuation had begun of the families of the
British contractors in the Suez Canal bases (bases main-
tained under the 1954 agreement with Egypt, by which
all British troops had been evacuated before the canal
crisis began). But the bulk of the British community
in Egypt, despite the advice of the Foreign Office on
August 2, continued to hope for the best, and saw
nothing in the internal atmosphere of Egypt to warrant
a hasty departure.

CAIRO, AUGUST 6

The Egyptian cabinet is discussing again to-night its reply
to the invitation issued from London four days ago to the conference on the Suez Canal question. Meanwhile, with British
warships on the move towards the eastern Mediterranean and the
first British families leaving Egypt in response to the Foreign
Office suggestion made last week, Egypt maintains a surprising
calm.

Paradoxically, one reason for this seems to be (though this reasoning contradicts the public statements of President Nasser) the enduring confidence of ordinary Egyptians in British respect for international law. "You admit we have the right to nationalise the Suez Canal Company," runs the argument. "You know you would not brand yourselves as aggressors by reoccupying the Canal zone unless the navigation of the canal was interrupted." And navigation through the canal continues normally, forty-one ships passing through on Saturday and thirty-five on Sunday.

The same is not said about the French—and in the press, of course, the worst motives are imputed to both countries. It is suggested that Europe's concern over the future of the canal is being exaggerated as an excuse to recover domination over Egypt, which was relinquished when the last British soldiers left last month.

Frequent meetings between President Nasser and the Indian ambassador during the last few days suggest that India's advice will have considerable influence on Egypt's attitude to the Suez Canal conference.

President Nasser was at Brioni with Mr. Nehru when the decision was announced in Washington to withdraw the offer of aid for the High Dam, the decision which launched this whole crisis.

President Nasser has also had several meetings with the Soviet ambassador, whose government's attitude to the London conference has not been made known either.

There is no hint here of what Egypt's reply will be, but it is probable that it will avoid saying yes or no and suggest a revision of the terms in which the conference is conceived. Unequivocal recognition of Egypt's sovereignty over the canal is a probable condition of Egypt's acceptance, with possible modifications in detail, such as the list of countries invited, and the date and place of the conference. Above all, Egypt is likely to demand that if the conference is to be held it should be held in an atmosphere free of economic or military pressures.

The Egyptian government may be right in thinking that by delaying its decision it is gaining time, for it is difficult to see

what British warships can do in the eastern Mediterranean until
there is more provocation for their presence than exists at present.

> *A broadcast by Sir Anthony Eden on the evening
> of August 8 did nothing to help the British cause
> abroad. The prime minister disavowed the intention to
> use force, but in terms which made it clear that he
> reserved Britain's right to do so if she could not obtain
> a "satisfactory" solution in any other way; and by a
> vigorous personal attack on the Egyptian president, he
> seemed to many listeners to bring the issue down to a
> level of personal animosity between himself and Presi-
> dent Nasser.*

CAIRO, AUGUST 9

Sir Anthony Eden's speech last night came too late to allow
much comment in to-day's Cairo papers, which restrict themselves
to quoting extracts. The prime minister's declaration that "We
do not seek a solution by force" received prominence, but the impression left here by the speech as a whole is that forcible action
by Britain and France remains a strong possibility.

Egyptians ask on what grounds the Western nations could
undertake such action, and criticise the continuing confusion in
Western pronouncements on the nationalisation issue and freedom of navigation. Mr. Nehru's speech was very fully reported
here, with emphasis on his insistence that India was only attending
the London conference on the understanding that the conference
would not infringe the "sovereignty and dignity of Egypt." The
Egyptian radio carried fairly full versions of both speeches, including Sir Anthony's personal attack on President Nasser.

The Egyptian attitude is now centred on these three points.

(1) Nationalisation is an accomplished fact which has the
approval of most countries, and against the legality of which even
Britain has adduced no convincing arguments.

(2) The crisis was precipitated by the insulting Western
communiqué which announced the withdrawal of Western aid
for the Aswan High Dam and the West must learn that it can no
longer use nineteenth-century methods to browbeat Egypt.

(In private responsible Egyptians will deplore the hostile

language used by President Nasser against the West in his speech announcing nationalisation, but they insist that the Western rebuff over the High Dam and its unnecessary and inaccurate references to the weakness of the Egyptian economy made a vigorous retort on President Nasser's part inevitable.)

(3) Egyptians say that if British concern is really over the continued freedom of navigation through the canal, why do they not wait for some sign that navigation is likely to be interrupted before taking diplomatic and military measures which practically amount to an ultimatum?

There is little doubt that yesterday's pronouncement by Mr. Nehru that "Egypt could not and would not participate in the London conference" accurately foreshadows the reply of the Egyptian government to the invitation from London. Egypt's reply will be delivered on Sunday morning, and elaborate preparations are now being made for the press conference which President Nasser is to give at noon on the same day. Ministry of Information officials say that they expect some 250 foreign journalists to attend.

Meanwhile the intense diplomatic activity which has gone on in Cairo ever since the nationalisation announcement continues. Last night President Nasser saw the Soviet ambassador, Mr. Kisselev, for the sixth time in ten days, and to-day the British ambassador, Sir Humphrey Trevelyan, has had meetings with his French and American counterparts. Diplomatists and political leaders of the Arab states are also very active these days, and a measure of the solidarity of the Arab world over the Suez Canal issue is the fact that a meeting of the political committee of the Arab League has been arranged for Sunday, though normally such meetings are canvassed for weeks in connection with particular issues and then very often fail to take place until the issue has passed beyond the veil of history.

> As the week drew to a close, some of the journalist's frustrations emerged in my next dispatch. It was exhausting, in the middle of the Egyptian summer, to be chasing rumours up and down the dusty city— but that was a journalist's business. What made it

depressing for many of us was the feeling that our own government was following a fatally wrong road, a road that could only lead to tragedy.

CAIRO, AUGUST 10

For two hot weeks only the breeze of speculation has stirred the torpid atmosphere of Cairo in August. While the diplomatists hurried invisibly to their various rendezvous and a swelling band of journalists chased the latest rumour, the people of Cairo—those of them not fortunate enough to have escaped to Alexandria or Europe—went about their business as though unaware that their country lay at the heart of a storm which was stirring the world.

Since President Nasser's original announcement of the nationalisation of the Suez Canal on July 26, the important moves in the resulting crisis have been made not in Cairo but in London, Paris, and Delhi. Here, Egyptians have watched and waited with a calm which may be attributed partly to their reliance on President Nasser as a political strategist, partly, too, to a surprising indifference over the fate of the canal. Western military preparations and attacks by British and French spokesmen on President Nasser have stirred indignation, but as far as the root of all the trouble, the canal itself, is concerned, their attitude seems to be "Why all the fuss?"

This mood of uncertainty, of indifference mingled with an imprecisely directed indignation, is likely to be radically altered at the week-end. On Sunday Egypt's reply to the invitation to attend the London conference will be announced (just four days before the conference is due to open). Immediately afterwards President Nasser will hold a press conference at which some hundreds of journalists from many countries are expected. On the same day the Political Committee of the Arab League is to meet in Cairo to concert a common Arab policy in support of Egypt's attitude.

Also on Sunday the Indian delegation to the London conference, led by Mr. Krishna Menon, will be in Cairo, where they are breaking their journey from Delhi, for consultations with the Egyptian government before the conference opens. Finally, on

Sunday evening, President Nasser will speak to the Egyptian people over the radio and explain his Suez policy. This will be the first official guidance that the Egyptians have received since the initial announcement of nationalisation, and it is to be hoped that the president will raise the question from the demagogic level on which it has been approached by the press (and in President Nasser's original speech in Alexandria) and tell Egyptians the facts of life about the canal.

At present they regard the canal as a kind of Aladdin's lamp, and for this President Nasser is mainly to blame, with his misleading suggestion on July 26 that the Aswan High Dam could be built with the revenues of the canal over the next few years. By adopting a realistic outlook towards the canal as a source both of revenue to Egypt and of concern to all maritime nations, President Nasser could strengthen morally a case which legally already looks stronger than anyone supposed in the first shock of surprise.

Unfortunately, moderation is not likely to be the keynote of the president's address to the nation, though he will probably adopt a much more reasonable tone when he meets the international press. The apparent solidarity of the Arab world on the Suez question might well break down if put to the test of action, but for the moment it looks unusually firm. Certainly any military action against Egypt would lead to varying degrees of unrest in neighbouring Arab states, with attacks on Western-owned commercial and oil installations a certainty (there have already been threats of such action in Syria and Jordan), and revolutions in Jordan and Iraq distinct possibilities.

Apart from the support of the Arab world the encouragement that Egypt has received from the Indian and Soviet governments makes any inclination on President Nasser's part to compromise with the London conference most unlikely. But Mr. Nehru's influence works both ways, and his criticism of Egypt's approach to the Suez question has not gone unnoticed here. In that influence seems to lie the best hope of a solution.

Finally the day came when President Nasser was to give his answer to the invitation to attend the London conference. But at the last moment there

was a delay of some hours, during which I tried to
assess the attitude of the Egyptians to the whole canal
dispute, and of their neighbours in the rest of the
Arab world.

While Cairo waited impatiently for Nasser's press conference
(which had been postponed for five hours) and a statement of
Egypt's intentions over the forthcoming London conference, two
important meetings took place here to-day.

Mr. Krishna Menon, on his way from New Delhi to attend
the London conference, saw President Nasser, presumably for a
last exchange of views between the Egyptian and Indian governments, whose consultations have been an important preliminary to
the conference; and the political committee of the Arab League
met this morning, under the chairmanship of Dr. Mahmud Fawzi,
the Egyptian foreign minister.

This meeting was attended by representatives of eight Arab
states, including Iraq and Jordan. Its purpose was to concert practical measures to be taken to support Egypt's stand over the Suez
Canal question. Whether these receive final agreement or not,
the convocation of a meeting at such a high level and in such a
short time represents an unusual triumph for the elusive principle
of Arab unity.

It cannot be too much stressed that the Suez question and
Western treatment of it have drawn the Arab world together,
strengthened President Nasser's position inside and outside Egypt
and placed Iraq, in particular, in a difficult position. This, in part,
is for spurious reasons which are not examined too closely in the
Middle East if they carry the seal of Arab nationalism.

But whatever weaknesses there may be in the arguments of
the Arab nationalists, the fact is that President Nasser has ma-
noeuvred Britain again into an untenable position, where she appears to be clinging to material interests and shreds of political
supremacy in this part of the world—and doing so in defiance of
the local desire for independence and a measure of prosperity.

How far the Egyptian people are behind President Nasser in
his dispute with the West no one can conscientiously say. Cer-

tainly many members of the professional classes in Egypt dislike his violence and are apprehensive about its results. Equally certainly, more and more of the working class, who at first resented President Nasser's displacement of the much more popular General Naguib, have been persuaded by his mounting successes that in him lies their salvation.

Of these two classes the former is anxiously aware of the critical nature of the canal question, and their largely European background of thought enables them to understand the importance of the canal to Western statesmen. The others, the workers, understand nothing of this, and most of them probably have not even a conception of what the canal is. But they have memories, which are frequently and bitterly refreshed, of European domination and European contempt, and when they see President Nasser repeatedly and successfully defying their old masters it is only natural that they should approve.

Of the present point of dispute they have no idea and they do not seem particularly interested by it. But they are interested in what they are told about British and French troop movements and by the easy explanation of these as evidence of the Western intention once more to impose alien domination.

In fact, these appear to lend colour to what they are always told is the basis of Western policy, and while, as a rule, they are apathetic in face of local press exaggerations and inventions, this whole crisis, starting from the abrupt withdrawal of the Western offer of aid for the High Dam, seems to have penetrated into the Egyptian consciousness to an unusual degree.

Only by the most scrupulous observance of her obligations as a member of the United Nations can Britain emerge with credit from the Suez Canal dispute—and in the long run that credit is more important to Britain than the canal.

An hour or two later, President Nasser met the press, and in stating Egypt's refusal to attend the London conference scored an unquestioned success by his moderation and good humour—which were inevitably compared with the increasingly ill-tempered outbursts of Sir Anthony Eden.

CAIRO, AUGUST 12

"The London conference has no right at all to discuss Egyptian affairs" President Nasser told some 250 journalists at an international press conference in Cairo this evening. But he added that, "true to its devotion to the principles of the United Nations," Egypt would be prepared

> ". . . to sponsor a conference of the other governments signatory to the Constantinople Convention of 1888, a conference to which would be invited the other governments whose ships pass through the Suez Canal, for the purpose of reviewing the Constantinople Convention and considering the conclusion of an agreement between all these governments reaffirming and guaranteeing the freedom of navigation on the Suez Canal."

The president's refusal of the London invitation was expected, but his presentation of Egypt's case was made with a mildness very different from the tone of his speech at Alexandria two weeks ago.

Speaking in English, he said that the Egyptian government had noted "to its complete surprise" that the United Kingdom had called a conference on a domestic Egyptian affair without consulting Egypt. He commented on the restricted nature of the conference, declared it incompetent for its purpose, and said that its avowed aim of internationalisation of the Suez Canal was "but a mild word for collective colonialism."

The communiqué of the three powers, issued from London last week, had "distorted fact to justify its interference in Egypt's internal affairs," he went on. He accused Western statesmen of misrepresenting the text of the Constantinople Convention when they tried to give the canal an international character.

After reading a prepared statement from the Egyptian government, President Nasser gave his personal commentary on the arguments of both sides in the Suez Canal dispute. There was no justification, he said mildly, for the headlines in Western papers reading "Nasser Seizes Canal" or "Egypt's Grab at Suez." He declared: "This is our territory, our canal."

The Suez Canal Company had never guaranteed freedom of navigation in the canal. "It was the Egyptian army which secured [meaning guaranteed the security of] the canal during the Second World War." Egypt would go ahead with the £20 millions improvement scheme for the canal planned by the old Canal Company.

Dealing with the finances of the canal in somewhat more realistic terms than those he used at Alexandria two weeks ago, President Nasser said the "ten million pounds distributed by the company to its shareholders" would now be used "not to build palaces or for any individual interests, but for the welfare of this country."

He rejected accusations that he or Egypt had broken its word. "I want to know details about any international obligation which Egypt has violated." He added that if, as he heard so often from Western statesmen, "We have no confidence in Nasser," Nasser could see no point in sitting down to a conference with them. Referring to threats of military action against Egypt, the president said "I know we are a small country, but we have to defend our rights to the last drop of our blood. We shall give an example of morale to the small countries of the world."

Answering questions later, he said the nationalisation of the canal had been considered more than two years ago, but that the decision had only been taken after the withdrawal of Western offers of aid for the High Dam. This withdrawal had seemed to the Egyptian government to be "an action against the Egyptian people to keep them poor," and the government had decided on nationalisation so that the profits of the shareholders should be devoted, instead, to the welfare of the Egyptian people.

Asked why he had not informed other interested parties of his intention to nationalise the canal, he replied that he had always been informed that there was a sort of conspiracy to prolong the Suez Canal Company's concession, so he acted without warning.

He refused to be drawn into discussion of affairs outside the scope of the press conference, answering with a smile when asked whether he thought his action would encourage other Arab states to nationalise, for instance, their oil industries, that he did not think they would look to him for permission before doing so. When asked if he thought other waterways in the world should be internationalised, he said: "For the meantime I am interested in the Suez Canal."

One of his most earnest passages came when he told one questioner, and through him the Western world, that he thought they missed something in observing events in the Arab world. That was Arab nationalism—"and Arab nationalism is the hope of every Arab, and if it is ignored there is no hope of solving any problems."

A moment later President Nasser brought a smile to the longest face when he read out the question: "Are you a dictator?" He replied: "I don't know." Perhaps some of his audience were sure of the answer but they did not sound like it.

Two days later the British foreign secretary, Mr. Selwyn Lloyd, in a broadcast to the British people, echoed Sir Anthony Eden's attack on Nasser, and held also to the prime minister's line that force would only be used "as a last resort."

The London conference was to open on August 16 (twenty-two nations finally sent delegations, while besides Egypt the Greek government refused the invitation), and a general strike was called throughout the Arab world as a gesture of solidarity in support of the Egyptian attitude.

CAIRO, AUGUST 15

Comment on Mr. Selwyn Lloyd's broadcast last night takes second place in this morning's Cairo newspapers to details of the general strike called for to-morrow to mark the opening of the London conference on Suez. But all newspapers report the speech fairly fully, without suggesting that it contributes any new idea to the controversy.

There was a slight hope here that the British foreign minister, in this first official pronouncement from England since President Nasser's press conference on Sunday, might have indicated some relaxation of the British insistence on international control of the canal, some willingness to consider the alternative proposals of the Egyptian president.

His attack on President Nasser receives prominence, and the extremist *El Gumhuria* says the foreign secretary was deceiving the British people in saying that force would only be used as a last resort, adding that behind this attitude of "false conciliation" Mr. Lloyd revealed his true identity as a "blood-sucking exploiter."

The general strike called for to-morrow will include employees of all but essential public utilities, such as power stations, water supply, and bakeries. Railway traffic, except for the movement of army supplies and essential foodstuffs, will be at a standstill. Dockers will be idle. Stores, banks, business firms (including British concerns like the Shell Company), and places of entertainment will all be closed. The public transport system will be out of action, petrol stations and garages will be closed, and, for the first time, Cairo Airport will also be affected, according to present arrangements, though airline operators have so far received no official notification of this and are at present in some doubt about to-morrow's schedules.

The situation is paradoxical, for unofficial strikes are illegal in Egypt, and yet this one is being represented as a spontaneous demonstration of public support for the government's stand over Suez and against Western intervention, as represented by the London conference. There is no evidence of government inspiration, though clearly the strike is part of the thorough and successful campaign of propaganda which has mobilised public opinion in Egypt at every strategic moment in the present crisis.

It is equally clear that the government could step in and order Cairo Airport to carry on as usual. Unless this happens the confusion among airline operators in the Middle East will be considerable to-morrow. There are twenty-seven firms using the airport, which is one of the busiest in the world outside the United States. Plans to divert air services to other Middle Eastern airports are complicated by the fact that Egypt's Arab neighbours plan a strike in sympathy: Damascus Airport, for instance, will probably also be out of action.

Meanwhile, after two and a half weeks of international tension, Cairo remains quiet, and there are no reports of unrest from elsewhere in Egypt. The training of reservists in the recently formed National Liberation Army has started, but this organization still looks more effective as propaganda than as a military weapon, to judge by the windy claims made for it.

The strike took place, with a surprising degree of unanimity, in the other Arab countries (except Saudi Arabia), but a more dangerous reminder came on the same day from Israel.

CAIRO, AUGUST 17

The incident in the southern Negev yesterday in which four Israelis were killed and seven wounded when a bus was ambushed fifty miles north of Eilath is a reminder that the Suez crisis makes more acute the danger of a flare-up along the armistice lines between Israel and the Arabs. If Egypt should be forced to climb down over the canal question, the temptation to regain face by an attack on Israel will be strong; and if President Nasser's gamble comes off there will be nowhere for him to turn for another prestige coup but Israel.

In yesterday's demonstrations in Beirut (which were part of the general Middle Eastern pattern of strikes to show solidarity with Egypt in the Suez question) banners were carried through the streets which read "After the canal, Palestine."

In Cairo there were no demonstrations, but the strike was completely effective, bringing the life of the capital to a standstill. Essential public utilities were excluded, but although, according to the morning papers, this was meant to include food shops, one large grocery shop which opened as usual received a visit at nine o'clock from the police, who suggested that it would be preferable if the shop were closed, which it promptly was. No public transport of any kind was in operation, and the streets, which are normally jammed with everything from station wagons to donkey carts, were almost completely deserted.

My Sudanese servant having generously lent me his bicycle, I made an extensive tour of the old and new cities. I found youths playing football in the streets and crowds wandering waywardly

along on the banks of the Nile as they do on any holiday whether
it has political overtones or not, but no suggestion anywhere of any
wish to demonstrate more actively their solidarity with the official
attitude of "mourning for the assassination of liberty at the London
conference," and certainly no sign of any hostility.

Explicitly or by implication two or three people voiced the
opinion that the strike, which lost the small man a day's pay and
the large operator of a store or place of amusement large sums of
money, was an illogical way of proving opposition to the Western
plans, but most seemed content to take one more holiday as a gift
from the gods and sit doing nothing in particular. One way and
another a lot of people not usually given to reflection had plenty
of time to sit and think yesterday, but until he is told what to think
the Egyptian is mostly content just to sit.

Many European employees of business firms accustomed to
organizing their lives around the office, the Gezira Sporting Club,
and the evening social round were left completely disoriented,
since, like the offices, the Gezira Club was closed, and since most of
their wives have been flown home even the social round has lost
its most ardent supporters. When all lights were extinguished at
9:45 P.M. for a practice air raid, a suitably impromptu ending was
provided for a day which had never got properly into its stride
anyway.

The Cairo papers this morning hail the strike as an unqualified success for Egypt and the Arab world. In commenting on the
opening of the London conference they are guardedly hostile, pre-
dicting that it must end in failure but reserving their shriller tones,
perhaps, until Mr. Shepilov has had time to indicate clearly the
attitude of the Soviet delegation. Alleging that freedom is being
murdered at the London conference *El Akhbar* writes editorially:
"In London there is a funeral, but there are rejoicings in this part
of the world."

*The London conference lasted a week, and while
it continued we enjoyed a brief respite in Cairo, where
the Egyptians were beginning to show some anxiety
about the effects of the financial restrictions enforced
by Britain since July 27.*

CAIRO, AUGUST 21

With all eyes on London and the Suez conference, Cairo is suspended in uncertainty like a village in no-man's land as the sands of an armistice run out.

In general Egypt's case is best served for the moment by playing a waiting game, but time is not altogether on her side. The effect of the economic measures that the British Treasury instituted against Egypt immediately after the nationalisation announcement is obscure but widespread. More than anything else these measures (which some competent judges consider more harmful to British than to Egyptian interests) are at the root of the present uncertainty in the business world here, an uncertainty which could lead to paralysis if it is not resolved before long.

. Most of Egypt's imports come normally from Britain or else are purchased with sterling. No one knows what to expect in the immediate future or even how the British restrictions affect contracts signed before the nationalisation but not yet put into effect. Certainly if the restrictions continue in force for a considerable time the effect could be to starve Egypt of essential imports or to drive Egyptian importers to seek alternative supplies.

Already it is reported that a government official has ordered importers of pharmaceutical goods to place orders with iron curtain countries for supplies which would normally have come from western Europe. Asked what steps importers should take to replace supplies of goods such as special drugs which are only obtainable from the West, the official is said to have replied: "Find alternatives—after all, how do the Russians live?"

Meanwhile an argument was developing about the attitude of the Suez canal pilots, of whom a majority were British or French. The Egyptians alleged that the British and French governments were putting pressure on their nationals to leave the canal, in order to provoke a crisis in its management and so provide an argument for the international control which President Nasser so strenuously opposed.

The delay in concluding the London conference has done nothing to lessen tension which is growing here as a result of conflicting statements about the attitude of the canal pilots. Whatever statesmen in one conference or another may decide or fail to decide, their influence on events will be less immediate than that of the couple of hundred men physically capable of getting ships through the canal.

While President Nasser's government has so far stood by every other section of the speech at Alexandria in which Nasser announced nationalisation, it has tried hard to gloss over his unfortunate threat to imprison those employees of the Suez Canal Company who refused to work for the new Egyptian Canal Authority. Since then it has been explained that all that was meant was that employees (of whom by far the most important are the pilots) would not be allowed to leave unless they had given proper notice—which almost certainly was not the original intention.

The official Middle East News agency reported here to-day that at the time of nationalisation the Suez Canal Company employed 205 pilots (250 is considered desirable for the most efficient running of the canal). Of the 205, 61 were French and 59 British. On July 26, the agency says, 43 were on leave and of these 27 have not returned, including 14 French and 7 British. At present 59 are reported to be away in all, which leaves less than 150 in the Canal zone.

In an exchange of accusation and counter-accusation about pressure brought to bear on pilots by both the old Canal Company and the new Egyptian Canal Authority, a spokesman for the Authority to-day denied the statement attributed to him by the Egyptian press this morning that if British and French pilots failed to return to duty the Egyptian authority might discriminate against British and French ships. Instead, he said that the Canal Authority would not be answerable for the consequences.

It is known that even before nationalisation the number of pilots employed by the company was far lower than the desirable minimum. The company's explanation of the shortage was that the Egyptian government had refused visas for foreign pilots in order to force the company to hire more Egyptians. Whatever the reason, it is obvious that if the new Authority loses the services of many pilots it may be unable to maintain a proper service in the canal, and since the Canal Authority now says that twenty-seven pilots have failed to return from leave in Europe, this point may be near. The shortage of pilots is one reason for the feeling here that the climax of the Suez Canal crisis is not far off. Another is the fact that whatever the conclusion finally arrived at in London, the Egyptian government gives no sign of being prepared to accept any terms which infringe its complete sovereignty over the canal.

This means that Egypt is prepared to enter into negotiation with the interested powers to affect the revision of the Constantinople Convention, but that she will not accept any form of international control, which the president has decried as "collective colonialism." The president's first move on his return to Cairo (after a few days' rest) was to hold a long meeting with General Hakim Amer, minister of war and commander-in-chief of the Egyptian army, and one of the president's closest political associates. Earlier in the day the Egyptian foreign minister, Mahmud Fawzi, had an interview with Mr. Kisselev, the Soviet ambassador in Cairo.

The third reason for supposing that some way out of the present deadlock must be found soon is the economic paralysis with which Egypt is threatened as a result of the restrictions imposed by the British Treasury immediately after the announcement of nationalisation. These have brought imports to a standstill and, if maintained for more than a few weeks, will cause serious shortages of drugs, consumer goods and especially spare parts for machinery.

The argument continued, with each side trying in advance to throw onto the other the blame for any breakdown that might occur in navigation through the canal.

CAIRO, AUGUST 24

The vice-chairman of the new Suez Canal Authority, Colonel Mahmud Yunis, announced at Ismailia yesterday that the authority had engaged thirty-one new pilots since nationalisation, of whom twenty-six were Egyptians.

He admitted a shortage of pilots, and said that this was partly due to the fact that the number of pilots employed by the company before nationalisation was insufficient and that the situation had been aggravated by the failure of twenty-seven pilots to return from leave since nationalisation.

Several points in Colonel Yunis's speech deserve consideration. First, in criticising the Suez Canal Company for allowing the number of its pilots to fall below 250, which is considered ideal, he made no mention of the fact that the company had wanted to hire more from outside Egypt but that the Egyptian government had denied them visas in the hope of forcing the company to employ more Egyptians. Second, in the matter of hiring Egyptians as pilots, the company had reached agreement with the Egyptian government in 1949 as to the qualifications which candidates must have before being appointed; and since 1949 every Egyptian candidate possessing these qualifications has been appointed.

This raises the third and vital question of whether the appointments announced yesterday by Colonel Yunis indicate any lowering of standards. If not, where did he find twenty-six Egyptians with proper qualifications?

Colonel Yunis said that applications had been invited from naval officers who wished to serve as pilots and that some of those who applied had been appointed. Presumably these were Egyptian officers, in which case they cannot have had experience in handling larger ships than destroyers, since the Egyptian navy has no larger ships; and handing a large, modern tanker in a cross-wind along the narrow Suez Canal is an exceptionally exacting job.

At the conclusion of the London conference, Mr. Menzies of Australia had been deputed to lead a five man delegation to Egypt, to explain to President Nasser the conference's plan for an international operating board for the Suez canal. This plan had been approved by eighteen of the twenty-two nations attending the

*conference, India leading a minority group (compris-
ing in addition the Soviet Union, Ceylon and Indonesia) in favour of a revision of the Constantinople
Convention of 1888, with certain provisions for United
Nations supervision and consultations between the
Egyptian operating authority and the user nations.
After some delay, President Nasser agreed to see the
delegation—but before it arrived in Egypt, a further
discouraging element was introduced into the situation.
Two British subjects were arrested in Cairo and charged
with espionage.*

CAIRO, AUGUST 29

No one from the British embassy has yet been allowed to see
the two Englishmen arrested on Monday and charged with espionage. A spokesman for the embassy confirmed this morning
that two first secretaries from the embassy, Mr. J. B. Flux and
Mr. J. G. Gove, had been declared *persona non grata* by the
Egyptian government, which had asked for their recall. The
spokesman said the embassy had no option but to comply, but did
so under protest, and that the two diplomatists would leave Egypt
within seventy-two hours.

At a press conference late last night the director-general of the
Egyptian Information Service claimed that the two men charged
with espionage, Mr. James Swinburn and Mr. Charles Pittuck, had
confessed to being members of a spy ring, and to passing information to Mr. Gove and Mr. Flux. A spokesman for the British
embassy denied categorically that the embassy was in any way
involved in the alleged activities of the two prisoners.

The director-general said that investigation of Mr. Swinburn
and Mr. Pittuck had led to the discovery of other agents working
for the British, and that more arrests had been made, "including
some British." No confirmation of this is available so far to-day,
except that a British subject named Mr. James Zarb is reported to
have been arrested on an unknown charge.

A spokesman for the British Embassy said to-night that a
protest had been registered with the Egyptian Foreign Ministry

over the fact that access to the detained British citizens had been denied.

Mr. Krishna Menon, whose government had led the minority group at the London conference, passed through Cairo on his way home from the conference. His talks with President Nasser helped to maintain the close liaison which existed between the Egyptian and Indian governments all through the Suez crisis.

Mr. Krishna Menon, who arrived at Cairo Airport at 8:45 A.M. this morning, had an interview with President Nasser at 11:30 A.M., at which the London conference on Suez and the mission of Mr. Menzies and his committee were discussed. Mr. Menon is expected to see President Nasser again to-morrow, before resuming his journey to India on Friday.

Replying to reporters' questions at the airport, Mr. Menon gave it as his opinion that the situation had improved and could be expected to improve further now that Egypt had given an affirmative answer to the initiative of the committee of five powers. This opinion is not widely shared here, where tension has notably increased during the long interval between Mr. Menzies' invitation and the Egyptian president's reply. But at least the two sides will soon be in negotiation again, and at the same time reports that the canal pilots have had further instructions to remain at their posts have at least postponed the likelihood of a breakdown of navigation.

The tone of the Cairo press does not suggest any willingness on the Egyptian side to compromise on the central issue of sovereignty over the canal, and there is no evidence to support the persistent rumours that Nasser's mood is growing more conciliatory.

This week, on the eve of Mr. Menzies' arrival in Cairo, was the darkest of the whole long crisis. British subjects were being imprisoned, the British government repeated its advice to British nationals to leave the country, there was fresh emphasis on British and French troop movements in the Mediterranean, and a "Liberation Army" was being mobilised in Egypt.

With the members of the Menzies mission arriving in Cairo, the situation over the Suez Canal remains fundamentally the same as it was a month ago. President Nasser has not changed his ground in the least and still insists on Egypt's full sovereignty over the canal, while the Western powers still assert that they cannot accept a situation where freedom of navigation depends on Egypt's goodwill.

But if the dispute itself remains as far as ever from solution, the atmosphere in which the next stage of negotiations must take place has seriously deteriorated. British and French military preparations have come into the limelight again with the news that French troops are arriving in Cyprus, and that Egyptian countermeasures are much in evidence.

Much of the publicity given by the Cairo press to the flow of volunteers from the whole Arab world and to the military training of such unlikely recruits as the sheikhs of El Azhar University can be discounted as propaganda; but it is now a familiar sight to see platoons of awkward civilians being drilled in the Cairo suburbs and military convoys rolling out towards that Western Desert with which so many Commonwealth soldiers were once familiar. A recent decree imposes strict penalties on anyone giving news of military dispositions, but any traveller on the desert road from Cairo to Alexandria can see the encampments which have sprung up along this 120-mile strategic artery.

On another level every effort has been made to discredit British diplomacy in the eyes of world opinion, and the "unmasking" of the supposed British spy ring in which two British diplomatists were alleged to be implicated must be seen as part of this campaign. Very little information has been released by the Egyptian authorities to support their accusations, and that little looks unconvincing, but for the moment this does not lessen the effect of the allegations on public opinion here. The expulsion of five British journalists and two oil company employees are further signs of the general emphasis here on that old bogy "security," which means, when you come down to it, that you jump every time the telephone rings after 11:00 P.M., and that when you go out by car you keep an eye on the driver's mirror to see who is following you.

From what one can see of it the Egyptian army is not an imposing force, still less the "Liberation Army" of volunteers which is being hastily mobilised under the minister of education (an odd choice at first sight, but then an army major was an odd choice as minister of education to begin with). Probably an all-out attack by Britain with whatever French levies can be spared from North Africa could quickly achieve the immediate objective of occupying the Canal zone, Port Said, and Suez.

In moments of depression it is even possible to believe that this is what the British government intends as soon as President Nasser has reaffirmed to Mr. Menzies his stand on the central issue of sovereignty. But more than this it is hardly possible to believe that the British government thinks the matter would end there, or that, finding it did not, it would contemplate the occupation in succession of Cairo, of the Delta, and of Upper Egypt, to say nothing of whatever military action it thought necessary to repress the sabotage operations that would certainly ensue.

Yet this, or something uncomfortably like it, seems to be the implication of the government's continuing military preparations, of the facilities being granted to French troops in Cyprus (if there is a better way of merging every Middle Eastern discontent than by mixing up Cyprus, Egypt, and French North Africa it has still to be devised), and of the warnings to British subjects in Egypt—and now in Syria and Jordan—to get out while the going is good.

This at least is how Egyptians see it, and to some of them the prospect is encouraging. These are mostly the dispossessed and discontented, as well as the few serious patriots who cannot compromise their liberalism by acceptance, even for a time, of President Nasser's police state—not even when you remind them that this regime is appreciably more honest as well as far more efficient than any of the seedy parliamentary regimes which preceded it. Such people as these to-day wring your English hand and say, "Go ahead, we're with you. This is the time to smash this dictator"—and if that's our object and we feel it is a legitimate one, probably they're right (only spare us Farouk).

But to the rest, the ordinary Egyptians—who may not have chosen their government but who at present certainly follow it with a greater degree of unity than from all accounts Sir Anthony Eden can claim—to them this is the moment of truth when to their surprise (and they are still incredulous about it) all that the Egyptian press has been telling them about Britain seems after all to be true.

If we attack Egypt without proper cause and in contempt of the United Nations, we shall in their eyes, and in the eyes of all ex-colonial nations for whom noisy nationalism is only a symptom of growing pains, be acting the part which cynical pamphleteers have already written for us of bloodsuckers, colonialists, and exploiters. And we shall know it, as they will, and we shall never be able to forget it.

Next day the Menzies mission began its talks with President Nasser, in circumstances as unpromising as they could well be.

CAIRO, SEPTEMBER 3

Members of the delegation led by Mr. Menzies, who arrived in Cairo last night, had their first meeting with President Nasser this morning at the Egyptian presidency. It is understood that the discussions were limited to procedural matters, and a further meeting, lasting twenty minutes, was held this evening. The meetings are to be resumed to-morrow morning.

Expectations of success for Mr. Menzies and his colleagues, which were never strong, have weakened since his arrival, partly because of the arrest to-day of one more British subject (without any communication with the British embassy, which indeed has still not succeeded in making contact with Mr. James Zarb, who was arrested almost a week ago) and partly because of the Egyptian government's attitude towards the visitors, which looks discouragingly casual so far.

The latest British subject to be arrested in Cairo—he is the fourth—is Mr. John Thornton Stanley, secretary of the life branch in Cairo of the Prudential Assurance Company. The reason for his arrest is not yet known, but it is assumed that it is connected with the investigation which is still proceeding into the existence of an alleged British espionage organisation.

Mr. Stanley was arrested at his home in the residential quarter of Zamalek and taken to his office under escort at four o'clock in the morning. The office was searched. Mr. Stanley is forty years old and has lived in Egypt for about four years. His Greek wife and their two-month-old child are at present in Crete, where Mrs. Stanley's family live.

Mr. Stanley was not a well-known figure in Cairo except among those who shared his two enthusiasms for sailing (he was treasurer of the Cairo Yacht Club) and music. To them and to his business acquaintances he was known as a quiet, friendly, open character, and the last person to be involved in espionage even if he had possessed a wider knowledge of Egypt or the Arabic language.

A possible explanation may lie in the fact that the Egyptian secret police are at present hypersensitive and the further fact that Mr. Stanley had a distinguished war record and, among other things, served in the underground movement in Crete, where he lived for a year disguised as a Cretan shepherd.

In this connection two answers given by President Nasser at the televised press conference organised by the American National Broadcasting Company last night are interesting. Asked whether he considered that those accused of espionage had been plotting a *coup d'état* against the regime in Egypt, he replied that there was no plot but that the accused had been collecting information about military subjects.

He was then asked why, if this were so and if the Egyptian authorities had known of this espionage for two years, they had waited until now to make any arrests. He replied that four or six months ago the matter had not seemed worth bothering about but that in the present tense situation it was serious. But four months ago the Egyptian government was engaged in a vigorous propaganda war against Britain, and it is most unlikely that if such a useful weapon as a well-authenticated charge of espionage had been available the Egyptians would have withheld it.

Until the government produces some concrete evidence

against against the accused men (and the scraps so far released have a very spurious ring), they must not be surprised at the assumption that this espionage furore is being built up as a means of discrediting Britain and the Western case over the Suez dispute.

The casualness of the Egyptian approach to the talks now going on was indicated at the airport last night, where the sketchiest arrangements had been made to meet Mr. Menzies, and the governor of Cairo, who was on hand as the president's representative, was lost in a crowd of reporters. The president, at his televised press conference, made it plain that the five man mission could not expect much help with their very difficult assignment. He was prepared to meet them but disclaimed any responsibility for the present critical situation, and disposed briskly of the possibility that he might consider a compromise on the question of Egyptian sovereignty over the canal. The talks with the mission, he said, should be considered as "discussions, not negotiations."

He said he did not like the idea of taking the dispute to the United Nations, where it would be subject to the "manoeuvring of the big powers and the veto," and emphasised his sense of reassurance at President Eisenhower's declaration on Saturday which had stressed America's "full respect for the sovereignty of Egypt."

President Nasser's position at the outset of the talks with the Menzies mission is unequivocal. He considers his case invulnerable on its basis of full Egyptian sovereignty, which he asserts is acknowledged, among other places, in the agreement of 1954 between Britain and Egypt over the Suez bases. He claims that Egypt alone can assure freedom of navigation through the canal to-day as in the time of the Suez Canal Company, and he refuses to acknowledge the anxiety of nations whose ships use the canal as a sufficient reason for the infringement of Egyptian sovereignty by the imposition of any international controlling body.

There is no reason to suppose that Mr. Menzies or anyone else can persuade President Nasser to budge from this position, especially since he is assured of wide support from outside Europe, and he is sincere in saying, both privately and publicly, that if he is attacked he will fight. In their present mood the Egyptians would fight with him, and what matters is not the question of whether they would be a match for any invading army, but the fact that with the first shot fired the invaders would have lost the moral battle and that temporarily, at least, they would lose their oil supplies as well.

As a point of incidental interest, President Nasser told me last night that he was amused to see Mr. Menzies was bringing with him a retinue of twenty or thirty people. "I have just three people who advise me on this subject," he said.

The remark perhaps illustrates both his strength and weakness. His self-confidence and lack of orthodox political upbringing give him a rare flexibility, but they lead him to oversimplication and leave him genuinely uncomprehending of the secondary but still relevant political considerations. This and a young nation's determination to savour to the full its new-found "sovereignty" are among the most formidable obstacles facing Mr. Menzies.

It was a thin week for the correspondents, since the talks between the Menzies mission and the Egyptian government were conducted behind a curtain of the most determined secrecy. In any case, much of our attention was diverted to the espionage investigation, whose ramifications grew from day to day, and of whose authenticity we remained sceptical. John Stanley, who was the fourth (and, as it turned out, the last) of the British subjects to be arrested, was a friend of mine. We had met first at the Cairo Yacht Club, and once or twice at dinner in the houses of mutual friends. While he was held incommunicado in the "foreigners' prison" (the Egyptians did not admit until September 5 that he was under arrest), it was difficult to keep an objective attitude to the developing crisis.

CAIRO, SEPTEMBER 4

Mr. Menzies to-day kept his promise to behave in Cairo like a Trappist monk, and news of his mission's discussions with the Egyptian government was limited to the fact that during the day both sides were reviewing their own arguments before they met again to-night.

Meanwhile the British community here is indignant at the Egyptian government's continuing silence over the disappearance of Mr. John Stanley in the small hours of yesterday morning. A British embassy spokesman told correspondents yesterday that he had been arrested, but so far the Egyptian authorities have refused to admit to knowledge of his whereabouts.

Two of the other three British subjects arrested during the previous week and charged with espionage, Mr. James Swinburn and Mr. Charles Pittuck, were alleged to have signed confessions and were later allowed to see British consular officials. The third, Mr. James Zarb, still remains incommunicado and no confession in his name has been issued.

President Nasser expressed on Sunday night his surprise at articles in some British newspapers about the activities of the secret police in Egypt which, he claimed, gave an entirely misleading picture of the atmosphere here.

It must be admitted at once that one or two articles published within the last week in London bore little or no relation to the facts, and that such irresponsibilities have done much harm and angered other correspondents here. But it is also true that the methods being adopted by the Egyptian police and the evasions of the information authorities here inevitably prompt comparisons with the political trials staged behind the iron curtain, and any foreigner who has at any time evinced curiosity about any but the most obvious facets of life in Egypt must now consider himself liable to arrest on some shadowy charge (or none at all).

A British embassy spokesman to-night said the consul-general, Mr. Basil Judd, had called on the consular section of the Egyptian Foreign Ministry and left an aide-memoire "registering a protest at the denial of consular access to Mr. Zarb."

The talks went on, behind firmly closed doors, and we tried to find grounds for hope in the fact that at least the two sides to the dispute were in touch with each other. For a time it seemed as though a compromise solution might be found.

To-night, when the Menzies mission and President Nasser began their fourth meeting, the discussions were expected to enter a new and more important stage. So far each side has stated its case, and, with the pieces now set out on the chessboard and the first formal gambits exchanged, it is time for the game proper to begin.

It is still too early to read encouragement or the reverse into the few hints which are available about the progress and atmosphere of the discussions (and the wisdom of Mr. Menzies' strong silent policy has the approval of all except perhaps the frustrated journalists), yet a perceptible flicker of optimism is noticeable here.

This is partly because for three days the two sides have at least managed to talk to each other and apparently with more than the formal minimum of goodwill, but also because, with this new breathing space, those who try to envisage the sort of solution which could emerge from the discussions agree for the most part that no vital principle separates the two sides.

Even the bugbear of Egyptian sovereignty, it is suggested, could be overcome in the framework of a new treaty, essentially a revision of the 1888 Convention (and President Nasser has agreed to such a revision) which would embody clear provisions for the running of the Suez Canal.

The point of such an arrangement would be that the provisions concerning, for instance, the proportion of the canal's revenues which should be devoted to maintenance, the profits which should accrue to Egypt, and the terms of service of the pilots, would be enacted by an international treaty, with Egypt exercising her sovereign rights.

In reality there would be a voluntary renunciation by Egypt of some measure of sovereignty, but if the terms were generous enough and the wording tactful, it is felt that President Nasser is enough of a realist to consider the idea. If an international loan were offered to guarantee needed improvements to the canal, this would be a further inducement. It would remove the fear that must otherwise remain, that even if Egypt gets her canal unconditionally in the face of strong Western opposition, she will at the same time lose all hope of access to the foreign capital which she needs for development schemes.

When asked on Sunday evening whether the British Treasury's restrictions on Egyptian use of sterling had hit Egypt hard, President Nasser replied, "No," and added, "Eighty-five per cent of our people live near the starvation level, anyway." (The implication was that they would get on as well or as badly without imported tinned meats, cosmetics, and cars).

The president may have underestimated the importance of economic weapons, but his answer was no mere debating point but a statement of one of the hardest truths about Egypt's situation and one which lies close to the centre of President Nasser's simplified view of his responsibilities to his country. To do something about it he might be content to trim off the last half ounce of his pound of flesh—especially if the parcel could be wrapped up to look like a pound anyway.

This, at least, is the theory which is gaining adherents here, and it is thought that the next two days should show whether it has any validity.

Meanwhile, the atmosphere remains quiet and the tension over the espionage allegations has been very slightly relaxed as the result of the announcement this morning from the British embassy that the Egyptian authorities had promised to allow consular officials to see three of the British subjects who have been arrested. The visit is expected to take place to-morrow morning, and in the case of Mr. James Zarb it will be the first time anyone has seen him since his arrest early last week.

The arrest of the fourth British subject, Mr. John Stanley, was confirmed late last night by the Egyptians nearly forty-eight hours after he had disappeared from his home. The Egyptian prosecutor-general has refused to allow consular officials access to him on the grounds that his interrogation is not yet complete.

These were frustrating days of "no comment" on all sides, and we picked over the bones of what facts there were like starving cats round a dustbin.

CAIRO, SEPTEMBER 6

Ever since the two announcements last night—the first that

President Nasser had invited the five members of the Menzies committee to dinner and the second that no meetings between the committee and the Egyptian president had been arranged for to-day—observers here have been putting different and anxious interpretations on the same few equivocal facts.

The dinner party was to one a sure sign that the discussions were coming to a fruitless end, while another saw it as a justification for renewed hope. In the same way the absence of any formal arrangement for a meeting to-day suggested to one that neither 'side had anything to say to the other, while to his neighbour it was an indication that proposals had been made which at least justified a day's careful consideration. In fact no one knows what to make of it all, and Mr. Menzies and his entourage are wisely not helping.

It appears that it is Mr. Menzies and his colleagues who want a breathing space, and President Nasser said last night that if they wanted to see him to-day he would be at their disposal. Meanwhile there is no sign that President Nasser plans any withdrawal from his prepared positions, and I was told this morning by someone in close touch with the president not to look for a solution in any face-saving formula. "President Nasser does not feel any need to save his face," said my informant.

The decision to allow French troops to land in Cyprus, and the particular moment chosen for this move, have done much harm here, giving Arab propagandists a fresh cudgel with which to beat the British government just when the impression of the earlier military moves had begun to fade. The French are a liability as allies in the Middle East, first as colonialists and second because they have already been chased out of almost all the territory they once ruled. To identify ourselves with them at this juncture is merely to make more certain the hostility of Syria and the Lebanon and convince all the Arab states that the reactionary policy openly advocated by the French government has strong support in Britain.

The offices of the British-owned Arab News Agency in Beirut were dynamited yesterday by unknown assailants who left a message calling on "British spies" to get out of the Lebanon. No casualties were caused. The attack was probably related to the arrest here of four British subjects as well as more than thirty others on espionage charges, since the alleged head of the supposed spy ring was the English business manager of the Arab News Agency in Cairo, Mr. Swinburn.

By the next day it was clear that the talks were ending, but more than that it was hard to say.

CAIRO, SEPTEMBER 7

In the hard currency of facts correspondents in Cairo are almost penniless to-day, and even when every "reliable source" has been tapped and every "informed circle" squared he is a lucky reporter who has two good rumours to rub together.

First, the facts: the Menzies committee met for three hours this morning and will meet again to-morrow morning. No arrangements have been made for another meeting between the committee and President Nasser. (The last time they met was when President Nasser entertained Mr. Menzies and his colleagues at dinner on Wednesday evening.)

No date has been fixed for the return of the Menzies committee to London, but it is known that Mr. Menzies himself aims at being in London by Sunday evening if possible. That is all—and all that emerges from it is that not more than one further meeting with President Nasser seems at all likely, and that unless Mr. Menzies receives fresh instructions there is little to keep him in Cairo beyond to-morrow.

Commenting on suggestions which have been made in the press that members of the committee have disagreed among themselves, a spokesman committed himself to the improbable assertion that "there is complete unity within the committee on all points." He added that no doubt each delegate had been in touch with his own government, if only to keep them informed of what was happening in Cairo.

When it comes to the soft currency of hints, rumours, and plain honest gossip, there is more to choose from. While there have been no official meetings between the Menzies committee as a body and the Egyptian government, two of Mr. Menzies' colleagues, the Ethiopian and Iranian delegates, have had private meetings with President Nasser, and last night the American delegate, Mr. Loy Henderson, dined with the president, who gave a farewell dinner in honour of Mr. Henry Byroade, the departing American ambassador.

Each of these separate meetings has been invested with significance of one sort or another, but none appears to have had any significant influence on the situation. It has also been reported that Mr. Henderson has been in touch with Washington, and that American aid has been offered as an inducement to President Nasser to accept the proposals outlined by Mr. Menzies.

This suggestion has its amusing side, since it was the withdrawal of the American (and then British) offer of aid for the High Dam which precipitated this crisis six weeks ago. Incidentally, that withdrawal was the second indication of Washington's new "firm" policy towards President Nasser (the first being the announcement that Ambassador Byroade was to be transferred to South Africa).

The best diagnosis in the case of the Menzies mission seems to be that the patient has a very slim chance of survival, and that relatives will know the worst by midday to-morrow. If it is any comfort to them, the patient (who has had the best of attention) was in a critical condition before he came under the doctor's care.

On Sunday September 8, one stage of the Suez crisis came to an end, though this was not immediately apparent, at least to us in Cairo. An attempt had been made to get the two sides to the dispute to thrash out their differences round a table, and the attempt had ended in thinly disguised failure. President Nasser had not in any way modified his stand over the canal, nor had most of us expected him to do so. But Sir Anthony Eden had said, and repeated, that the canal "could not be allowed to come under the control of a single state." And British and French naval units were "somewhere in the Mediterranean."

CAIRO, SEPTEMBER 9

After a final meeting with President Nasser to-night, the first since Wednesday evening, members of the Menzies committee will leave Cairo to-morrow morning. The committee and

the Egyptian president yesterday exchanged memoranda dealing
with the discussions between the two sides at four meetings last
week, and it is clear that, on the present basis, they feel they have
nothing more to say to each other.

This is not quite the same as saying that the talks have ended
in failure, since their objective was to find out whether the proposals endorsed by eighteen nations at the London conference
would be accepted by President Nasser as a basis for further
negotiation. Clearly, they learned that they were not. But it
seems likely that the committee will leave Cairo with a clearer
idea of what President Nasser would consider a reasonable basis
for negotiation—or, to put the situation in its starkest terms,
whether any basis at all exists on which President Nasser and Sir
Anthony Eden, to say nothing of other interested parties, could
and would negotiate.

Mr. Menzies, commenting on the talks which ended this
evening, said: "These two documents [the memoranda issued by
the two sides in the Cairo talks] are completely comprehensive
and will give, I believe, a complete picture of the week's discussions." Mr. Menzies, whose purpose in meeting the press was to
explain why he had thought it best to withhold any news of discussions as they took place, said: "We wanted to discuss the most
serious problem the world now has before it, and we wanted to
discuss it as quietly as possible."

Mr. Menzies, who seemed full of bounce, did not succeed
with these few comments in dispelling the impression which is
current here among journalists (admittedly frustrated by a week
of "no comment") that the talks with President Nasser had been
unproductive of any substantial result or that the Suez problem
remained at least as intractable as it was before Mr. Menzies set
foot on Egypt's sands.

That both sides wanted to keep the ominous word "failure"
out of the headlines when Mr. Menzies finally left Cairo has
been evident from the activity of Mr. Menzies and his colleagues
and President Nasser and his close circle of political advisers
during the last three days. Yesterday, while the Menzies committee was meeting at the Australian legation, President Nasser
was closeted with the foreign minister, Mahmud Fawzi, the minis-

ter of war, Hakim Amer, and Ali Sabry, the director of the president's political office.

The minister of war left the presidency after three hours, but the meeting went on until 8:00 p.m. After that President Nasser spent an hour with the Indian ambassador, Ali Javar Jung. The Indian embassy here, when asked whether there was any truth in reports that President Nasser would have a further meeting with Mr. Nehru this month, merely confirmed that Mr. Nehru would be in King Saud's capital for three days during the last week of September and pointed out that if President Nasser wanted to see him it would not be difficult to arrange a meeting.

During the past week the presence of the Menzies committee here has turned the spotlight on Cairo, but in fact Cairo has not been the true centre of gravity of the Suez crisis. As soon as Mr. Menzies and President Nasser had gone beyond the first formal exchanges of views, it became clear that the Egyptian president was prepared to consider any plans for operation of the canal provided (as he had said so often since nationalisation) they did not infringe Egyptian sovereignty. In other words, he was ready to discuss any solution to the crisis except the one which in some shape or other Mr. Menzies had come to ask him to consider.

Faced with this not unexpected steadiness on the part of the Egyptian government, the committee has plainly been casting about for a more promising approach, and this has meant looking for guidance to London and Washington. In spite of the fervent denials of press officers for the Menzies committee, it is thought here that this guidance has caused dissension within the committee which has occupied a large part of its discussions during the last three days. If this is not true it is difficult to see what they have been discussing since they last met President Nasser on Wednesday evening.

The next move came from the Egyptians, who revived a suggestion thrown out by President Nasser at his press conference on August 12 and elaborated it into a proposal for a wider international conference on Suez.

As the B.E.A. plane with Mr. Menzies on board crossed the Egyptian coast this morning on its way to London, the Egyptian government seized the initiative in the Suez crisis. A note embodying Egypt's suggestions for solving the crisis was delivered at ten o'clock to the embassies and legations of all the countries with which the Egyptian government maintains diplomatic relations.

The note was devoted to a review of the developments which followed President Nasser's announcement of the nationalisation of the Suez Canal Company on July 26. The London conference and the talks in Cairo, which ended last night, are briefly mentioned, as are what the note describes as "displays of force and inducements from certain quarters to cause the defection of technical personnel with the intention of hampering navigation in the Suez Canal."

The note comes to the point when it says: "It is to be noted that no negotiations with Egypt have yet taken place." And it goes on to recall that President Nasser, at his press conference on August 12, had expressed the willingness of the Egyptian government "to sponsor, together with the other governments which were signatories to the Constantinople Convention of 1888, a conference for reviewing the convention and considering the conclusion of an agreement reaffirming and guaranteeing freedom of navigation."

This proposal the Egyptian government is now reviving in the belief, as it says, that "without prejudice to Egypt's sovereignty or dignity, solutions can be found for questions relating to (1) the freedom and safety of navigation in the canal, (2) the development of the canal to meet the future requirements of navigation, and (3) the establishment of just and equitable tolls and charges."

Maintaining its usual tortuous policy concerning the dissemination of information, the government summoned a restricted press conference at lunch time to-day, at which one of its few authoritative spokesmen answered questions put by a score of correspondents, who had been chosen, apparently at random, from representatives of European and Asian newspapers.

The spokesman explained that the Egyptian proposals en-
visaged two stages of negotiation. First, there should be discussions between the nations interested in the problem, at which
questions of the procedure to be adopted at a larger conference
should be debated and the date, venue, and composition of that
conference decided. Then the full conference would be summoned and entrusted with the task of reviewing the 1888 Convention and providing guarantees satisfactory both to Egypt and
the nations using the canal.

The larger conference, he said, need not be restricted to those
whose ships passed through the canal or even to those whose trade
depended on it. For, he said, "the Philippines may not use the
canal to-day but may to-morrow." When asked whether these
proposals were intended as an alternative to raising the question
at the United Nations, he said that Egypt was not in favour of
taking it there "because it might drag on," but that, of course,
Egypt, as a member of the United Nations, would join in any
discussions there and would never object to such discussions.

The spokesman said that these proposals represented an independent initiative by the Egyptian government on which no
other government had been consulted. (Some of the correspondents thought they detected the hand of Mr. Nehru at work, and
the Indian ambassador has been a fairly frequent visitor in the
inner circles of the Egyptian government since the crisis began.)
Nor had they any direct relation to the talks which had ended
yesterday with Mr. Menzies and his colleagues in the five-power
committee. (There had been speculation about individual visits
paid to the presidency by the Ethiopian and Persian members of
the committee.)

The ideas embodied in to-day's note, he said, "had been in
our minds before," and this initiative had been taken "now that
we have learned more about the other points of view" on the
Suez question. When asked what the Egyptian government expected to happen next, he said they were waiting now to get the
reactions and views of other governments on these proposals. If
enough nations supported the ideas contained in the note, the
first, so to speak, constituent assembly would be formed and
charged with the task of convening a larger conference.

How many other governments would be "enough," asked a correspondent. The spokesman declined to commit himself to anything more precise than a "substantial" number, but he said that equal importance would be given to the views of all governments irrespective of the degree of their interest in the canal. No conditions or reservations would be imposed on any nation attending the conference nor would Egypt herself go to it with any reservations. When asked specifically if Egypt had ruled out international control of the canal as a solution for the problem, he replied, "Oh, yes."

The Egyptian government's note does not represent any new approach to the problem, but it is possible to detect in it some slight advance towards a realisation of the vital interest of other nations in the security of navigation through the canal. The original Egyptian attitude that this was a purely domestic concern in which no other nation had the right to interfere has been modified, at least to the extent that the need for international discussions has been recognised.

The Egyptian proposal was turned down at once in London, on the ground that President Nasser had demonstrated his unwillingness to negotiate over the canal. This was both unfair and unwise, and the situation took another turn for the worse.

CAIRO, SEPTEMBER 11

In the Egyptian press to-day the main point of interest is the note which the Egyptian government yesterday sent to some eighty nations suggesting a further conference on the Suez question. The frosty reception given to the note by the Foreign Office spokesman is quoted, and it is hard not to feel here that with it Whitehall conceded yet another round in the tactical struggle which is going on in the world's eyes.

Since President Nasser had just received the Menzies committee and spent a week at their disposal for the discussion of proposals which everyone knew were unacceptable to him, surely the Foreign Office (it is thought here) might have waited at least until Mr. Menzies' aircraft had touched down in England before rejecting what after all was a formal counter-proposal.

From the way the Suez crisis has been handled it does not look as though the British government sees the problem in these terms, but if it banks on the support of those elements which it presumes to be friendly to Britain in Asia and the Middle East it might make it easier for them to show their support without looking like traitors to their neighbours. At the forthcoming meeting of the Arab League, which has been announced as taking place in Cairo next Monday, Iraq (and probably Saudi Arabia) will have inward reservations about giving full support to Egypt over the Suez question. But for the landing of French troops in Cyprus so would the Lebanon and even Syria, which would like to see the Arabs concentrate their attention on Israel. But none of these is likely to introduce a discordant note into the Arab League meeting at this juncture, and the usual clichés can be confidently expected in the meeting's final communiqué.

The United States ambassador, Mr. Henry Byroade, left Cairo last night to take up his new post in South Africa. Before leaving he had an interview lasting nearly an hour with President Nasser, with whom, said Mr. Byroade in a parting message, he had always found it possible, "even when our views did not coincide, to exchange opinions in a spirit of mutual respect and goodwill." Mr. Byroade also called on the Egyptian foreign minister, Mahmud Fawzi, and the British ambassador, Sir Humphrey Trevelyan. The new American ambassador, Mr. Raymond Hare, is expected in Cairo at the week-end.

PART 2   Only as a Last Resort

*Once again, with a lull in the wrangling of the
politicians, attention turned to the canal itself. The
number of ships using the canal had remained steady
during the six weeks since the nationalisation decree,
but now came an announcement which caused some
shipping lines to reroute ships round the Cape of Good
Hope, and led to an increase in insurance rates for
those still using the Suez Canal.*

CAIRO, SEPTEMBER 11

The news that the Suez Canal Company has advised all its
non-Egyptian staff to make arrangements to be repatriated suggests that the real crisis is beginning.

Egyptian propagandists have, of course, anticipated this move
by saying that if the pilots leave their posts as a result of pressure
from outside Egypt, the world will understand that any resulting
interference with navigation will be the fault of those exerting
the pressure and not of the Egyptian government, whose spokesmen have claimed that even if all British and French pilots left
it would be possible for the present canal administration to maintain traffic through the canal.

This is, to say the least of it, doubtful, since British and
French account for more than half the pilots now working the
canal. But President Nasser himself gave this answer when I
asked him about it at a press conference a week ago. Probably
at a pinch there are plenty of experienced merchant captains who
could take their ships through the canal, at least in the good
conditions that prevail at this time of year.

If the British and French pilots leave (fourteen Norwegians
are also reported to be restive), it would not be possible to find experienced pilots for all ships using the canal, and though the
Egyptian government has claimed that there have been many

applications from abroad for jobs on the canal since nationalisation, it would be about six weeks on the most optimistic estimate
before they could be ready to take ships through. Even then they
would only be able to take small ships unless the old company's
standards were completely ignored.

*The question of how many pilots would be needed,
and with how much training, to maintain the normal
traffic through the canal, was one which only the experts could answer—and the experts, as so often
happens, disagreed. I went down to Ismailia to try to
sort the matter out, and found the British pilots (who
were to leave at the end of the week) insisting that
once they and most of the other European pilots had
gone, it would be impossible to keep anything like the
normal number of ships moving through the canal.*

*The Egyptians were obviously determined to do
without them if it were humanly possible—and if the
job was only half as difficult as the pilots said it was,
this looked like a sporting effort.*

ISMAILIA, **SEPTEMBER 12**

Mr. Mustafa Niazi, a spokesman for the Egyptian Suez Canal
Authority, told me this morning that "arrangements have been
made which will ensure that transit through the canal continues
in all eventualities." When I asked whether this applied even
if all the British and French pilots should leave at the week-end,
he said categorically and confidently: "Yes, in all circumstances
navigation will continue at the same rate as at present."

He did not expect any legal action would be taken against
personnel leaving their jobs. "Those who wish to leave are free
to leave," he said. "We know the price of freedom, and we never
wish to impose it on anyone."

Mr. Niazi said that he knew the methods which would be
adopted to meet the emergency to be expected this week-end, but
was unable to say what they were. He did, however, leave no
doubt in my mind that he and his chief expected to be able to
avoid a breakdown of canal operations.

Talking later to two British canal pilots at Ismailia, I was told that they could not see how this could be done, since the withdrawal of all European pilots except the Greeks (of whom there are about nine) and three or four others would leave only forty or fifty fully qualified pilots. Besides these it appears there will be the twenty-six Egyptian pilots appointed two weeks after nationalisation, one Greek appointed at the same time, between fifty and sixty apprentice pilots who would not normally be allowed to take ships through the canal, and ten new pilots who have just arrived—the last two yesterday from Holland—in response to recent Egyptian appeals for pilots from abroad.

The present daily average of ships using the canal is just over forty, but since the transit is made in two stages with the journey broken at Ismailia this means that over eighty pilots are at work each day apart from those who take ships in to Port Said harbour and roads before handing them over to more senior pilots in the canal proper.

Yesterday there were two north-to-south convoys containing in all twenty-two ships, and one from south to north also containing twenty-two. To-day traffic is normal, and as I write a northbound convoy is moving out of the Bitter Lakes into the northern section of the canal where, a few miles from Ismailia, it will meet the second southbound convoy of the day.

The problem of maintaining navigation through the canal is not confined to the pilots: apart from the pilots the Canal Company employs an engineering and administrative staff totalling almost 1,000, of whom 530 are Europeans; and in addition a labour force of over 4,000 of whom nearly 1,000 are foreigners. These are affected by the Suez Canal Company's advice yesterday, and as far as I could establish almost all of them are also likely to leave this week-end.

The two pilots to whom I spoke were emphatic that the feeling among the employees of the old Canal Company, pilots and others, was "almost unanimous" in favour of leaving the canal. The chief reason was that nobody had any confidence in the new Canal Authority—neither in the security of tenure for foreigners working for it nor in its technical ability to maintain the standards of operation of the canal.

The British and French pilots were to leave on
September 15, and as that date approached the whole
wretched canal crisis, now seven weeks old, took on for
a moment the more cheerful air of a sporting contest,
a wager in which the stakes were horrifyingly high, if
you stopped to think about them, but in which the
issue might still be decided by skill and human en-
durance. Had the old Suez Canal Company played
a trump card in ordering its pilots to leave, or would
the remaining pilots, most of them Egyptian, manage
to pull the game out of the fire?

Just before the test came, the politicians claimed
our attention once again, with the least promising of
all the solutions proposed at one time or another for
the future administration of the Suez Canal. The
Suez Canal Users' Association, that unhappy product
of Mr. Dulles' imagination, never looked as if it would
develop into a workable organisation, especially since
it was clear amost from the start that Mr. Dulles had
a very different conception of the form it should take,
and the responsibilities it should assume, from those
of the British and French leaders who joined in spon-
soring it. They were talking in terms of an organisation
which would have its own pilots and collect its own
canal dues—in effect forcing the Egyptian Canal
Authority out of business—and there were even suggestions that SCUA should run a convoy through the
canal with its own pilots and challenge Nasser to put
himself in the wrong by trying to stop it. Mr. Dulles,
on the other hand, began at once to water down the
original conception, until his version of SCUA became
merely a negotiating body. But if the statesmen who
designed SCUA were uncertain about it, the Egyptians
were not.

CAIRO, SEPTEMBER 13
The headline "Nonsense," splashed in red across the front
page of the Cairo daily, Akhbar el Yom, gives concise expression to

the Egyptian opinion of the plan for a users' asociation to or-
ganise traffic through the Suez Canal.

The Egyptian communication to-day to Mr. Hammarskjold
states that the Egyptian government is taking steps to maintain
navigation through the canal after the withdrawal of the non-
Egyptian pilots; if navigation should be interrupted for reasons
outside its control "responsibility for this will fall on those who
have provoked this situation."

The plan for a users' association seems from here to combine
the worst features of most of the solutions so far advocated for
the Suez crisis. To begin with, it is even more offensive to Egyptian feelings than the international authority outlined in the
London talks, and it gets the sort of welcome one would expect in
the Egyptian press to-day. It is provisional in character and so
leaves the real issue unsettled.

It would create an authority which would have no legal
standing and which would inevitably be in conflict from the
start with the Egyptian Canal Authority. It could be put into
effect only by force or a show of force, and it looks most unlikely
that it would be workable anyway.

A statement issued last night by the director-general of the
Egyptian Information Service described the plan for a users' association as "simply an act of provocation aimed at unleashing
war. The plan's obvious aim is to create a situation which would
lead to armed aggression against Egypt." This opinion is widely
shared here and not only by Egyptians.

*The critical week-end arrived, uncomfortably
heralded by several incidents on the border between
Jordan and Israel, and by another repetition of the
British embassy's advice to British subjects to leave
Egypt.*

CAIRO, SEPTEMBER 14

As pilots of the old Suez Canal Company make their last
journeys through the canal this afternoon Egyptians at all levels
remain confident that traffic will be maintained at a normal rate
to-morrow. President Nasser has spoken of seventy pilots who
will work overtime to see that the usual forty ships go through,

and this figure was confirmed to me to-day by one of the president's few confidants.

At the new Egyptian Suez Canal Authority's headquarters at Ismailia the same confidence prevails, and it is echoed by newspapers and by individuals who know nothing of the canal or its operation but who have growing confidence in President Nasser's ability to keep one jump ahead of his opponents.

The figure of seventy pilots must include twenty-six who would not normally be considered fully qualified to take ships through the canal, but who have been training now for a month, doubtless with a sense of urgency which for the old company was never necessary. Whether, under the spur of this emergency and to meet the challenge to which President Nasser has committed them, these seventy can indeed keep traffic at its normal rate is the question of the day here. At present the same task keeps more than twice their number occupied to the point where they complain, with good faith, of exhaustion. But the pilots who are leaving to-night have not had the same incentive to work themselves to a standstill.

For most of those who will carry on (of whom two-thirds are Egyptian) the stake will be Egyptian sovereignty, and the critics to whom Egyptian sovereignty and patriotism are empty words may find themselves surprised in the event. The number of ships seeking to pass through the canal may, in fact, be less than the normal average of forty, since some ships like the P. & O. liners are being rerouted round the Cape, and the big liner presents one of the most exacting challenges to a pilot's skill.

If so, and if pilots in rotation work two ships daily instead of one, they could probably avoid a serious hold-up for two weeks, perhaps for a month. By that time the Egyptian authorities hope to have trained some of those who have applied for jobs—reportedly from Germany, Russia, China, Spain, the United States, among other countries—since nationalisation. The Egyptians feel that they can defeat any peaceful manoeuvre from abroad to impose alien control, whether it is international, tripartite, or hybrid. If it is a matter of fighting, that is another question—but they will fight.

The Cairo press to-day gives extensive reports of yesterday's debate in the Commons, with emphasis on the arguments of the opposition. *Akhbar el Yom*, whose editor is one of President Nasser's closest associates, parodies Mr. Dulles' landlord and tenant argument about the Suez Canal users. Commenting on the proposed Users' Association, it suggests that under this plan Egypt would be in the position of a landlady, one of whose lodgers runs the household, collects rents, and hands over to the landlady whatever share he is kind enough to grant her. This, says the paper, is "plain robbery."

The same paper goes farthest in condemnation of the prime minister's proposal in saying that "any attempt to implement the Users' Association means war." The general tenor of comment in the Egyptian press is that war is Sir Anthony Eden's aim and that his only alternative is resignation. From Egypt's Arab neighbours promises of support continue to pour in, and a meeting of the Arab League's Political Committee, which has been called for Monday in Cairo, will back Egypt's stand against Britain, France, and (presumably) America, whose latest shift to a policy of support for the Users' Association has lost her the fleeting popularity earned by President Eisenhower's earlier pronouncements about peaceful solutions.

Such support is *de rigueur* for Arab countries to-day, but behind it there is clearly much uncertainty, and the present consultations between Iraq and Saudi Arabia, normally the most bitter enemies in the Arab world, suggest that in private, at least, counsels of moderation will be urged on President Nasser. Iraq and Saudi Arabia, as the two oil-producing countries in the Arab League, stand to lose most if the suggestions for sabotage of oil installations are translated from loose talk into fact.

In this connection the president of the Federation of Arab Labour Unions yesterday declared that in the event of an attack on Egypt, Arab workers would put into effect resolutions adopted at a congress on August 10, including one to blow up Western oil installations and pipelines on Arab territory.

The danger of war in the Middle East is not, of course, confined to the Suez issue. Thursday's highly unconventional denunciation by the Foreign Office of a retaliatory attack earlier this week by Israelis against a Jordanian police post confirms that

Britain is exerting all her influence to restrain the Israelis from fishing in the present troubled waters.

Even without the Suez crisis this would have been considered an exceptionally dangerous week in the Middle East, with six Israelis and twenty Jordanians killed in two border incidents and the further incident reported to-day by the Arab Legion spokesman.

The British embassy in Cairo has repeated once more its advice to British subjects who have "no compelling reasons" for staying to leave Egypt. This is the third warning since the Suez crisis began seven weeks ago, and there are now only some 2,000 United Kingdom citizens left in the country. Such life as there is among the British community here is now of a gloomily spartan and celibate character, since even the British embassy has sent home almost all dependents, and within a few days only four wives (including Lady Trevelyan, wife of the British ambassador) and one child will be left.

Next day I drove down to Ismailia again, to see what would happen when the Egyptian pilots took over from their British and French colleagues, and if possible to get myself onto a ship passing through the canal. At the Canal Authority's headquarters in Ismailia everyone seemed tired and harassed. There was an "information officer," whose instructions had obviously been to tell no one anything. Journalists were definitely unwanted, and when I bypassed the information officer and managed to penetrate into the central planning room (where I had been courteously received a week or two earlier), I was quickly bundled out and told that if I had any questions to ask, they should be addressed to the information officer. So I went wearily back to him, and for some hours tried everything I knew to enlist his support in getting me onto a ship. I joked with him, pulled his leg about the fact that he obviously knew less about what was happening than most of the journalists; I lost my temper with him, and told him it would be his fault if the

*world got a one-sided picture of what was going on;
I apologised, and commiserated with him on his mis-
fortune in having to deal with a lot of hotheaded and
unsympathetic correspondents.*

*For a long time he held out, saying it was quite
impossible for anyone to get onto a ship that day, and
why didn't I come back the next day, when everything
would be different. But in the end he began to weaken,
and before I left him that evening he had promised to
telephone to me at 10:00 P.M. with a definite answer.
The British consul had kindly asked me to dinner, in
the midst of his many preoccupations, and we had just
finished dinner when the call came, and I was told to
be ready at 6:00 A.M. to go aboard a tanker bound for
Suez.*

*I was up at five after a hot night in an uncom-
fortable hotel, but when I presented myself at the
Canal Authority's offices there were further delays.
Characteristically, the information officer had mistaken
the time of the convoy to Suez, which in fact was due
four hours later. But more serious was the fact that no
one else was prepared to accept the scrap of paper he
had left for me as an authorisation to join one of
ships in the convoy, and I spent further hours going
from one police post to another and cajoling reluctant
officials into telephoning other and more important
officials. By the time all this had been straightened
out, and I had finally been taken out on a tug to
scramble up the gangway of the tanker "East River,"
I felt as though I had done a hard day's work—and
the calm air of detachment on board was like a tonic.*

IN TRANSIT, SUEZ CANAL, SEPTEMBER 16

This is the eye of the storm whose peripheral gusts are rattling
windows as far afield as Washington, Moscow, and New Delhi.
Here, by contrast, all is quiet—blissfully so for anyone who has
been involved, however remotely, in the diplomatic and political
and propaganda campaigns of the past two months. Here a line

of ships steams gently, silently through the desert, and instead of slogans or threats or political catchwords all you hear is a murmured "Ten points to port—five—steady as she goes," * and the nostalgic plaint of a Neapolitan love song from the crew's quarters in the afterpart of the ship.

The "East River" is a tanker of just under 13,000 tons, bound from Genoa to the Persian Gulf. She is registered in Liberia, but her crew are Italians under Captain Giorgio Peiretti, from Camogli, in Liguria. Fully loaded she can carry 18,600 tons of oil from Kuweit or Kharamshar to the ports of Western Europe; but to-day, on the outward run, she is in ballast and riding high in the narrow waters. For the passage of the Suez Canal from Port Said to Suez she is in the hands of Captain Gamal Mongued, an Egyptian pilot with five years' experience on the canal.

I joined the East River at Ismailia, and since then I have watched Captain Mongued nudging her round the bends in the canal with gentle orders (which he must be able to give in the crew's own language) of "Dieci a sinistra—cinque—via cosi" and sometimes "Avanti adagio" when he sees the Norwegian tanker ahead stealing away from us. Every ship has her peculiarities, Captain Mongued says, and the Norwegian tanker's is that at the required canal speed of about seven knots she vibrates. So the pilot who is taking her through goes alternately a little faster and a little slower, imposing corresponding adjustments (and close attention) on the following pilot. Behind us is a trim Italian liner with white hull and clean lines, and behind her again follow the rest of the twenty-two ships making up to-day's south-bound convoy. The northbound convoy consists of fourteen ships, including six British, three Norwegian, two French, one Russian—a rare sight in the canal, Captain Mongued remarks as the two convoys cross in the Bitter Lakes, an hour south of Ismailia.

Normally a pilot takes a ship only half-way through the canal, which gives him six hours of continuous responsibility.

* "Ten points to port," was my own translation of "Dieci a sinistra," which is what the pilot said, and it revealed my ignorance of navigation and elicited a letter in the next day's paper, which read, as nearly as I remember: "Dear Sir, If your correspondent really heard the pilot say 'Ten points to port,' he was lucky not to finish his journey on a camel."

To-day, as part of the measures to overcome the shortage of pilots, Captain Mongued is taking the East River right through—and yesterday he did the same thing in the other direction, taking a loaded German tanker from Suez to Port Said. To-morrow, after doing what is normally four days' work in two, he is to have a day off in Ismailia. He is not tired, he says, and he does not look tired, unlike many of the administrative staff at the Egyptian Canal Authority's headquarters at Ismailia, whom I could believe when they said they had not slept for three days.

To take a ship right through the canal instead of only half-way does not really double his working day, he points out. For whereas normally a pilot spends about twelve hours getting to his ship at, say, Suez, taking it to the half-way point at Ismailia, getting off and returning to his starting point, now he spends twelve hours on board but on arrival at Suez or Port Said spends the night there before taking another ship back next day. In any case Captain Mongued and the authorities at Ismailia told me that this is not a rigid system and sometimes a pilot will work only half the canal as before, according to his experience and to the requirements of the service. Captain Mongued tells me that there were four or five spare pilots at Port Said when he left this morning who could have taken ships if any more had been ready to pass through the canal. He added that the full twelve-hour passage of the canal, which was not too much of a strain for him, might tax a less experienced pilot for whom even six hours from Ismailia to either end of the canal can be exhausting work if he is still new to the job.

Of seventy Egyptian pilots now operational on the canal, twenty-six were on the old company's strength as fully qualified pilots at the time of nationalisation (in various grades which allowed them to take ships of different sizes). A further fourteen were acting as pilots in Port Said roads, ready to start taking ships in the canal proper as soon as there were vacancies. The remaining thirty were on a reserve list and have been put through a special training course since they were engaged five weeks ago. In addition there are ten Greek pilots who agreed to stay on when all other foreign pilots left this week-end. The problem for these eighty, of whom only about half have much canal experience, is the formidable one of keeping a daily average of forty ships passing through the canal until replacements from the foreign pilots now reaching Egypt are ready to take their places.

Of all the thousand and one rumours distracting Ismailia over the week-end, the wildest turned out to be true. The fifteen Russian pilots who arrived on Saturday did not have snow on their boots, but the red and white labels on their suitcases (Aero-transport Moskva) seemed almost as improbable to eyes screwed up against the desert glare. Gratefully shedding their heavy jackets, they showed with one exception no unwillingness to talk about themselves. Aged between twenty-eight and fifty-two, they were all experienced seamen, though only one of them had been a canal pilot (in Leningrad). But this did not cloud their optimism, and Feodor Pankov, *doyen* of the team, declared gaily that given two days to study the regulations and signals in use on the Suez Canal he would be ready and willing to lead a convoy of fifteen tankers piloted by himself and his colleagues from the Mediterranean to the Red Sea.

These new-comers, who were accompanied by four Yugoslavs, arrived as the bulk of the foreign staff of the former Canal Company made their final preparations for departure. The French, who seemed the best organised, left for Cairo on Sunday, where charter planes had been arranged. Most of the British, for whom the embassy in Cairo seemed reluctant to take responsibility, are now expecting to leave to-morrow, also by air. These pilots are leaving furniture stacked in their houses, but little else, except in some cases bank balances which cannot be taken out of Egypt until final income-tax clearance, which in Egypt tends to be a long drawn-out process. For the Maltese (of whom there are more than a hundred former canal employees in Port Said) things are more complex since they have their homes in Egypt, and in many cases have never seen Malta. Their evacuation will leave potential headaches for the already weary British consular staffs.

The British pilots here are indignant at suggestions that they have been bribed or coerced into leaving the canal. Their decisions to leave were in most cases taken before the Canal Company announced the financial help it would give to those retiring, and they were only prevented from putting these decisions into effect earlier by requests made to them by the Company that they hang on until the London and Cairo talks were concluded.

Now Suez is in sight, and behind it the sun is sinking, throwing deep shadows across the pink hills of Sinai on our left. In the bay ships are gathering for to-morrow's northbound convoy—seven or eight tankers and a couple of small freighters past which the leading ships of our own convoy are already steaming out to sea. Up on the bridge of the East River Captain Mongued looks unruffled as ever in his white shirt and shorts as I take leave of the friendly Italian captain and third mate and hurry down the gangway, leaping into a cutter as the ship approaches the mouth of the canal. Already I can feel that I am leaving the quiet eye of the storm, and as I spring ashore I brace myself again for the storm itself, of which the first intimations come with guards on the gate, inspection of passes, and presently the sound of an Arabic news bulletin from a café radio. Perhaps the canal itself cannot long escape the turmoil—for the moment it seems the quietest place in a troubled world.

Back in Cairo the storm was still raging, but its centre was shifting, away from the canal and onto the frontiers of Israel. The Egyptians' success in keeping the canal open with their own pilots had virtually finished the chances of the Canal Users Association as a practical weapon, and little more was to be heard of it.

CAIRO, SEPTEMBER 17

Thirty-five ships passed through the Suez Canal again to-day in two southbound convoys of eight and four ships and one northbound of twenty-three. The reversion to a system of running two convoys daily from north to south does not mean any radical alteration in method.

The intention of the Egyptian Canal Authority, as explained to me at Ismailia, is to keep operation methods fluid so as to avoid putting more strain than necessary on the limited number of pilots available. There may be a subsidiary reason in the wish to avoid committing anyone to a definite system of organising navigation, so that critics will have as little as possible to fasten on. This flexible policy has been successful in avoiding any delays, and it is reported from Suez and Port Said that no ships have so far been held up at either end of the canal for want of pilots to take them through.

As long as this is the case it is very difficult to see how the plan for a users' association could be brought into operation on the canal. If it could work at all it could only do so with the co-operation of the Egyptian authorities on land, since the timing of convoys (which can only meet and pass each other either in the Bitter Lakes south of Ismailia or in the bypass north of Ismailia) is a vital part of the canal control system.

While the Egyptians are running their own convoy system and doing so in a way that imposes delays on no one, the case for setting up a rival control system, even if legally plausible, seems so impractical as to be absurd. This, of course, is the view of the canal authorities in Ismailia as well as the Egyptian pilots, except that they deny categorically that the proposed users' association would have any legal standing at all.

An Egyptian pilot who took me through the canal yesterday told me that to him and his colleagues the Users' Association was simply a disguised way of making war on Egypt, presumably with the aim of getting Egypt to fire the first shot. He thought Egypt would be ready to do this since her sovereignty would be invaded by any ship attempting to pass through the canal without authorisation.

Mr. Krishna Menon, who arrived in Cairo early this morning, had an interview with President Nasser at midday and is expected to see him again this evening. The Indian minister without portfolio said he had brought no new proposals for a solution of the Suez crisis, but he had come "to see how things were going." He will spend two days in Cairo and expects to go on to London.

The Political Committee of the Arab League met in Cairo this evening for the second time since the nationalisation of the Suez Canal Company. The meeting was attended by the foreign ministers of most Arab countries and by Sayed Tewfik el Suedy, ex-premier of Iraq. Originally the purpose was to discuss only the Suez crisis and the steps so far taken to solve it, but it was announced here to-day that the meeting would also discuss the situation on the Jordan-Israel border, where a series of grave incidents last week caused the death of some thirty Jordanians and ten Israelis.

An Iraqi military mission is in Amman to-day to discuss with Jordanian military leaders measures of co-operation against Israel. The meeting is understood to be the result of an interview last week between King Hussein of Jordan and his cousin, King Feisal of Iraq.

> *The tension continued, and helped to draw the Arab states together, although where the canal was concerned they were showing signs of their usual disunity.*
>
> *In London, the eighteen nations who had backed the fruitless Menzies mission were still trying to give SCUA a workable shape, but it was clear that if SCUA survived at all, it would only do so in a much modified and relatively inoffensive form. In Cairo we felt that the West was beginning to realise that its only hope lay in a negotiated settlement, and the tension slackened accordingly.*

CAIRO, SEPTEMBER 23

When the European pilots were leaving the Suez Canal and an undefined users' association was on the drawing board, the British in Egypt were thankful to know that their wives and children were safely home in England. Now the talk is rather of how many dreary weeks or months of negotiation must pass before the wives and children can return.

Already the interest of the Arab world shows signs of shifting back to its most enduring preoccupation, Israel. This is prompted, among other things, by the news that Canada is to deliver twenty-four jet fighters ordered by the Israeli Government some months ago. *El Gumhuria* concludes that the Western powers, having "failed" over Suez, are taking another path towards their main objective in the Middle East—the "shattering of Arab nationalism, which is becoming a serious menace to imperialistic plans."

Tension on the Israel border, aggravated by a number of serious incidents in the last two weeks, certainly finds Arab governments in more prompt unanimity than does the Suez problem. King Saud, who last week played host to King Feisal of Iraq (a descendant of that Hussein whom King Saud's father drove out of Arabia), is to-day entertaining President Nasser and President Kuwatly of Syria. To-morrow he expects the visit of Mr. Nehru. All these visitors are likely to find King Saud vehement in denunciation of the Israelis, of whose repeated frontier violations the Jordan government has just complained to Mr. Hammarskjold. The Israelis, in turn, accuse Jordan of no less than 160 violations since April.

President Nasser may have more difficulty in persuading King Saud to give active support to Egypt over the canal. King Saud, more than anyone in the Middle East, depends on oil for his existence. If opposition to Western policy took the form of sabotage of oil installations, it could mean the end of King Saud, as, for that matter, it could mean the spread of Nasserism to Saudi Arabia—and King Saud is the nearest thing to Farouk left in the Middle East.

The next most directly threatened among Middle Eastern rulers by the possibility of interruption of oil operations is King Feisal, and whatever it is that has brought King Feisal and King Saud to speak to each other (the last direct contact between the rulers of Iraq and Saudi Arabia was more than thirty years ago) it is less likely to be love of Nasser than anxiety lest his stand over Suez should cut their precious pipelines.

Arab unity is still a delicate plant kept alive principally in recent years by the fertiliser of anti-Israeli sentiment. The Suez crisis, which at first (largely through clumsy handling by the West) promised to give it new strength, is more likely in the long run to weaken it, since unlimited victory for Nasser would benefit only Egypt at the cost of Western investment in the Middle East as a whole. And whatever mobs may feel, Middle East governments still depend largely on Western trade and capital.

It is not known yet whether President Nasser will stay in Riyadh long enough to meet Mr. Nehru. If Mr. Nehru shares his roving emissary's optimism, he is likely to feel that events of the past week, both on the Suez Canal and in London, have paved the way for reconsideration of the proposals that the Indian government put before the first London conference. Those proposals were never far from President Nasser's own idea of a conference to negotiate a new Constantinople Convention. They now seem little farther from the modified conception of the function of the Users' Association which has emerged from the second London conference.

The same day the British and French governments asked for a meeting of the Security Council, to consider Egypt's action in bringing to an end the system of international control of the canal. This was not likely to lead Egypt any nearer to compromise, but the feeling was growing that some of the other Arab governments were becoming less enthusiastic in their support for Egypt's stand. Nasser's visit to Saudi Arabia seemed to confirm this feeling.

CAIRO, SEPTEMBER 24

President Nasser returned to Cairo this afternoon after his two-day visit to Saudi Arabia. Contrary to expectation, it seems that he did not stay to meet Mr. Nehru, who was due to arrive within an hour or two of his departure.

A communiqué issued from Riyadh dealing with the meetings between the Egyptian, Syrian, and Saudi heads of state contained no surprises but dwelt on their complete coincidence of views on all important political questions, particularly the question of the Suez Canal. It was not to be expected that the communiqué would confirm reports that King Saud wished to put the brake on President Nasser on behalf of himself and King Feisal of Iraq, but the general opinion here stands by this interpretation of the central theme of the talks. It is felt that Mr. Nehru will add his voice to those urging President Nasser to go to the limits of conciliation with the Western powers.

It remains unlikely that the Egyptian president will see those limits as including any interference with undisputed Egyptian control of canal operations. If the question is raised before the Security Council of whether Egypt will reverse her present policy of refusing passage to Israeli ships (and thus obey the earlier injunction of the Security Council), Egypt will stand firm on this too

—and with the full support of the Arab States, who are united on this issue as on no other.

In fact, introduction into the question of Israel's point of view will only complicate the issue and prolong discussions, since the Egyptian government believes it has a strong case in disputing the justice of the Security Council's ruling over Israeli shipping, and the relevant clauses of the Constantinople Convention are far from explicit.

Article 4 of the Convention says the canal shall remain "a free waterway in war-time even for the passage of ships belonging to combatant countries." But another article says that Article 4 shall not apply in case of measures taken "to defend Egypt and maintain the public security therein."

Egypt's case in refusing to obey the Security Council's resolution is that she is in a state of war with Israel and considers herself threatened by Israel. The point is one which could occupy lawyers for some time and so hold up consideration of the point now at issue of whether and in what sense the Suez Canal is an international waterway.

Another Israeli attack on a Jordanian frontier post on the night of September 25 put the Egyptian government in an awkward position.

CAIRO, SEPTEMBER 26

Last night's Israeli attack comes at a moment when suggestions are rife that in spite of its vehement protestations the Arab world is less united in support of President Nasser's Suez stand than it would like others to think. For this reason it is the more dangerous, since it leaves Arab states the choice between giving substance to the oft-repeated slogan about Arab unity and sitting down under a particularly severe blow from the Israeli enemy.

Egypt, for obvious reasons, would not welcome any full-scale military operations on the Jordan-Israel border at the moment. In fact since President Nasser's speech of July 26, in which he announced the nationalisation of the Suez Canal Company (and attacked Israel in strong terms), Israel has received far less attention than usual in Egyptian policy statements and in the press.

It is likely that most Egyptian forces have been withdrawn from the Gaza area and other posts on the Israel border in case they were needed for the defence of the canal.

To the rest of the Arab world, Israel remains the first preoccupation, and if Egypt tried to oppose this tide of feeling this could endanger her position of leadership in the Middle East. Already there have been indications of restiveness on the part of other Arab states at the way President Nasser takes it on himself to speak and act for the whole Arab world. The indications are still very imprecise, but the interests of Iraq and Saudi Arabia in safeguarding operations in the oilfields is one element in them and another is the feeling that Nasser's headstrong policy inevitably means a drift towards Communist infiltration, which makes the insecure Middle Eastern monarchs—not to mention presidents—feel nervous.

Up to now Israel has provided one sure rallying point. If that goes, the vague ghost of Arab unity would be blown away with it. The urgent message which King Hussein of Jordan sent to President Nasser yesterday (before the Israeli attack) may have been a reminder of this. It is one which in the present circumstances Nasser can hardly ignore.

For the moment, the canal seemed to be almost forgotten, and the Israeli attack of the twenty-fifth (in which thirty-eight Jordanians had been killed) had thrown the Arab world back into its customary discord.

CAIRO, SEPTEMBER 28

Since the attack by Israeli forces against a Jordanian frontier post on Tuesday the usual assurances of unfailing solidarity are being exchanged throughout the Arab world, revealing more than anything else the continuing disunity of its member states.

The accusation is also freely made, especially in Syria but also in the Egyptian press, that the Western powers encouraged this attack, like others made by Israel. And the presence of French troops in Cyprus lends special bitterness to the charge of Western hostility to the Arab states, as well as the recent announcement that Canada would supply Israel with jet fighters.

Not surprisingly, Jordan shows signs of resenting the fact that she bears the brunt of frontier incidents, while her Arab neighbours confine their share in Arab unity to protestations about loyalty to their unfortunate sister nation and promises of aid. The Jordanian newspaper *El Jihad* wrote yesterday: "Jordan considers it is futile to offer its youth as cannon fodder unless the Arab states hasten to present genuine and earnest aid. We hope the Arab leaders will not confine themselves to mere manifestations of sentiments and compliments which can repel no aggression. We here in Jordan are tired of such talk."

Certainly Egypt's reaction to the most recent incident was almost absent-minded by comparison with her fury when a similar Israeli attack in the Gaza strip in April killed a comparable number of Egyptians. President Nasser's telegram to King Hussein after Tuesday's attack said: "I feel grieved and I offer you the condolences of Egypt." Such language hardly bears out the claim of the Beirut newspaper *El Hayat* that "Jordan is a thorn in the conscience of the Arab states."

The plain fact is that Tuesday's incident caught the Arab states preoccupied, as usual, with their separate interests, to which talk of Arab unity supplied no solution. Egypt was preparing her case over the Suez issue for the Security Council; Saudi Arabia and Iraq were alarmed lest the Suez crisis should interrupt oil operations and reduce their revenues; Syria and the Lebanon, while perhaps resenting Egypt's acting in the name of the Arab world without consulting her Arab partners, had their attention riveted on the French troops in Cyprus.

In the circumstances no concerted action was likely. Nor is it likely after the meeting of heads of the Arab states which King Saud is reported to be suggesting for next week, for beyond these immediate and conflicting interests lies the wider issue—the struggle for leadership of the Arab world. As far as the Arab peoples are concerned President Nasser is an easy favourite, but for the Arab rulers he is a less promising candidate, since Nasserism, by its very nature, is a threat to the survival of the old regime in the Middle East, and it is the old regime which manages to keep in being monarchies like that of King Saud in the twentieth century.

For the moment, only Egypt has the moral standing or material resources to give a lead in the Middle East, and to-day Egypt has plenty to think about without looking beyond her own frontiers. The economic restrictions imposed two months ago by the West are making themselves felt—the fact is underlined by the spate of statements from government authorities denouncing hoarding and explaining nervously that all is well—and though not likely to be crippling, they can only be circumvented by swift measures of reorganisation, which at present look inadequate and which are already causing much grumbling in the business world.

None of this is likely to be lost on the Israelis when they make their cool calculations of the profits and losses of border "incidents."

The Security Council was to meet on October 5, and this helped to ease the tension, since the British and French governments, now that they had at last turned to the United Nations, would hardly be rash enough to attack Egypt while the Council was debating their complaint against her; and for Egypt, obviously, the best policy was to maintain an attitude of scrupulous correctness—and keep the ships moving through the canal.

Meanwhile Egypt was faced with a problem in her relations with the rest of the Arab world, where her leadership seemed to be threatened by her failure to deal with the Israeli threat.

CAIRO, OCTOBER 1

Last week's retaliatory attack by Israeli forces near Jerusalem, in which thirty-eight Jordanians were killed and eleven wounded, has sparked a new series of inter-Arab meetings whose avowed aim is to strengthen the common Arab defences against Israel.

In Beirut to-day representatives of Syria, the Lebanon, Jordan, and Egypt—the four Arab states having borders with Israel—met to discuss the terms of a common complaint which their governments will make to the Security Council against Israeli aggression. In Amman the Jordanian prime minister had talks with the Egyptian ambassador about measures of assistance to be given to Jordan by Egypt and other Arab countries. It is also announced from Amman that a military conference will be held there next week, to be attended, it is hoped, by the commanders-in-chief of the four Arab states having common borders with Israel.

The Iraqi commander-in-chief is already in Amman, where he had discussions over the week-end with Jordanian officers over the implementation of the defence pact signed by Jordan and Iraq in 1947. In Bagdad, too, there have been consultations between representatives of Jordan and Iraq, this time on the political level, with King Feisal taking part at a long meeting on Saturday at which the Iraqi premier, Nuri el Said, and the Jordanian foreign minister, Abdel Hadi, were present.

No communiqué has yet been issued about the results of these talks, and when one is issued the Arab weakness for overstatement will probably cloud its importance. Still, one gets the impression from here that there is a more genuine core to the present Iraqi-Jordanian co-operation than to most inter-Arab dealings. And it is significant that after last week's Israeli attack on Jordanian positions, Jordan turned at once to Iraq rather than to Egypt for reassurance.

Taken in conjunction with King Feisal's recent visit to King Saud, this suggests that the present tendency amongst Arab states is to bypass Egypt in their deliberations, and Egypt's absent-minded reaction lately to the battle cries of Arab unity help to explain this. There is probably more to all this than the simple preoccupation of Egypt with the Suez crisis. It looks as if the Arab governments are beginning to think for themselves.

Unobtrusively the Egyptians were holding their own on the canal (which was hardly newsworthy any longer), and as the first of their new pilots completed their training it was clear that the West could no longer hope for a breakdown in the operation of the canal to strengthen their case for international management.

CAIRO, OCTOBER 2

The first twelve apprentice Suez Canal pilots are taking their written examination on canal signals and regulations to-day and if successful will be qualified to take ships through the canal from to-morrow.

Among them are four Russians who arrived on September 15, the day that most of the old foreign pilots stopped work, and four Germans, two Spaniards, a Dutchman and an Egyptian. All twelve have already passed the practical examination in canal navigation. A further thirty-nine new pilots will take the same examinations during the coming week, an Egyptian Canal Authority spokesman said in Port Said to-day.

Two weeks seems to be the training period set by the new Authority, and an American pilot with whom I talked at the week-end said that after spending two days on the canal he was expecting to undergo a further ten days' training before being ready for the examination which all new pilots must pass before "going solo."

The daily average of ships using the canal is gradually creeping back towards the normal figure of about forty-five daily. During the early days of purely Egyptian management the average was in the mid-thirties. Now it is just under forty. Figures for tonnage passing through have not been made available but they are certainly a good deal lower than normal, since the largest ships normally routed through the canal are mostly going round the Cape.

This fact has a direct bearing on the amount of dues paid (of which it is estimated that the Egyptian Authority is now getting more than a third), since dues are calculated on the basis of freight capacity and the number of passengers carried. Until yesterday the largest ship to pass through since the Egyptian authorities took over was the Dutch liner "Oranje," of just over 20,000 tons, but yesterday a super-tanker belonging to Spyros Niarchos and bearing his name was in a convoy of twenty-seven ships passing through from Suez to Port Said.

The "Spyros Niarchos" has a gross tonnage of 30,000 and fully loaded can carry over 40,000 tons of oil. It will have carried less yesterday since the canal is not deep enough to allow the passage of such a large tanker fully loaded.

*My leave was overdue, and with the canal dispute
going to the Security Council on October 5 and the
prospect that the discussions there would last at least
two or three weeks and probably lead to some further
negotiation between the parties, I suggested to my
editor that I might take a holiday. He agreed, and
on the fourth of October I left Egypt, hoping to have
three weeks' rest after a hard hot summer in Cairo.
Before I went, I put together some ideas on a theme
that had been much discussed during the Suez crisis,
and which had played an important part in the strange
processes by which public opinion is formed. The
original point at issue, of whether or not President
Nasser was within his rights to nationalise the Suez
canal, had long since been overlaid by all sorts of
relevant but secondary considerations. Above all—and
this seems clearer when one looks back on that disastrous summer—the British people's attitudes to the
crisis had been largely influenced by what they knew
(or did not know) of the Egyptian people, and by the
image of Gamal Abdul Nasser that had been created
in the public mind.*

CAIRO, SEPTEMBER 25

During the dispute over the Suez Canal parallels have been
drawn openly or by inference between President Nasser and
Hitler. Sir Anthony Eden has said that our recent dealings with
the Egyptian president have reminded him of the course of events
in the 1930's, and the obvious conclusion is that we should halt
this new dictator before he leads the world into a fresh disaster.

Superficially the parallel is an apt one. Like Hitler, President
Nasser is an absolute ruler, whose claim to authority is not
strengthened in the eyes of the democratic world by a plebiscite
giving him 99.9 per cent of the votes cast. Like Hitler, he has
championed Irredentist movements in surrounding countries and
by so doing has sown suspicions (none of them as yet proved) that
he has territorial or imperialist ambitions. Like Hitler, he controls
the sources and dissemination of information, and has used this

power to spread violent propaganda against states with which he maintains normal diplomatic relations. He has expelled a number of foreign journalists who criticised his regime. Lastly, and most important, he has pursued a foreign policy ("vigorous" or "aggressive" according to the point of view) which has taken as its first aim the removal of alleged grievances, and in doing so has damaged the interests of the Western powers—of Britain in particular—in the Middle East.

But in one respect Nasser's approach has been very different from Hitler's. Hitler told us in *Mein Kampf* what he intended to do, and then set out to do it. Nasser, too, has published, mercifully on a much smaller scale, his reflections about "the objectives we [the Egyptian people] should aim at, and the energy we should mobilise to achieve those objectives." His *Philosophy of the Revolution* is a very personal document, and not an easy one to understand without some knowledge of its author and of the historical circumstances in which he came to power. But whatever else it does, Nasser's booklet certainly does not give us a clear idea of the course he intended to follow when he came to power or (in spite of its title) of the philosophy behind his revolution. In fact, it reveals unconsciously one central fact about the Egyptian revolution: that it started out without any underlying philosophy—and it has never developed one. It started as a movement to disrupt a certain established social and political framework, and it has not yet decided what to put in its place. This has given Nasser a useful flexibility and freedom of action which he might not otherwise have enjoyed; but it has also involved a preoccupation with negative aspirations—"Down with imperialism!" "Down with Israel!"—at the expense of the constructive tasks which face him in building the new Egypt and which are at least as acute now as when he came to power.

This absence of a philosophy is not all loss for Nasser. At least the movement he initiated has not become clogged with the kind of phony philosophy, the unattractive rationalisation, which made *Mein Kampf* so daunting a book and National Socialism so disagreeable a credo in democratic eyes. There is no suggestion in Nasser's approach that Arabs or Egyptians are better people than anyone else, and no search for scapegoats among his own people.

(It is a remarkable fact that the Jewish community in Egypt, in spite of Egypt's violent antagonism towards the state of Israel, is not subject to any official or unofficial discrimination.) The Egyptian revolution was achieved without bloodshed, and the only lives lost for political reasons in its first year were those of two ringleaders of a riot near Alexandria. (Seven members of the Moslem Brotherhood were sentenced to death in 1954 after an attempt on Nasser's life.) And just as there have been no purges, no pogroms, none of the sadism and brutality which degraded Nazi Germany, so the Egyptian revolutionary leaders have steadfastly avoided the outward pomp with which Hitler and his associates surrounded themselves, as well as (and in contrast to the preceding Egyptian regime) the libertinism which so often accompanied it.

These are important but secondary points of difference between Nasser's regime and Hitler's, between "the course of events in the 1930's" and the troubled world of to-day. The main consideration must be whether Nasser in his conduct of foreign affairs has followed the same unscrupulous course by which Hitler led the world to disaster in 1939.

Nasser's foreign policy had from the start two main preoccupations, both of them inherited from the previous regime in Egypt. There were Egypt's relations with Britain, who still maintained forces on Egyptian territory; and there were her relations with Israel, whose triumph in the Palestine war in 1948 had shaken the morale of the whole Arab world.

With Britain there were two points of contention, the occupation of the Canal zone and the future of the Sudan. Both had been cleared up by October, 1954.

It was felt on both sides at the time that the agreement for the British evacuation of the canal base would open up the way to a new and fruitful relationship, since it removed the factor which had bedevilled Anglo-Egyptian relations for thirty years. Instead, this proved to be a turning point, but in the opposite direction, leading to estrangement more complete than any that had existed before, until only two years later the two countries faced the thought of war with each other over the Suez Canal. To the Western governments, looking back over those two years, the explanation seems a simple one. Nasser, having won his immedi-ate objective, set out to undermine once and for all the Western imperialist influence in the Middle East, by lending moral support to the nationalist movement in French North Africa; by stirring up trouble wherever Britain still maintained garrisons or treaty rights in Arab states; by his violent opposition to the Bagdad Pact; and by his unscrupulous use of the "Voice of the Arabs" radio to spread anti-Western propaganda. Seen in this light, the national-isation of the Suez Canal Company appears as simply another step in a master plan for the elimination of Western interests and the creation of an Egyptian-Arab empire in the Middle East.

This explanation would be more satisfying if there were any evidence that such as master plan existed. In truth the evidence all points the other way.

The signing of the Canal Base Agreement left Nasser one major problem of foreign policy—Israel. Until he had made Egypt strong enough to avoid a repetition of the 1948 fiasco, no ruler could feel secure in Egypt, especially since the Arab world was now hopelessly shaken and divided by the memory of new betrayals to add to the old. President Nasser confidently expected that as an earnest of the new spirit which was to animate Anglo-Egyptian relations after the 1954 agreement had been signed (and Nasser had agreed to maintain the British base in the Canal zone with civilian technicians looking after it), he would obtain from Britain the arms he needed to cover his eastern flank. When these arms were refused, Nasser took it as a breach of faith, and re-acted strongly in his nature of soldier-conspirator. If the West would not give him arms, he said, he would find them where he could—and he turned to the East and put through the famous arms deal which for the first time brought Russian tanks and fighter planes into the Middle East.

But this turning to the East was again no part of a deep-laid plan, though once it had begun it might prove difficult to stop, since Nasser was dealing with more experienced conspirators than himself. It was the Western refusal to give him arms (arising out of the West's misunderstanding of the burning reality for every Arab state of the "Israeli menace") that turned Nasser to Mos-cow—though it did not go so far as to persuade him to stop imprisoning his own Communists as often as he could catch them. And when at last he had got his arms and the last British soldier had left the Canal zone, and Nasser belatedly turned his attention to Egypt's domestic problems, the West's withdrawal of its promised aid for the High Dam challenged him to turn again to Moscow. But this time Nasser chose another and still more dangerous course.

The nationalisation of the Suez Canal Company was plainly an act of hostile intent, planned in resentment at the Western rebuff. To Nasser, that rebuff was also a hostile act, intended to undermine his ascendancy in the Arab world, and it is difficult to dispute this judgment. (The fact that its effect on the Arab world was the opposite is not proof of its innocuous intent, but only of the bad judgment which prompted it.) But no one has yet succeeded in challenging the legality of nationalisation. It may be that its consequences for Egypt and for Nasser's own regime will be disastrous, but that does not convict Nasser as a treaty-breaker, or justify us in calling him a new Hitler. He is a nationalist ruler, an opportunist, whose objectives of strengthening the Arab world and establishing its full independence of outside influences are painful to us but arouse the natural enthusiasm of his own people, and the sympathy of all the ex-colonial nations in Asia and Africa. Perhaps the West's tendency to jump to the worst conclusions about Middle Eastern nationalism has its roots in our nostalgia for the days when, if we pulled the strings in the Middle East, the important people danced. Those days are gone—and gone for good.

During most of October, as I had hoped, the crisis remained in abeyance. The Security Council's session started with the expected exchange of arguments, which were followed by a series of secret meetings. Then the first part of a British-French resolution (much modified from the original version) was passed by the Council, with even the Egyptian foreign minister speaking in favour of it. This included the provision, so often cited later and so empty of practical meaning, that "the operation of the canal should be

insulated from the politics of any country." But the second part of the resolution, endorsing the principle of international control and calling for a settlement on the basis of the conclusions of the London conference, was vetoed by the Soviet Union. However, at least the representatives of Egypt and of the Western powers had met each other round the conference table, and had narrowed the area of disagreement. It was thought that they would meet in further discussions soon after the end of the Security Council's session.

In the Middle East there was plenty of tension, but it was centred in Jordan. On October 11 the Israelis made another vigorous "reprisal" raid on the Jordan frontier, and Iraq promised her support in case of further attacks. Then in the middle of the month a general election was held in Jordan, in what all agreed was an atmosphere of unusual freedom, and pro-Egyptian and anti-British elements gained a clear-cut victory. From this followed two important results: the formation of a leftist government under Suleiman Nabulsi (who comes into this story at a later date), and the establishment of a joint army command including the forces of Egypt, Syria and Jordan, under an Egyptian commander-in-chief. Israel's policy of merciless reprisal raids in return for the minor infiltrations of the Arabs had not had the desired result of cowing the Arabs, but had genuinely alarmed them—and now the Arabs' counter-measures alarmed the Israelis.

I had planned to be back in Egypt on the twenty-seventh, but my plane was delayed and then another "solidarity strike" in the Arab world left me stranded in Athens until the strike ended at midnight on October twenty-eighth. I caught the first plane that left for Cairo, and arrived at five o'clock on the morning of the twenty-ninth. After a sleepless night I thought I would go to bed for a few hours, and get up around midday to pick up the threads once again. Fortunately, I decided first to wait until an hour when people would

*have reached their offices, and then make a couple of
phone calls, to reassure myself that there was nothing
immediately dangerous in the rumours I had heard in
Athens of an Israeli mobilisation.*

*From the first call I learned that the American
embassy had advised American citizens to leave Egypt
at once—and it was some time before I caught up on
that missing sleep.*

CAIRO, OCTOBER 29

There is no confirmation here of Tel Aviv reports that two
squads of Egyptian fedayeen (commandos) were captured in Israeli territory last night near the Erez settlement northeast of the
Gaza strip. Such reports can be expected (and of course may well
be true) since Israel would be careful to have some pretext for an
attack and so confuse the issue as far as the implementation of
the tripartite agreement is concerned. It is, to say the least of it,
unlikely that Egypt would encourage the activities of the fedayeen
at this juncture, when Egypt's strength on the border is thought
to be below normal and when it looks as though Israel might be
glad of such a pretext. On the other hand the activities of the
fedayeen have before now seemed to run ahead of official authorisation.

Acting in conformity with President Eisenhower's statement
on Sunday about the dangerous situation (the president spoke of
Israel's "heavy mobilisation of its armed forces") the American
embassy in Cairo to-day "urgently advised" American citizens who
had no compelling reasons for staying to leave Egypt. The official
announcement stated that this action was taken on receipt of instructions from the State Department in Washingon and added
that "dependants of American officials and employees will be
evacuated as soon as possible." Some thinning out of non-essential
official staff would also take place.

This advice to American citizens, which is more urgent and
forthright in tone than three similar warnings issued by the
British Embassy during the early stages of the Suez crisis, has taken
Cairo by surprise. The question inevitably asked is whether this
step has been taken purely in reaction to Israel's mobilisation

measures or whether it is also evidence of a new American intention to come into line with the British and French in their approach to the Suez question. The only undisputed conclusion is that since this step, with its inference that war is again a strong possibility in the Middle East, is likely to damage the Republican administration's prospects in next week's election, it can only have been taken reluctantly and after anxious consideration.

Agency messages from Washington, quoting official sources, speak of 150,000 to 200,000 Israeli troops deployed along the Arab borders, which would indeed come close to full mobilisation, though the Israelis, in announcing the mobilisation measures, qualify them as "partial."

Clearly these reports, if true, have the most serious implications on a border in a permanent state of extreme tension. But if the State Department's conclusion is that the Israelis are contemplating a full-scale attack on the Arabs, it is suggested that the more logical reaction would be a stern restatement of the American determination to fulfil its obligations under the Tripartite Pact which binds the United States, Britain, and France to render military assistance to Arabs or Jews if either should be attacked by the other.

Against this must be restated the ever-cogent fact that in an outbreak along this inflammable border it might be impossible to decide which side had been the aggressor—and that in a matter of hours a determined Israeli attack could swallow up that part of mandate Palestine which lies between the present border and the river Jordan and forms the west bank portion of King Hussein's broken-backed kingdom. The Tripartite Pact received only passing, and almost accidental, mention in President Eisenhower's statement yesterday when he said he had given instructions that developments in the Middle East should be discussed with Britain and France "which joined with the United States in the tripartite declaration of May 25, 1950."

American anxiety about Israel's intentions may well be justified, since the present offers what may be Israel's best opportunity for some time to come of swift victory over the Arabs. Not only is Egypt's attention still on her own Suez problem, but both the United States and the Soviet Union have their present preoccupations—the Americans with their election (in which the preservation of peace is so vital a counter to Mr. Eisenhower and the Republicans) and the Russians with events in eastern Europe.

Until these two factors are out of the way—and with the election, at least, that does not leave long—Israel might feel safe to count on a breathing space sufficient to give her a swift victory.

On the evening of October 30 I was sitting in the office of the Arab News Agency, trying to make some sense out of the conflicting accounts that had reached us of the fighting in Sinai, when someone put a slip of paper in front of me. It contained a few lines torn off a Reuter ticker machine. I read them once, and hoped I had misunderstood them. But there was no mistaking the sense of the news flash, which announced that Sir Anthony Eden had told the House of Commons that afternoon of his ultimatum to the Egyptian and Israeli governments. The ultimatum called on both parties to withdraw their forces ten miles from the Suez Canal, and said that Anglo-French forces would occupy Port Said, Ismailia and Suez, if this was not done within twelve hours.

It seemed that our government had taken leave of its senses. Even when every allowance was made for the differences of opinion that had torn the British people apart, even if one could accept the argument that since negotiation seemed impossible the use of force could be justified where something as vital to Britain's security as the canal was concerned—it was still inconceivable that anyone in authority could fail to realise the fatal consequences of an intervention which ranged us on the side of Israel.

CAIRO, OCTOBER 31

After a confused night of partial blackout, sporadic anti-aircraft fire, and scurrying rumours, Cairo this morning looked surprisingly normal.

Rumours, of course, ran thicker than ever—British troops had embarked from Cyprus and were landing at Port Said, the Royal

Navy was off Alexandria, Mr. Eisenhower had managed to hold up the invasion plans, roads were open, then closed—and of the fighting in the Sinai peninsula nothing was known except that the Egyptian authorities claimed to have halted an Israeli attack near Nakhl, roughly midway between the border and the Suez Canal, and to have shot down eight or nine Israeli planes without loss.

The forecourts of the British and American embassies presented an extraordinary sight. In front of the British embassy files were being burned in eight large wire incinerators, and the ashes floated out on the fresh breeze towards the Nile beyond the compound wall. The lawn in front of the American embassy looked like a rallying point for a picnic, with dozens of Embassy secretaries sitting on suitcases or chatting in groups as they waited for transport to take them on the first stage of their evacuation journey.

As yesterday, the plans for evacuation were dependent on a highly uncertain situation as concerns communications in Egypt.

The British embassy, which plans to evacuate the less essential embassy staff by way of Alexandria to-morrow, was uncertain this morning whether a convoy would be allowed over the desert road. It was reported that a Greek ship was in harbour at Alexandria which could take the party (consisting of about seventy or eighty people, or over half of the present embassy staff), and the Egyptian authorities were reported to be ready to grant exit permits without delay at the port. It is not known whether or when further transport will be available after that.

The population of Cairo, which was greatly excited last night by the first air-raid warnings and black-out (no planes were overhead, but it is reported that two made reconnaissance flights over the coast), is calm to-day, but the flying rumours are inevitably creating tension.

The idea which yesterday was no more than a widespread theory, that the Israeli attack had been made in collusion with, if not at the instigation of, the British and French, is to-day universally accepted as fact. Britain's remaining friends here are disillusioned, and her enemies not, as might be expected, bitter or savage, but coldly contemptuous.

Britain, of course, has many enemies, but until to-day she

still had friends as well—but even these cannot stomach France or Israel, the one (in Egyptian eyes) a vengeful ally, and the other a willing tool. The astonishment which last night greeted the news of the British and French ultimatum and which certainly was not confined to Egyptians is expressed in this morning's issue of *El Gumhuria*, where Anwar el Sadat writes: "This man Eden must have completely taken leave of his senses if he ever imagines that Egypt will consent to the landing of British or French troops in the Suez Canal zone."

Two newspaper editors to whom I suggested that whatever they thought of the ultimatum Egypt's best course might have been to accept it, said privately that if Britain alone were concerned it might be possible to consider such a course, but that no Egyptian leader could survive for a minute who accepted such treatment at the hands of France, let alone Israel.

Even to those still willing to credit Britain with some sincerity in her attitude to the Suez crisis, the new Anglo-French approach seems to unite all the most fatal characteristics of every so-called solution proposed in the last three anxious months, through the early gun-boat era of the first London conference, though the phase of the Menzies accept-this-or-else mission, and later the plan to put a guinea-pig ship through the canal to test the power of the Users' Association. Egypt's attitude to-day remains as firm as ever in the face of what is seen here as the most openly aggressive Western initiative of all.

For a few days we remained at liberty, though our usefulness as correspondents had gone, and we could only report the official news of the fighting (in Sinai it was virtually over by November 2) and the Anglo-French air attacks.

CAIRO, NOVEMBER 2

Military censorship is now in force here. Official communiqués from Egyptian military headquarters give no news of land fighting in the Sinai Desert but are restricted to details of British and French bombing raids, which continue night and day.

Anti-aircraft batteries in the Cairo area have been active intermittently throughout the past thirty-six hours. An Egyptian official communiqué yesterday claimed that six British bombers had been shot down in raids on Alexandria and Cairo. Apart from the nine wounded reported yesterday, the communiqués give no news of casualties.

British and French civilians are still at liberty but were advised this morning that they must register with the Egyptian authorities during the next three days. All members of the British embassy staff are still here, though ready to depart. Evacuation arrangements are being negotiated with the Egyptian authorities through the intervention of the Swiss legation.

On November 4 nine British correspondents were detained by the Egyptian authorities, myself among them, and the next day we were transferred to the Semiramis Hotel, where we spent the next eighteen days in a topsy-turvy land of our own, ostensibly guests of the hotel like anyone else, but in fact closely watched by security police (with whom we were soon on the best of terms) and confined for most of the day to our own rooms. We were not allowed to leave the hotel, and were supposed to have no contact with anyone else at all, though the ingenuity and kindness of our American colleagues found ways of circumventing this restriction. The hotel staff, to their credit, made absolutely no distinction between us and the other guests, and when we were allowed to use the bar and the dining room at mealtimes they accorded us the same courteous inefficiency as anyone else. If this helped to accentuate our mental discomfort, that was certainly not their fault.

At dawn on November 5 Anglo-French paratroops landed at Port Said, and our remaining hope—that public opinion in Britain might force the government to abandon its fatal course—was destroyed. Of the events that followed, the battle for Port Said, the diplomatic exchanges between London, Washington and Moscow, and the cease-fire, I knew next to nothing at the time, and they are not within the scope of my purpose here. With the landings, one-half of the British people (for whom the Manchester Guardian *had been a mouthpiece) had lost the battle. All we could do now was to wait until the dust had settled, and then start out to see what could be salvaged from the wreckage of Western hopes in the Arab world.*

From the Semiramis we were able to send cables to our papers, though we had no idea whether they reached their destinations or not. One of these I reproduce here, which did get through, and which mentions three of the factors which were to be of importance in the Middle East during the next phase—the problem of clearing the Suez canal, the cutting of the oil pipelines across Syria, and the formation of the United Nations Emergency Force.

CAIRO, NOVEMBER 16

Just two weeks after the start of Allied bombing raids on Egyptian airfields and ten days after the British and French landings at Port Said, the first party of the United Nations police force arrived in Egypt yesterday. Mr. Hammarskjold arrived in Cairo to-day, after travelling with the second detachment and talked with President Nasser and Dr. Fawzi, the foreign minister, presumably about his object of "tying up loose ends."

There are plenty of these, and they account for Cairo's continuing mood of watchfulness. Military traffic through the city, which was heaviest during the first days of the cease-fire, has diminished, but military precautions are maintained. So is the blackout, and an occasional air-raid alarm still finds Cairo lying dark and still under the growing moon.

The position of British and French nationals in Egypt remains uncertain. Registration with the police and the carrying of special identity cards are now compulsory. There is talk of a further evacuation, and the Swiss legation is negotiating with the Egyptian authorities over this.

Evacuation, which was almost a physical impossibility until a couple of days ago (except by the long overland journeys to Libya or the Sudan) is now feasible again with the reopening of Cairo Airport and the arrival of the first ships in Alexandria harbour since hostilities began. The port authorities have stated that they expect harbour traffic to become normal again within a few days. Permission has also been given to some foreign airlines to resume services to Cairo.

Accommodation for 1,000 men of the United Nations force is being prepared at Abu Suweir, near Ismailia. It is not clear yet on what terms Egypt is prepared to accept their presence, but it is certain that she will resist any suggestion that they or any other foreign forces should remain in the Canal zone once the present confused situation there has been resolved.

It is equally clear that Egypt does not intend to allow any progress to be made towards clearing the canal or the resumption of traffic until the British, French, and Israeli forces are completely evacuated from Egyptian territory. Censorship makes it impossible to determine how much work needs to be done to clear the canal, but one large ship which was attacked by a French plane at its mooring off Ismailia is now known to be sunk where the canal debouches into Lake Timsah. Other sinkings are unconfirmed. The use of explosives on the wrecks is probably impossible owing to the danger of subsidence. Some twenty ships of the last convoy attempting passage are moored, not sunk, in the canal. Their crews are now in Cairo according to the Egyptian authorities.

Press comment here centres on two themes; the solidarity of the Arab world as demonstrated by support for Egypt's defence against the Anglo-French attack, and the almost unanimous world opinion behind Egypt's stand. For the first, its extent was largely as predicted by most commentators here. Promises of support from governments received publicity, and there were practical offensive steps, such as the blowing up of pipelines, by groups of active sympathisers.

The net result, also predicted, was greatly to strengthen the idea of Arab unity, which President Nasser remarked last week had before been mostly words. The Arab heads of state, meeting in Beirut, have for the first time concrete evidence of their power to withstand pressures from the West and will not forget the lesson.

As seen from here, Mr. Hammarskjold's task in "tying up loose ends" will be first to enforce a complete and unconditional withdrawal of all foreign forces; secondly, to arrange the policing of the Israeli border and the return of prisoners captured in Sinai; and, thirdly, to assure the Egyptian government that outside pressure has finally been removed and that work on the canal can begin.

If the United Nations then feels able to attack the problems involved in reaching a complete Middle Eastern settlement, the world can expect to face many weary months of negotiation. If not, the Middle East must be expected to relapse into its habitual state of persistent uneasiness and suspicion—with the difference for Britain that she will have lost her remaining bastions of political and economic influence.

Ten days later our evacuation was arranged, through the good offices of the Swiss legation in Cairo, and I returned to England once more, feeling gloomy and frustrated, but cheered at the last by a leave-taking as unexpected as it was characteristic of Egypt.

LONDON, NOVEMBER 27

The poinsettias were out all over Gezira Island, scarlet flags in the soft November sunshine, when an Egyptian security officer drove me to my home and gave me half an hour to pack my belongings, before leaving Egypt last week. Before I could open the front door Said, the laundryman from across the way, spotted me and came running across to ask how I was. We had not seen each other for three weeks, during which I had been luxuriously interned in the Semiramis Hotel. "How are you?" he asked enthusiastically. "Are you coming back to stay?" Sadly I explained the position, with a nod in the direction of the officer, and said that I should have to leave Egypt next day.

A few moments later, as I was throwing things hastily into a couple of suitcases, people began to drift into my bedroom— Said and his two assistants, a jobbing gardener, small shopkeepers from along the street, the children whose pictures I had once taken and given to them, to their undying delight and local fame—these and their friends and odd passers-by who had heard the news that

the "Ingleezi" was going, and who looked in out of the characteristic Egyptian blend of curiosity and human sympathy. Finally
what could be packed was packed, and the rest distributed, hastily
and often inappropriately, among the bystanders, one of whom
looked doubtingly at a beret, while another lifted his *galabiyeh*
(robe) to test the length of a pair of blue jeans. Willing hands
seized the suitcases, and we all drifted out into the street. Here
there were protracted farewells, since every hand had to be shaken
and the conventional Arabic phrases of well-wishing at least at-
tempted. The security officer was goggle eyed and a shade im-
patient. When we drove off, with forty or fifty people waving
and small boys running alongside the car, he turned to me in
astonishment: "You have so many friends here—and you must
leave the country?"

Behind that scene (which was being duplicated in one form
or another all over Cairo) lay all the futility bred of recent events
in Egypt. It would be absurd to gloss over the resentments which
have sprung from Britain's long connection with the country,
and which are so studiously kept alive by a vindictive minority—
but it would be equally wrong to forget the immense fund of
goodwill accumulated, the lifelines which have been kept open,
through good times and bad, by friendship, and plain dealing
between business associates, as well as by the formal agency of
such organisations as the British Council (whose Cairo reading-
room remained crowded with Egyptians until the day it was
closed). When history, in considering our action at Port Said,
draws up the balance sheet of its results, all this will form an
item—perhaps the largest item—on the debit side. For through
all the vicissitudes of three-quarters of a century, it still remained
true until a month ago that the Englishman, with all his faults
(and these have always been well advertised in Egypt), was in
Egyptian eyes the least imperfect of mortals, whether as administrator, businessman, diplomat, soldier, or friend. There will
be many heavy hearts, as well as much jubilation, at the brusque
ending of the English connection.

The recent ruling that all British subjects must leave Egypt
is only a formalisation of a process which had already started.
When the British government, during the early stages of the

Suez crisis, advised those who had no pressing reasons for staying to leave the country, the Egyptian authorities made it plain that those who did so could not count on being allowed to re-enter Egypt. When British and French forces began their air attacks on Egypt before the landings at Port Said, a number of nationals of both countries were placed under house arrest, and in isolated cases taken to prison. (Most of those imprisoned were later allowed to return to their homes.) After the landings these measures, hitherto arbitrary and erratic, became more systematic, and were extended to the large Jewish community in Egypt, which has always enjoyed a rare degree of toleration, even at the height of the Palestine war.

Now all British, French, and Jewish residents have been ordered to leave Egypt,* and while this will cause material hardship as well as sadness to many Europeans who have spent up to thirty and forty years in the country (and often devoted to it a great deal of unselfish work, especially in the fields of medicine, welfare, and education), the blow will fall most hardly on the non-Europeans. For most of these, who may hold British or French passports (in the case of Jews even those holding Egyptian passports are affected), but whose ancestry may be Maltese, Armenian, or any one of those complicated Levantine blends that are characteristic of the eastern Mediterranean, expulsion means ruin, a sudden step down into the desolate status of permanent refugees. Their lives, their homes, their businesses were in Egypt, where in many cases their families had lived for several generations. Many of the Maltese, for instance, for whose future the British government will now become responsible, have never seen Malta, let alone Britain; some of them can hardly speak English, though they probably have a cloudy command of half a dozen other languages. All these will now have to leave Egypt with whatever they can carry and twenty Egyptian pounds, abandoning behind them shops, savings, furniture, and all the familiar background of a lifetime.

There has been little warning for these unfortunates. Apart

* After various contradictory orders had been given, the Egyptian government only expelled a small minority of the Jewish population of Egypt, though since that time a good many Jews have left Egypt of their own accord.

from the isolated arrests, especially of Jewish persons, which had taken place during the weeks following the British and French intervention in Egypt, the first clear sign of what was in store came in a decree published in the name of the Egyptian president on November 22. This set out the qualifications which must be fulfilled by anyone claiming Egyptian nationality, and among the details of how Egyptian parentage should be established came an important negative clause: "These conditions do not apply either to Zionists, or to those who have been convicted of crimes throwing doubt on their loyalty to the country, or to those convicted of treason." The fact that the word "Zionists" is used, rather that "Jews," suggests that the clause may be brought into operation against people whose Jewish ancestry may be hard to establish but against whom an allegation of disloyalty has been preferred. In this way it represents a looser and more comprehensive threat to anyone who has incurred official, or even private, displeasure. On any interpretation the clause represents a departure from the previously tolerant Egyptian tradition.

Of course there is worse than this, too—the stories of individual ill-treatment (especially of Jews), of physical violence, and of the threat of the concentration camp—none of which I could verify in my genteel internment, but of which accounts reached me in the whispered comments of friends brushed against in the corridors of the hotel, or in conversations overheard in the office of Swissair, where an anxious crowd jostled for places on one of the transport planes which were bringing the United Nations police forces to Egypt. From another angle there is the loss to Britain of assets in Egypt variously estimated at between three and four hundred million pounds sterling in the shape of British businesses taken over by the Egyptians—and taking no account of private property abandoned or sequestrated. All this, with the blocking of the Suez Canal, and the temporary stoppage of our oil imports, involving petrol rationing and an undetermined amount of disruption in our economic life, is part of the price to be paid for recent British policy in Egypt.

For many Egyptians all this will be cause for rejoicing. How could it be otherwise when Egyptian lives have been lost and Egyptian property destroyed in a quarrel in which the Egyptians felt their cause was sound—and saw that almost all the rest of the world thought so, too? Those who had doubts (and there were many) about the wisdom of their own government's policy over Suez can scarcely be expected to retain their detachment after watching British bombers from their Cairo roof tops. Yet, as that visit to my Gezira home showed, the planned retaliation of an angry government should not be mistaken for a people's wrath. Happily the Egyptian is so used to regarding his own government as something only remotely related to himself that he sees the recent British action in Egypt as the work of a government and not of a people. And even his bewilderment and resentment at this betrayal of the standards he had always (however unwillingly) attributed to the British are pale and academic beside the feelings of the British themselves in Egypt. For the great majority of these this is the inglorious end of an era; for them the loss of home and property is sad—but sadder is the loss of moral standing, the knowledge that in a part of the world with which England's destiny has been so closely linked an Englishman cannot now hold up his head without shame. There will be many Egyptians to regret it, too.

PART 3 America Takes Over

When we left Egypt, our passports were stamped with the words "No return," so when I went back to the Middle East a few weeks later, it was in the Lebanon that I made my headquarters.

The Lebanon is half-Christian, half-Moslem, Western by inclination, oriental in undertone, a refuge in the past for the outcasts of a score of neighbouring tyrannies both civil and religious, and to-day—an anxious misfit in the Arab world, struggling to find a safe perch between the upper and the nether millstones of Arab nationalism and the American way of life. Its capital, Beirut, which likes to think of itself as the ville lumière of the Middle East, sparkles like a piece of cheap tinsel on the drab hem of the Arab world.

It was certainly a change from Cairo—and whatever else it might prove to be it was more cheerful.

BEIRUT, JANUARY 1

Sunshine and shadow were chasing each other across the brown and green hills about Beirut; the sea was a deep, smooth blue, and the Middle East presented an unfamiliar smiling face to a traveller whose last experience of it was in Cairo.

"Happy New Year," said a customs official; "it could hardly be worse than the old one," and to the tally of recent events present in both our minds he added floods, the disastrous earthquake of last spring, and a smallpox epidemic. The porter loading my bags into the car a few minutes later added a less conventional but equally genial "Merry Christmas."

I drove into the town past groves of ripening oranges, and beside tamarisks bordering the cliff road where modernistic apartment buildings are extending Beirut's southwestern outskirts, with the feeling that here at least the Englishman still finds a welcome. But, as one Arab warned me: "Don't build too much on those easy smiles. You have made the divisions in the Middle East deeper than ever by what you've done in Egypt. People here don't want to take sides, and so far they have managed not to, but don't think that because the Lebanese would rather cultivate their own gardens they are not affected by what has happened in the Middle East."

Britain's recent showing in the Middle East came near to forcing the Lebanese into a rigid position which they would much rather avoid. But for the moment the crisis is past and there is still "a happy New Year" for all comers.

The new year was only five days old when the idea of the "Eisenhower Doctrine" was presented to the Arab states.* For most of them this provided something of a dilemma.

BEIRUT, JANUARY 6

President Eisenhower's new Doctrine for the defence and rehabilitation of the Middle East has had a mixed reception, in which respect for American sincerity and a willingness to share in any handout are tempered by suspicions of what is loosely called the "new colonialism."

The fact is that Britain and France have driven all Arab governments into a position where support for Egypt's lead is obligatory, and no one wants to be pilloried as a deserter from the Arab cause. But, as always, no one is quite sure what the Arab cause is, and the only certainty is that no immediate or long-term objectives of the Arab countries can be achieved without outside help.

Discussion abroad on whether American or Soviet influence shall fill the power vacuum left by the eclipse of Anglo-French influence leads the Arab nationalists to say that the Arabs must fill it themselves. This they are not in a position to do, and the crucial question for the Middle East remains whose help they can get—and whose they will accept.

* For a summarization of the eventual form of the Eisenhower Doctrine, as embodied in a resolution of Congress, see p. 149.

FORE !

World copyright by arrangement with the Manchester Guardian

The fact that the Suez crisis had reached its climax in a renewal of fighting between Arabs and Israelis underlined the old truism that the Palestine question, still unresolved, remained the principal obstacle to the settlement of the Middle East's problems. But the Arabs, even the most moderate among them, refused in public to acknowledge that the time had come to tackle it.

BEIRUT, JANUARY 6

Dr. Charles Malik, the Lebanese foreign minister, said on Saturday that his government was "in agreement with the sister Arab governments" to defer the raising of the Palestine question at the United Nations. He added: "We believe that the aggression

on Egypt has created a new situation in which it is not possible to
go into any general settlement, and that in view of existing United
Nations resolutions on the subject any new discussions as to the
essence of the matter would be superfluous."

Asked whether this did not suggest an unprofitably negative
attitude to the problem which lies at the heart of all Middle East
discontents, Dr. Malik said this was an illogical deduction, adding:
"We are exceedingly positive in every approach we have to every
problem." The validity of the dictum seems to rest on what is
meant by "positive."

Dr. Malik leaves to-morrow to lead the Lebanese delegation
at the new session of the General Assembly where, he says, the
Lebanon will "strongly insist" on the necessity of Israel fulfilling
the United Nations decisions on a complete and unconditional
withdrawal of Israeli forces behind the armistice lines. On his
way to New York, Dr. Malik will call at Cairo for two days'
talks with President Nasser, and also at Rome, Paris, and London
to discuss "problems of common interest." The talks with President Nasser will complete the round of diplomatic contacts he
has had with all Arab governments with the aim of presenting
a common Arab front at the United Nations.

Pressed again on the subject of Palestine, he said that before
any solution to the problem becomes a practical possibility two
conditions must be fulfilled. First, all parties must comply entirely with United Nations resolutions on the Middle East. Since
November 1 these had been straightforward enough. Then there
must be a "clear and absolute indication on the part of everyone
concerned that there is a real determination to be absolutely just
and impartial in dealing with this issue." If the world is to wait
until this condition is met, there will never be any possibility of
settling the Palestine problem; and until the Palestine problem
is settled there is no hope of stability in the Middle East. If the
Arab governments are truly agreed on wishing to defer again discussion of a settlement with Israel then some other government
must show them where their interest—and the world's—lies.
That government could hardly be British but could be American.

Dr. Malik will carry with him a personal message from
President Chamoun to President Eisenhower expressing Lebanese

appreciation of "the position taken by the United States **and** President Eisenhower in the recent trial through which Egypt and all of us have gone." American stock still stands high in **the** Arab world as a result of her unexpectedly stern attitude to **the** Suez adventure.

The Soviet Union, too, had strengthened its po-sition with the Arabs by championing their cause in the autumn, and by threatening at the time of the attack on Egypt to bombard London and Paris with rockets. While America, with the Eisenhower Doc-trine, was now promising military support and eco-

"WHAT HAPPENED? A COLLISION OR A COLLUSION?"

PETROL PROSPECTS
World copyright by arrangement with the Manchester Guardian

nomic assistance to the Arabs if they felt themselves threatened by communism, the Soviet Union was giving them practical help in countering the effects of Western economic pressure.

With the assurance of Russian help, Syria was gradually asserting her claim to be the most intransi-gent of the Arab states in her defiance of the West.

The Syrian government, by blowing up the pipeline of the Iraq Petroleum Company where it passed through Syrian territory on its way to the Mediterranean, had been the only Arab government to give practical support to Egypt at the time of the Anglo-French attack. This action, combined with the blocking of the Suez Canal by the Egyptians, had practically stopped the supply of Middle Eastern oil to Europe, causing oil rationing in almost every country in Western Europe and a threat of industrial dislocation which was only averted when the American oil companies banded together to fill the gap with supplies from the Western hemisphere.

But the Middle East, too, was dependent on the flow of oil. Saudi Arabia and Iraq stood to lose a large proportion of their national incomes as long as it was interrupted—and now Syria was only saved by Russian help from the consequences of its own action in cutting the pipeline.

BEIRUT, JANUARY 9

It is now officially reported that a Soviet tanker is on the way from Banias, in Syria, to Tripoli, in the Lebanon, with 9,000 tons of crude oil for refining.

But for this Syria would have been facing a complete stoppage of her oil supplies. The refinery at Tripoli from which Syria obtains her refined products was to have ceased operating this week, when, it was expected, the stocks of crude oil would have been exhausted.

It is two months since the cutting of the pipeline in Syria stopped the flow of oil from Iraq to Syria and the Lebanon. But until now there has been enough crude oil in the storage tanks at Tripoli to keep the refinery running. There are still 170,000 tons of crude oil in storage at Banias, where the Iraq Petroleum Company pipeline has the larger of its two Mediterranean outlets. But at Banias there is no refinery, so that the Syrians have to find means of getting the crude oil down the coast to Tripoli to keep the refinery working. Reports that Egypt would lend them a tanker have so far proved insubstantial. But their new-found friends, the Russians, have come to their aid.

> *On the same day Sir Anthony Eden resigned, a tragic victim of events which proved beyond his understanding or control. His passing removed one of the obstacles to a* détente *in the Middle East—but many remained.*

BEIRUT, JANUARY 10

Sir Anthony Eden's resignation is the topic of the day here and throughout the Middle East, but comment is generally

SUNK OFF SUEZ
World copyright by arrangement with the Manchester Guardian

milder and less recriminatory than might have been expected.

Little surprise is shown, and the general assumption is that though the ex-premier's health is involved too, the real reason is the failure of his Suez policy and the need to regain American confidence. One Beirut paper even sees the resignation as a corollary of the Eisenhower Doctrine for the Middle East.

Certainly the resignation will make easier the task of picking up the pieces in the Middle East. It was Sir Anthony who made the Egyptian issue a personal one with his broadcast last August saying that Britain's quarrel was with Nasser, not with Egypt. From that moment Sir Anthony became the embodiment for Egyptians of what they had been taught to believe—that the Western policy was one of repression and exploitation. It seemed inevitable that whatever the outcome of the Suez crisis might be it could not leave both Sir Anthony and Nasser in power.

The present Egyptian line is that only the complete replacement of the British government which launched the attack on Egypt can be the prelude to further negotiations on the canal; but Egypt is in economic straits, and the guarded support of some Arab countries is likely to temper this extremist attitude.

Much depends at present on the future of the Syrian government. Syria is Egypt's one firm support in the policy of keeping the West at arm's length; indeed Syria's rejection of the new Eisenhower approach to the Middle East goes far beyond Egypt's sceptical wait-and-see attitude. Jordan and Iraq have welcomed the American initiative; the Lebanon is always anxious to avoid disputes which are bad for business; and Saudi Arabia's economy is dependent on American goodwill. The weakening of the Syrian Government in its present "neutralist," anti-Western, fellow-travelling policy could cut the ground from under Egypt's feet, for many Arabs have had enough of a crisis which endangers the interests of all for the ends, primarily, of Egypt.

The Israelis, after their victorious campaign in Sinai, had evacuated most of the Egyptian territory they had occupied, the United Nations forces taking over in their wake. But without guarantees that there would be no renewal of Egyptian fedayeen raids on the border, they refused to give up the two critical areas of the Gaza strip (which they claimed had been the fedayeen base) and, in the south, Sharm el Sheikh (which commanded the approaches to the Gulf of Aqaba and the Israeli port of Eilath).

As long as the Israelis defied the United Nations by holding onto these points, the Syrians refused to allow the repair of the oil pipeline and urged the Egyptians not to allow the clearing of the Suez Canal.

Meanwhile the Syrians and Egyptians together set themselves to win the allegiance of those Arab states which still had ties with the West, and in particular of Jordan, whose army was maintained by a subsidy paid by the British government. The new Jordan government of Suleiman Nabulsi was committed to putting an end to the British tie (completing the process that had begun with the expulsion of Glubb Pasha, the Arab Legion's commander, nearly a year earlier). But first Nabulsi had to be sure of replacing the British subsidy, and of the Arab governments who had promised help, only Saudi Arabia could in fact afford it.

BEIRUT, JANUARY 16

The Middle East to-day is in its usual chronic state of confusion and instability with two questions urgently to the fore. Will Egypt, Syria, and Saudi Arabia provide a long-term subsidy to replace the £12 millions a year at present being paid by Britain under the terms of a treaty which the Jordan government is committed to abrogating? And will the Arab states agree on a common policy to pursue if the Israelis refuse to evacuate Sinai and the Gaza strip?

King Hussein of Jordan to-day flew from Amman to visit King Saud to discuss the implications of the new Eisenhower Doctrine for the Middle East and see whether Saudi Arabia is prepared to give more precise expression to the offer of financial aid first made at the Cairo "Big Three" conference last spring. To-morrow King Saud is due in Cairo for talks with President Nasser, where the same agenda is likely, before going on to visit the United States.

Reports in some Beirut papers that King Hussein and the Syrian prime minister, Sabri el Assali, will also go to Cairo seem unfounded, and in spite of the optimism of the Jordan foreign minister, Abdullah Rimawi, who is reported from Cairo as saying yesterday that the talks about financial aid to Jordan have been crowned with success "as far as matters of principle are concerned," few observers here expect the principle to be swiftly translated into economic fact. Egypt and Syria are too near bankruptcy themselves to play convincingly the role of fairy godmother: King Saud is unlikely to want to pay the whole bill himself.

This leaves three possibilities: that the Arab governments will pay the subsidy after themselves borrowing the money (Arab nationalists know that Moscow is ready with "unconditional" aid for its friends); that Jordan may apply for an American subsidy (of course without conditions); or that the British taxpayer may be allowed, in *The Economist's* graphic phrase, to go on buying hate at £12 millions a year. Whichever it chooses, the situation of the Jordan government will remain precarious.

The government was elected in October with a mandate to abrogate the treaty with Britain, and three months' delay has not lessened the Jordanians' desire to end the British connection. Soviet aid would probably finish the Middle East's shakiest monarchy altogether. Substitution of American for British aid would be characterised by nationalist elements as a disguised continuance of the colonial system—and not only in Jordan. A cartoon in to-day's Beirut paper *El Siyassah* shows the Americans wheeling a Trojan horse labelled "Eisenhower Doctrine" into the Middle East stronghold.

The other danger point is Syria, where repair of the oil pipelines sabotaged in November is still held up by the Syrian government's insistence on a full Israeli withdrawal from Sinai and Gaza first. Syria was saved last week from imminent economic breakdown as a result of the oil shortage by the dispatch of a Soviet tanker. This tanker, which left Tripoli in the Lebanon early yesterday morning after unloading its second cargo of crude oil for refining, is under contract to run a shuttle service between the Syrian port of Banias, where crude oil is stored, and the refinery at Tripoli.

If the service is maintained until Syrian stocks are exhausted, it will cover Syria's needs for three months. (Jordan also relies on the Tripoli refinery for its oil products.) Before that the question of the Israeli withdrawal from Gaza and the approaches to the Gulf of Aqaba will have become acute, and Arab delegates to the United Nations are certain to press for complete observance of the Security Council's resolutions in November calling for unconditional withdrawal. Even the Lebanese government, which has firmer ties with the West than other Arab states, is adamant on this point.

Three days later an "Arab Solidarity Pact" was signed in Cairo, by which the governments of Egypt, Syria and Saudi Arabia undertook to pay to Jordan £12.5 millions a year, and it looked as though Jordan had passed into the Egyptian orbit. The Eisenhower Doctrine seemed to have found no takers except little Lebanon (whose defection Egypt could afford to take lightly). But Saudi Arabia's attitude remained equivocal, and King Saud, after signing the agreement in Cairo, set out for Washington as the guest of the American government.

BEIRUT, JANUARY 21

This promises to be a critical week in the Middle East, with the Israeli withdrawal complete except from the Gaza strip and points in southern Sinai controlling access to the Gulf of Aqaba.

Meanwhile, a tug-of-war is going on throughout the Arab world over the attitude to be adopted to the Eisenhower Doctrine for the Middle East. The Doctrine has been denounced by official spokesmen in Syria and by the Egyptian press as implying improper interference in an area which refuses commitments to East or West. In the communiqué announcing Saturday's agreement between Egypt, Syria, Saudi Arabia, and Jordan on the provision of financial aid to the latter to replace the British subsidy, the four governments opposed the Eisenhower Doctrine, though the initial reactions in both Jordan and Saudi Arabia were not unfavourable.

The pact will be ineffective until ratified by the four signatories, but it is almost certain to lead to negotiations for the abrogation of the treaty between Britain and Jordan under which Britain pays Jordan £12 millions a year and maintains three bases

MID-EAST SNACK
World copyright by arrangement with the Manchester Guardian

in Jordan. The renewal of the subsidy would be due in March, and the Jordan government is likely to press its Arab allies for something on account before refusing further British contributions.

The abrogation of the Jordan treaty will leave Iraq more isolated than ever as the only Arab state whose defence plans involve commitments to and by Britain.

The "Arab Solidarity Pact," as it is styled, was described by Cairo Radio, quoting the Syrian premier, as a slap in the face for the imperialists. But if it assures Jordan's solvency while saving the British Exchequer £12 millions a year, this will be a false judgment. The treaty with Jordan, whose aim was the buttressing of King Hussein's uncertain little kingdom, lost after the Suez adventure what little value it retained for Britain. British bases in Jordan were useless, indeed almost besieged during the critical days of November, while the British subsidy only bought the ill-will of the Jordanian people.

The ending of the treaty will remove one encumbrance to British Middle East policy, which certainly needs all the help it can get these days. For Jordan the results of abrogation might be less satisfactory. If and when the Arab Solidarity Pact is ratified, Jordan's finances will be less secure than they were under the British guarantee; and the ending of the treaty means that Britain will no longer be committed to the support of Jordan against an Israeli attack. Egypt's showing in the Sinai campaign is unlikely to commend her in Jordanian eyes as an equally valuable protector.

Unfortunately the fact that Britain appeared to the Arab world to support the Israeli attack makes these arguments academic, and whatever the Jordanian leaders feel in their hearts about the wisdom of putting themselves in the hands of President Nasser, the pressure of public opinion in favour of ending the British connection is likely to be decisive.

The Eisenhower Doctrine could provide a way out of this difficulty, and King Saud, who has left Cairo on the next stage of his journey to Washington, is likely to discuss the problem with the American president and Mr. Dulles. The main subjects under discussion during King Saud's visit will be the tenure of the American base at Dhahran and a settlement of the Suez Canal question, which is of acute interest to King Saud because the present blockage cuts into his oil royalties.

But if King Saud, who is believed to be favourably disposed to the Eisenhower Doctrine, can get the Americans to underwrite an "Arab Solidarity Pact," Jordan's anxieties may be allayed while the façade of Arab solidarity is preserved. For America the problem is one of timing and method, for Britain's Suez adventure has heightened the old suspicions and complicated policy-making for Britain and her friends.

Talk of "filling a power vacuum" has not helped, for Arabs, though aware that a vacuum exists, prefer not to recognise it—or their own inability to fill it. In the Lebanon, which is only technically an Arab state, the facts are seen more clearly than elsewhere in the Middle East, and the newspaper *El Amal* writes that for the moment the Arabs "are content to fill the vacuum with resounding speeches, patriotic songs on the radio, and newspaper articles." But it says that what they have to face is not a balancing game but a choice of civilisations. Remarking that one civilisation respects the individual while the other mistrusts him, the newspaper asks in which one Egypt wishes to live.

King Saud and his backward autocracy would seem an odd vehicle for the furtherance of trans-Atlantic democratic ideals in the Middle East—but apart from the Lebanon (whose far-seeing foreign minister, Dr. Malik, is in New York now) and Iraq (whose crown prince, Abdul Illah, follows King Saud to Washington) Saudi Arabia has the strongest reasons for co-operating with the Americans since her oil industry, under American management, provides almost her entire national income. And King Saud's regime has for the moment the advantages of being unassailably Arab and relatively secure.

For the moment Jordan seemed to be the centre of interest, and remembering the riots that had taken place in Amman a year earlier when an attempt was made to bring Jordan into the Bagdad Pact, I flew down there towards the end of January to see how the signing of the Arab Solidarity Pact had been received.

AMMAN, JANUARY 27

"Welcome to the rock-throwing capital of the world." That was my welcome when I visited Amman last spring, soon after the dismissal of Glubb Pasha. It was in my mind when I drove last week into this stormy little capital less than a week after the

signing in Cairo of the Arab Solidarity Pact (which coincided
with the public hanging here of a man convicted of spying for
Israel).

The Solidarity Pact's chief aim was to pave the way for the
termination ("abrogation" is not considered a nice word, I was
discreetly reminded) of Jordan's treaty with Britain, by which
Britain provides an annual subsidy of £12 millions and maintains
three military bases on Jordanian territory. The signature of the
Arab Solidarity Pact was greeted in Cairo and Damascus as a
slap in the face for Britain, and it seemed reasonable to expect
rocks to fly in Amman. On the contrary, though most Jordan
papers rightly saw the Cairo agreement as an important step
towards giving reality to Arab unity—which for once appears in
a positive light, shouldering new responsibilities instead of merely
advertising old animosities—both the government and the people
of Jordan appear to take a sober view of the new step.

It is undoubtedly welcome, because Jordan has come to feel
deeply her dependence on Britain and to resent the continuance
of a treaty relationship which, however theoretical it has become
as the result of recent developments in the Middle East, still bears
the stigma of imperialist domination. But once the Arab Solidarity Pact was signed, instead of brusquely denouncing the
treaty with Britain as might have been expected, the Jordan
government quietly set in train negotiations for its termination,
and statements in both Amman and Whitehall on the subject
have made graceful reference to the long and warm relationship
between Jordan and Britain.

It is a relationship whose advantages for both sides are
easily forgotten to-day when the structure of British policy in
the Middle East lies in ruins, and when Jordan is ardently pursuing the path of Arab nationalism, but it is one which in more
tranquil retrospect will be seen to have served its purpose both
in the development of this uneasy little kingdom and in the
preservation of peace in the Middle East.

It has been officially announced that negotiations for the
termination of the Anglo-Jordan treaty will take place next
month, and since both sides appear eager for a divorce there

seems no reason to expect delay. For Britain the termination will mean the saving of £12 millions a year, a relief from the need to maintain three costly and useless bases in Jordan, and the elimination of one more advantageous position for sniping by the "anti-colonial" propagandists.

It is bound also to leave a lingering doubt about the security of Jordan, which, of course, is primarily something for the Jordan government to worry about, but which is also of concern to any power interested in the wider security of the Middle East. The Jordan government appears to be satisfied that the promises by Egypt, Syria, and Saudi Arabia of aid to replace the British subsidy will be redeemed.

But Syria is bankrupt, Egypt survives chiefly because the needs of her poverty-stricken peasants are so elementally slight, and the Saudi Arabian king is known to be liberally overdrawn on the massive oil revenues which provide the bulk of his country's income. Of course, an income of close on a million dollars a day gives a man a certain standing with his banker, but still King Saud's reluctance to follow the Iraqi example, by devoting a larger proportion of his oil revenues to productive schemes, raises doubts about his qualifications to act as the senior partner in the new Arab banking firm to which Jordan proposes to entrust its affairs.

Realism has never been a strong point of the Arabs. One of their most percipient critics, himself an Arab, has remarked: "It is a characteristic of the Arab mind to be swayed more by words than by ideas, and more by ideas than by facts." * This was never brought home to me more sharply than in Jordan, where I found an astonishing, and, it seemed wilful, ignorance about a number of topics of very pressing interest to the Jordanians themselves. But even though they overrated the value (in a purely military sense) of the Egyptians as allies, and refused to admit that Russian policy might have any but the most unselfish

* Atiyah, Edward, *The Arabs*, Pelican Books, 1955.

*aims, they failed to hide altogether their doubts about
the future of Jordan once British support was withdrawn. And they had committed themselves to insisting that it should be withdrawn.*

AMMAN, JANUARY 28

Negotiations for the termination of the 1948 treaty between
Britain and Jordan are expected to begin here within two weeks.
In informal conversations it is impossible to miss the undertone
of anxiety over the effects of this step on Jordan's political and
economic future, but official spokesmen are unanimous in expressing their confidence that the severance of the British connection will leave Jordan's security unimpaired.

For the moment the press and public opinion are more
concerned with the debate in the United Nations about Mr.
Hammarskjold's report on the Israeli withdrawal. Jordanian
newspapers stand unreservedly by the Egyptian thesis that the
United Nations has no right to discuss safeguards for Israeli
interests in Gaza or the Gulf of Aqaba until the Israelis have
retreated from every foot of the territory they occupied in
November. The newspaper *El Difaa* yesterday called on the
United Nations to impose economic sanctions on Israel if she
refused to withdraw, and to-day it observes that "Israel would
not be in a position to defy the United Nations resolutions unless
she were supported by some nations in the world."

In fact, the West, and Britain in particular, is held responsible
for Israel's attitude for two reasons: first, because Britain is considered the chief architect of the Jewish state, from the creation
of which the Arabs date their present discontents; and secondly,
because Britain's intervention in Egypt in November is taken as
proof of the old-established Arab theory that Western imperialists
created and maintained Israel as a hostile base in the heart of
the Arab homeland.

Most Jordanians are unaware of Egypt's poor showing in the
Sinai campaign, and those aware of it are unwilling to admit it.
The danger of this blindness lies in the fact that, just as the
Arabs' defeat in 1948 was disguised and is still explained here
as the result of machinations by the British leaders of the Arab

Legion, so now there are Arab voices which say "if the United
Nations will not compel the Israelis to withdraw the Arabs must
attempt it." For the moment the Egyptians are unlikely to wish
to take Israel on again, but the legend of Egypt's heroic campaign
in the face of an Anglo-Franco-Israeli conspiracy has lent a false
and dangerous bravura to extreme elements among Arab nationalists.

In the dispute over the Israeli withdrawal the opposing
arguments are on two separate planes. On the legalistic plane
Mr. Hammarskjold, like the censor of a gangster film, must
clearly show (and be seen to show) that crime does not pay.
This argument makes a strong appeal to the Arabs, who have
recently come to view the United Nations as a possibly subversive
but potentially useful branch of the Egyptian Ministry of Foreign
Affairs.

The other plane is the less elevated one of practical politics,
on which Israel has to try to defend herself (and the peace of the
Middle East) against the renewal of the Arab blockade and the
threat of fedayeen attacks. So far no one has suggested a way
of bringing these disparate arguments into focus.

America might have had the best chance of putting forward
a workable solution, for since her condemnation of the Anglo-
French attack on Egypt she has gained much credit with the
Arabs. But the Eisenhower Doctrine, with its insistence on the
danger of overt Communist aggression as the principal threat to
the Middle East, makes little appeal to Arabs, who refuse to
believe in this danger.

"We are Moslems and communism is contrary to our re-
ligion," they tell you, or else "We know we need help, but we
will never accept foreign influence again." And it is a waste of
breath to remind them that you don't need to ask for Communist domination to get it.

To the Arabs, Israel is the danger, and, because they identify
Western policy with support for Israel, they will remain fundamentally hostile to the West until the Israeli problem is settled
or the moon turns blue.

Only a few Arabs recognise that Russia has fish of her own
to fry in the Middle East. To most, Russia is a disinterested

friend who has gained credit for supplying arms which the West refused, at a time when Britain especially was identified with opposition to Arab interests. Russia's services to Israel are forgotten or ignored by those who should know better.

A government official here asked me yesterday who was the third power to recognise the state of Israel when it was proclaimed. "The third?" I asked puzzled. "I suppose it was Britain."

"Right," he said triumphantly, with the air of a man playing an ace.

"You remember who was the second?" I gently asked. But he thought the question irrelevant and I am not sure he believed me when I said that it was the Soviet Union.

> *With every crisis that overtakes the world one or two unfamiliar names emerge, to become for a moment household words and flicker with an uncertain distinction, until they sink back into the obscurity of the gazetteer. One such that emerged from the Suez crisis was Aqaba, a desolate seaport on the fringe of Arabia, which now found itself a meeting place for two cross-currents of international argument. And when the eyes of the world, after a good deal of preliminary searching, came to focus themselves on Aqaba, they found that, to complicate matters further, Aqaba was occupied by a British garrison.*

AQABA, FEBRUARY 3

At this remote outpost in the rocky Arabian Desert the frontiers of four countries meet by the headwaters of the narrow Gulf of Aqaba. Purple hills border the gulf on two sides—the eastern in Saudi Arabia and the western in Egypt. Between them the gap is just wide enough to admit the narrow tongues of Jordan and Israel to lick at the sea.

At present two main currents are agitating the political waters of the Middle East, both affecting Aqaba. The first is Israel's refusal to evacuate Gaza and positions dominating the entrance to the Gulf of Aqaba until, among other things, she obtains guarantees of free access to Eilath, from which in the past

Egypt has barred ships approaching from the Red Sea. The second is the pressure exerted on Jordan by her Arab allies to end her treaty relations with Britain and obtain the evacuation of British forces from Aqaba and Mafraq. Negotiations to this end are to begin to-morrow in Amman, but meanwhile the British are here under the terms of the 1948 treaty with the object of safeguarding the Jordan frontier. And in the present state of tension in the Middle East their presence is a stabilising factor.

The force at Aqaba consists of an armoured regiment, the 10th Hussars, with auxiliary forces and headquarters staff—in all about 1,700 men with forty-eight tanks. (One squadron is at Maan, some sixty miles north near the railhead of the old Hijaz railway.) Conditions here have eased slightly since November, when Jordanian hostility over Britain's intervention in Egypt virtually sealed off Aqaba from the outside world. Since then hardly any of the British garrison have been out of Aqaba except on military exercises into the desert hinterland, but sorties are now being arranged once more to near-by Petra, the "rose-red city" carved in a rocky depression south of the Dead Sea. Jordanians meeting British troops are less likely than they were a month ago to spit or throw rocks at their vehicles.

I flew down from Amman, an hour and a half southward over Jordan's desert. A strong south wind funnelled up the gulf and drove waves up the beach, scattering sand over everything—tents, equipment, stores, bedding, and workshops. Next morning it was raining, a noteworthy event in Aqaba, clouds rolling up at dawn over Sinai, raining on Eilath during breakfast, on Aqaba half an hour later, and by nine o'clock (with perfect impartiality) on the Saudi Arabian coast as well.

The British soldiers grinned at my discomfiture both in the driving sand and the mud which followed the rain. "It's summer that's fun here," they said, "when the winds from the north are blowing out of the desert and the temperature doesn't fall below a hundred for weeks on end. Then with hostile tribes all round you and perhaps one ship a month coming up the gulf from the Red Sea, you really know you've come to the end of the world."

Aqaba's lifeline now is the R.A.F., which flies in mail and replacements three times a week. From Middle East Land Forces

Headquarters in Cyprus it is less than three-hundred miles to
Aqaba—but now, thanks to Syrian intransigence, planes must fly
well over a thousand miles by way of Turkey, Iraq, and Jordan to
reach this lonely outpost.

In these circumstances, and against all reason, those who
know the British soldier would expect his spirits to be high—and
they would be right. Living in tents and without their families
(who were evacuated in the Suez crisis and have not been allowed
to return), with the beach and one tiny cinema as the only dis-
tractions, with nature as hostile as surrounding mankind (though
there is a mite of compensation in the colours that paint the
evening hills), they grumble richly but seldom complain. For this
all credit is due to the commander of the Aqaba garrison and his
officers, who appear gladly to accept their challenging situation
and who, after exacting days, dress for dinner with urbane equa-
nimity as if they were going to spend the evening in Pall Mall.

But once this week's negotiations have made the British
evacuation of Aqaba a certainty—and both sides seem set on the
swiftest dissolution of their union—a long and difficult period
must elapse before the evacuation can be completed. Aqaba is
Britain's last land base in Arabia, except for those on the fringes
along the Persian Gulf and in the Aden Protectorate and the
Aden Colony. Here are equipment, stores, workshops, ammu-
nition, and spares to the tune of £4 or £5 millions, whose disposal
will be arranged presumably during the forthcoming negotiations.
Jordan would certainly like them but equally certainly could not
pay for them.

The bulk of the equipment of Aqaba could and should be removed by sea, though loading facilities here are poor and once the
hot weather starts in May work is virtually impossible after
11:00 A.M. That the need for this evacuation comes as a surprise
to the British is shown by the fact that married quarters were
only completed a few months ago (just before their occupants-ap-
parent were evacuated from Aqaba), and that an electronic organ
for the church, which was ordered in the now-remote past from
England, arrived round the Cape last month and was duly if in-
congruously installed last week.

Meanwhile, across on the opposite hillside, Eilath is growing apace, each week seeing more foundations laid for workers' houses and progress on what looks from here like an hotel or hospital and waterfront buildings. There is every evidence that Israel means to make something of Eilath and will insist on ensuring free access to it through a channel eighty miles from here down the Gulf of Aqaba.

The future of Aqaba is, of course, affected by that of Eilath, and there is a strong impression here that the withdrawal of the British will mean its eventual absorption either by Israel or by Saudi Arabia, which claims it as rightfully hers. The border between Jordan and Saudi Arabia is undemarcated and local Arabs come and go freely, so that to them it would not make much difference. But Aqaba is Jordan's only outlet to the sea.

A story which I brought down from Amman (where it was told me with every evidence of sincerity by an officer in the Jordan army headquarters), that British troops here are accustomed to visit an Eilath night club on Saturday nights, has had an immediate success with the British garrison, for whom new jokes are rare. The single strand of barbed wire which marks the border on the beach is not a formidable obstacle, but two British soldiers who ventured across against the strictest orders last year were manhandled by the Israelis and court-martialled by the British on their return.

Any information here on what's going on in Eilath comes from an observation post where a British sentry with field glasses watches the border—a border which Jordan will be hard put to it to defend once the present British garrison is withdrawn.

Aqaba's isolation was graphically demonstrated to me by a storm which raged for several days and which cut us off completely from the outside world. This delayed my return to Amman, and by the time I got there the negotiations to end the Anglo-Jordanian treaty were under way. The long summer of British influence in Jordan was ending; ahead, the winter looked bleak.

AMMAN, FEBRUARY 9

In the summer of 1955 it still looked as though Jordan represented one of the surest supports for British policy in the Middle
East. Yet within eighteen months events have moved so fast that
now negotiations are in progress to dissolve a union that goes back
to the days of the Arab revolt in the desert. Of the British bases
in Jordan, one (the airfield at Amman) has already been abandoned, while the other two are only maintained in an isolation so
complete that at times it has come near to being a state of siege.

What finally destroyed Britain's position in Jordan was our
apparent alliance with the Israelis against Egypt. This important
fact is still imperfectly understood. It was not the attack on Egypt
that lost Britain her last supporters in Jordan but the taint of collusion with Israel. For Jordan the existence and the ambitions of
Israel have a significance more urgent than for any other Arab
state. After the Palestine fighting of 1948-49, Abdullah's little,
paternal, desert emirate of Transjordan was suddenly transformed
into the kingdom of Jordan, a broken-backed creature of circum-
stance and dynastic rivalries, its natural outlet to the Mediterranean blocked, its frontier marching with that of Israel for 350
uneasy miles. To its population of less than half a million mainly
Bedouin Arabs were suddenly added twice that number of Palestinians, most of them more sophisticated (both socially and politically) than the original Transjordanians, and all of them burning with the desire for revenge against Israel. The murder of King
Abdullah in July, 1951, marked the unhappy coming-of-age of the
Hashemite kingdom.

Economically, Jordan has made slow but appreciable progress
since the east and west banks were thrown into their uneasy union.
Light industries have been developed, the export of phosphates
increased, agricultural production improved and expanded. Until
the Suez crisis, tourism was playing a significant part in redressing
Jordan's chronic imbalance of payments. But to-day the shops and
hotels of Jerusalem are empty, the guides and taxi-drivers and
tourist agents are idle—and the same blight of anxious inactivity
hangs over every kind of commercial enterprise in the country.
Investment, whether foreign or domestic, has been discouraged by
political uncertainty, and those responsible for development plan-

ning in Jordan now see the country's future as depending more than ever on outside sources of aid such as the Point Four organisation and the continuance of Britain's development loans.

Such considerations explain the hesitant attitude of the Jordan government towards the Eisenhower Doctrine for the Middle East. Torn between its loyalty to Arab nationalism and its need for all the help it can get from abroad, the government in Amman has resisted the urge to echo the denunciations of Cairo and Damascus, and has asked for a greatly increased allocation of Point Four aid. In the expectation of this and other Western assistance, public and private development plans are going forward for a deep-water harbour at Aqaba (Jordan's only outlet to the sea), an all-weather road to link Aqaba with Amman, and an oil refinery at Zerqa (at present Jordan, which has no oil of its own, depends for its refined products on the Lebanese refineries and so on the goodwill of Syria, through whose territory they must come). And the largest development project of all, as well as the most remote in the present political circumstances, is the Yarmuk valley irrigation scheme, which again depends on the co-operation of the Syrians.

In the circumstances it would not be surprising to find in Jordan to-day many misgivings about the wisdom of severing the country's connection with Britain, who has given Jordan what economic assurance it has known since the war. In truth, one finds few such misgivings (and then expressed only privately and with reluctance), and the reason perhaps lies in the fact that Jordan has never yet had to stand on its own feet, and that its people have in consequence a capacity, rare even in the Arab world, for confusing hopes with facts. To the outsider who likes to think his view is unclouded by nationalist polemics or outdated talk of "exploitation," the effects on Jordan's future of the termination of the treaty with Britain look more serious.

The most obvious danger appears to be that, without the British guarantee of military assistance and without the British land and air forces at present stationed on her territory, Jordan will be in a much worse position to defend herself against an attack from Israel. (To this the Jordanians' answer—and in view of our intervention in Egypt is not a surprising one—is that they no

longer believe in our willingness to help them against Israel.)
Whether the alliance and the financial assistance of the other
Arab countries will be able to maintain the Jordan army on its
present high standard remains to be seen; but it is certain that the
army will have to accept reductions in pay, since at present its
soldiers receive appreciably more than those of its new paymasters
—and are noticeably smarter and more efficient. In the economic
sphere, apart from the question of the continuance of the British
development loans (which is not governed by the treaty), Jordan
will no longer be able to call on grants-in-aid from Britain, which
in the past have always helped to balance the budget of Jordan,
and Transjordan before it. In addition it will lose several "invisible" assets which resulted from the British connection.

Behind and encompassing these dangers is a larger and a less
tangible one—the danger that in breaking away from Britain Jordan will become a prey to the rivalries of its neighbours. The
original Transjordan was an artificial creation, but the Transjordanians slowly learned to nurse their loyalty to their Hashemite
ruler. The addition of the west bank areas in 1949 brought under
the Jordanian crown twice as many Palestinians, who owed no
natural loyalty to Abdullah or to his grandson, the present King
Hussein. Saudi Arabia in the south nurses an old claim to the
territory around Aqaba (where a British armoured regiment is now
stationed) and as far north as Maan. In the north, the frontier
between Jordan and Syria is a purely arbitrary one, and the Syrians,
by occupying the northeastern arm of Jordan, could link up with
Saudi Arabia and complete the isolation of Iraq (incidentally
gaining control of the Iraq Petroleum Company's now inoperative
pipeline through Jordan to Haifa). And in any partition of Jordan, of course, the Israelis would be eager to swallow up the area
of old Palestine on the west bank of the Jordan.

To any such arguments, the answers in Amman to-day are
that Jordan prefers to trust herself to her sister Arab countries,
rather than continue in disguised colonial dependence on Britain,
and that there is no danger, internal or external, which has such
immediacy for the Arab peoples as that of Israel—against whom
Britain's alliance no longer offers any assurance of protection. To
the West these seem unrealistic answers, and for Jordan they may

prove fatally so. But that they should also be natural and even inevitable answers is something for which the West must share the responsibility.

At this point I left Jordan, with the feeling (so soon to be borne out) that it would not be long before I was back. An application I had made earlier for an Egyptian visa had been granted, and a few days later I was on my way south once more, in some excitement.

I was excited because Egypt was still the focal point of the Middle East, and because events elsewhere in the Arab world (in Jordan, for instance) were largely conditioned by what had been happening in Egypt. And since the ill-fated intervention at Port Said, Egypt had been hidden from British eyes by a curtain of suspicion and uncertainty. I was eager to look behind that curtain and try to find answers to a dozen questions that hung in the air, and that were important if one was to understand the new pattern that was unfolding in the Middle East. Had the mood of triumph persisted after the withdrawal of the British and French forces (but not, as yet, the Israelis)? Had President Nasser's position been strengthened by what had happened in October and November? What of the rumours that circulated constantly in Beirut, of plots against his regime? What progress had been made with the clearing of the Suez Canal? And, more personally, what would be the attitude of the Egyptians towards a returning Englishman three months after those nightmarish days when British bombers were over Cairo and British paratroops were fighting in Port Said?

This last question was soon answered.

CAIRO, FEBRUARY 13

Below the aircraft the Mediterranean coastline of Egypt appeared as a vague line of sandbars between saltflats and the open sea. The saltflats gave place to the neat green fields of the delta, then as we flew south the delta narrowed and desert appeared on either horizon until we dropped down on Cairo Airport and I stepped out into the warm February sunshine. My British passport caused a flutter of interest, and I was politely ushered aside and entertained with tea and desultory conversation while my visa was checked and my entry to Egypt authorised. By the time this was done the other passengers had gone off in a bus and I was put into a creaking Cairo taxi to drive in past El Maza aerodrome, which, when I last saw it in November, was littered with wrecks of Egyptian aircraft destroyed by British bombers.

For a time we drove in silence; then I made some conversational opening in scratchy Arabic. A pause, then "Are you French?" asked the driver. "English," I replied, and with an Egyptian's automatic sense of hospitality he said *"Kwaiyis"*—good. Then a thought struck him and I watched his mind working as he wondered whether he ought to take the word back. Instead he turned, stared at me over his shoulder, and a slow grin stirred the three days' stubble on his cheeks. *"Maalesh,"* he said, with a generous wave of his hand, "Never mind." It was a declaration of peace.

Cairo is a strange place for an Englishman to-day, strangest perhaps because it is not unfriendly. The taxi driver's spontaneous reaction was a characteristic one among poorer Egyptians, while in more sophisticated quarters the events of the last three months have caused sadness as well as resentment, but seem to have left little rancour. To almost everyone it seems that the sight of a returning Englishman is welcome, if only as a reassuring indication that the worst is past.

For Egyptians have been afraid, and still are, though they are not sure what it is they are afraid of. Last November Egypt found herself in the front line alone for the first time. (In the Palestine fighting of 1948 she had "allies" with whom to share the credit or blame for the undertaking—and the British garrison in the Canal zone to counter any threats to Egypt's territory). It was an unnerving experience, but when they found they had come through it and heard the plaudits of the Arab world ringing in their ears and saw that for once opinion in the wider world beyond was on their side, Egyptians felt they had triumphed. Since then disillu-

sionment has set in, as the world's sympathy, though finding
formal expression in the United Nations repeated resolutions, has
proved powerless to obtain the withdrawal of the Israelis from key
points on Egyptian territory.

Outwardly things have changed little in Cairo since October.
Traffic flows as thickly as ever (there is no petrol rationing here)
and with the same desperate urgency. Hotel standards and prices
remain unchanged, though in food shops imported goods are 20 to
50 per cent more expensive. The bazaars are quiet but not dead,
with the Germans and the Americans keeping the wolf from the
door. And for the great majority of Egyptians, whose horizons for
better or worse exclude the world the tourist sees, and whose lives
revolve around the simplest of homes and work at four or five
shillings a day—for them there is hardly any difference at all.

The newspapers are full of reassuring pronouncements that
there is no shortage of drugs, that kerosene is plentiful (which is
true), that "Egyptianisation" of business concerns can only
strengthen the country's economy. But these only encourage a
vague malaise which is prevalent all through Cairo and which has
its origin in an accumulation of disheartening details: in the dearth
of tourists from whom so many Egyptians indirectly benefited; in
the sudden appearance of air-raid shelters in central Cairo; in the
blue paint which is still flaking from most car headlamps and
which recalls the dark days of last November. The legend of
Egypt's brave stand was tarnished by the stories of soldiers returning from Sinai, and even Port Said's hour of glory has faded
amid the counter-claims of the propagandists. The press, officially
uncensored, tells Egyptians of the country's unity and strength—
but makes no mention of the rumours which circulate unceasingly
of plots against the regime, or of the continuing exodus of foreigners, whose part in Egyptian economic life has been a vital one
but who see no future for themselves in a country whose nationalism has gone to extremes. The result is an atmosphere where
everyone fancies that his telephone is tapped—which is perhaps
more important than whether it is really tapped or not.

Amid all this a handful of British subjects remain in Cairo
who were unaccountably left out of the general expulsion order or

else successfully resisted it. Their businesses are sequestrated and
their telephones disconnected, but otherwise they lead normal
lives, have suffered no victimisation, and speak with feeling of the
loyalty of Egyptian servants who have stayed with them. The
Swiss flag flies over the Chancery building of the British embassy,
whose grass is now green again (when last I saw it it was ankle
deep in the ashes of burning files), and here a special staff from
the Swiss legation handles the interests of the remaining British
subjects in Egypt. The embassy flower-beds are well trimmed and
beyond the garden wall the Nile flows by just as it did in Cromer's
day, until watching it you forget for a moment that an era has
ended, and a special relationship, and that whatever replaces them
will be very different.

Looking elsewhere in Cairo you see one aspect of this in the
way other interests are filling the economic and commercial
"vacuum" left by the sequestration or withdrawal of British businesses. Hotels are full of Germans preparing for a mammoth trade
fair in Cairo next month. A troupe of Russian dancers at the
opera house are rapturously (and deservedly) applauded, and there
are Russian books and magazines on sale everywhere and a Russian
film festival at a Cairo cinema—but to the Egyptian on the street
corner, who has never seen flesh-and-blood Russians, they are no
better than the rest, even if it did look for a time as though they
meant to help the Arabs against "the Anglo-Franco-Israeli conspiracy."

Now it is only Israel that counts, and the Egyptians, who for
a rare space of time after the invasion felt they could count on the
world's support, find themselves back in the familiar position of
being outmanoeuvred by the Israelis. One thing that has not
changed is the implacable hatred of Israel and all its works, and if
the returning Englishman's reception in Cairo is less frigid than
might be expected, it is partly because Israel's defiance of the
United Nations order to withdraw has underlined the fact that
Britain obeyed when world opinion turned thumbs down on the
November invasion. More than that it is hard to explain, except
by the thesis that in their long and stormy association there has
been much hostility between Britain and Egypt but more than a

little understanding, too. Whatever the reason, not all of Britain's standing has been lost as far as Egypt is concerned, and in Cairo to-day it does not seem fanciful to suggest that an intelligent approach from our side to problems which now divide the two countries might meet with an unexpected response from the Egyptians.

> *The question of the day was when—and whether —the Israelis would withdraw from the Gaza strip and the approaches to the Gulf of Aqaba. The Egyptians felt that it lay within the power of the American government to force the Israelis to withdraw, and when the American government failed to do so, its stock— which had stood so high with the Arabs as a result of America's opposition to the Anglo-French intervention in the autumn—fell rapidly.*

CAIRO, FEBRUARY 15

Mr. Dulles is in trouble with the Egyptian press, which unanimously condemns his reported attempts to bargain for an Israeli withdrawal from Gaza and the Gulf of Aqaba.

No official version of the proposals he is supposed to have made to the Israeli ambassador in Washington has been published here yet, but editorial comments characterise the proposals (in *El Gumhuria*) as "a flagrant violation of the principles of international law as well as of all accepted moral and equitable rules." The Russians do little better with their draft plan for the Middle East, which prompted *El Qahirah* to say: "It is really strange that both East and West should draw up schemes acceptable or otherwise about the Middle East behind the backs of the peoples of the region."

The Egyptian attitude, that a complete Israeli withdrawal must precede any discussion of the future status of Gaza or safeguards for freedom of navigation in the Gulf of Aqaba, shows no sign of relaxation. The director-general of the Egyptian Information Service last night issued a statement relating these questions to the central and abiding Arab grievance—the United Nations failure to enforce its recommendations regarding the rights of the

Palestine refugees. Part of the statement read: "The question of the passage of Israeli ships in Arab or Egyptian territorial waters is really part of the Palestine problem and not of the recent aggression against Egypt, and before asking that her ships be granted passage through Egyptian territorial waters, Israel should first implement the United Nations' resolutions on the rights of the Arabs of Palestine."

The fact is that the Arabs, who for the first time in the long and sordid history of the Arab-Israeli dispute have felt the world's sympathy behind them during recent months, now see that sympathy deserting them—the present American attitude, in particular, is a crushing disappointment—and the triumph they thought was in their grasp when world opinion forced the abandonment of last November's attack now appears to be fading into the familiar bitterness of defeat.

In the circumstances desperate remedies are proposed, though they are unlikely to be adopted. An article in *El Akhbar* lists three possible courses for the United Nations. The first is the imposition of sanctions against Israel and the second her expulsion from the United Nations. But since both are unlikely to receive sufficient support, the Arabs should insist on the third, which is that the United Nations "should give Egypt carte blanche to drive out the aggressor, in which case Egypt would not strike alone since all the Arab countries which share her point of view would join her."

The writer concludes by saying: "I have told the Arabs before to make war. I repeat it to-day with the same emphasis—take arms and fall on them." In view of Egypt's present military situation in relation to Israel, such rodomontades may seem laugable (though a Jordan government spokesman declared himself in similar terms a few days ago), but that they arouse no laughter here nor any official rebuke is an indication of the mood of dangerous unrealism which still pervades the Arab world.

The American State Department was evidently optimistic about the attitude and influence of King Saud, who had just visited President Eisenhower and had expressed in Washington a guarded approval of the Eisenhower Doctrine.

CAIRO, FEBRUARY 17

King Saud, who on his way back from Washington is visiting Spain, Morocco, and Libya, is expected here at the end of the week for a meeting with President Nasser, President Kuwatly and King Hussein. This meeting may be decisive in setting a new tone for relations between the United States and the Arab world, for, while Egyptian comment on American policy shows a growing cynicism, King Saud is thought to be taking a more generous view since his meeting with President Eisenhower. The American hope is that this week-end he will persuade his Arab colleagues to take a chance on the strength of American sincerity.

Meanwhile, Mr. Raymond Hare, the United States ambassador here, who recently returned after a month of consultations in Washington, has been preparing the way for King Saud by holding a series of meetings in Cairo with the ambassadors of Persia, Jordan, India, and the Lebanon, and on Thursday had an interview lasting three and a half hours with President Nasser.

In the spate of official and unofficial comment here on the question of an Israeli withdrawal from Sinai, and the related question of guarantees for Israel's security in Gaza and the Gulf of Aqaba, it is possible to detect hopeful signs that Egypt, if her demand for complete withdrawal is met and the principle recognised that as the victim of aggression she should not be asked to give ground to the aggressor, would be prepared to accept a realistic settlement of Israel's claims. If this happens it will be a triumph for America's new policy.

But time is getting short, and Egyptian exasperation with Israel and with the United Nations failure to do more than pass resolutions against Israel leave the government little room for manoeuvre in the eyes of public opinion here and in the other Arab states.

The General Assembly of the United Nations was to take up again the question of the Israelis' refusal to withdraw from Egyptian territory, and the Egyptians had to decide whether to use the only weapon left to them—the Suez Canal, which had been partly cleared by a United Nations salvage team under General

Wheeler, but where a number of wrecks still prevented the passage of ships.

No one at the United Nations office in Cairo was quite willing to accuse the Egyptians of holding up the clearance operations, and I decided to travel the familiar road to Suez and see for myself. It was not difficult to establish the facts.

SUEZ, FEBRUARY 20

A 1,390-ton tug, the "Edgar Bonnet," threatens soon to become as famous as the "Mayflower" or the "Marie Celeste." The "Edgar Bonnet," which lies squarely in the centre of the Suez Canal below the French hospital at Ismailia, with only fifteen feet of mast showing above water, is the most formidable of the three remaining obstacles which prevent resumption of traffic between here and Port Said.

So far the Egyptian authorities have withheld permission for the United Nations salvage team to start work on it. The reason given by the Egyptians is the presence of explosives aboard, which they say must be removed by Egyptian naval experts before the wreck can safely be handled by the salvage team. Egyptian frogmen first examined the "Edgar Bonnet" six weeks ago, but if there are, in fact, explosives aboard, and if they have any intention of removing them, they are taking things very easy.

I looked down from the French hospital on the placid scene yesterday. Beside the tug's mast a naval launch was moored, with half a dozen men sunning themselves on the gunwales and gossiping with a constable in the police boat at its side. No activity of any kind seemed probable until a press photographer approached and took a picture. This only stung the constable into vociferous protest, leaving his naval companions unmoved and unmoving. When General Wheeler, the director of the United Nations clearance operation, approached last Friday and was recognised, however, his presence prompted someone to start up the launch's engine and a frogman went flying over the side.

At United Nations headquarters no one is willing to comment on the deliberation with which the Egyptians are tackling the problem of explosives aboard the "Edgar Bonnet," or even to hazard a guess as to why there should be explosives aboard a Canal Company tug. But the impression is inescapable that the Egyptians, recognising that the canal is their last weapon in face of Israel's recalcitrance, are stalling on the question of its clearance.

From Ismailia south to Suez the canal looks much as it did last September—when I made the journey aboard an Italian tanker the day after the Egyptian pilots took over from their departing British and French colleagues—except that the humble feluccas, which then crept furtively up the sides of the canal outside the buoys marking the main channel, now sail proudly up the fairway, lording it over the vanished and impotent steamers. To them, at least, the present impasse brings this slender advantage.

The surface of the Great Bitter Lake, which when I last saw it was a mass of ships as the northbound and southbound convoys passed each other, was yesterday empty, save where an ugly island proved on inspection to be the stern of the blockship "Akka," which was filled with concrete and sunk in the main channel at Ismailia. A German salvage team, consisting of the lifting craft "Energie" and "Ausdauer," raised the "Akka" last week and beached it here in shallow water well out of the way of navigation. This was the most ambitious of the clearance operations so far handled by the international team under General Wheeler's direction.

From there until a point about four miles north of Suez there is no sign, for the uninitiated eye, of anything abnormal about the canal—except that there are no ships. But at Kilometre 156, within sight of Suez and the desert hills of Sinai beyond, the admirable and unsightly German twins are working again, raising a bucket dredger whose removal should be completed within a week.

After that only the "Edgar Bonnet" and the Egyptian frigate "Abukir" will still be blocking the main channel, and if they can be removed within a further ten days General Wheeler will have kept to the schedule which foresaw the opening of the canal to ships of 10,000 tons by March 10. At present this looks unlikely, but General Wheeler yesterday told me he was confident that if he got an immediate green light from the Egyptians to start work on the "Edgar Bonnet" the job could be completed by the German twins within seven days. Without them it would take the best part of three weeks.

The "Abukir" presents a less formidable obstacle, though it is lying completely invisible in the centre of the channel only a few hundred yards from the southern mouth at Suez. Here, too, there is the problem of obtaining Egyptian permission, since the Egyptian authorities say there are mines aboard. At present no attempt is being made to remove them, and the position of the "Abukir" is marked only by warning buoys and the swirling of the current as it passes over this warrior, whose first and only battle is being fought unexpectedly from under water.

All around, on the canal banks and out in the waters of Suez Bay, are signs of the unprecedented clearance operation which the United Nations team has so successfully executed until now. Within a stone's throw of the "Abukir" are half a dozen wrecks, which have been raised by Dutch, Danish, German, Belgian, Swedish, Italian, and Yugoslav experts.

One of the Canal Company's two lifting craft, "Castor," which with its twin "Pollux" (now sunk at Port Said) had a lifting capacity of 4,000 tons, now lies near the empty British consulate, its engine-room torn open by explosives, which will necessitate its rebuilding. Across the canal two Danish lifting craft, the "Odin" and the "Thor," hug between them the tug "Atlas," which they brought to the surface on Sunday, seaweed growing on the chart-room walls and limpets speckling the plate glass of its searchlight.

Near by are the jagged remains of a rockbreaker raised from a few miles further up the canal (again the signs of the explosions which sank it are unmistakable), and out in the harbour Dutch vessels are dragging away sections of the Egyptian freighter "Zamalek" from the grave where it blocked the entrance to Port Ibrahim.

Inside the port is the Italian ship "Alcantara," which struck a mine in Suez harbour two weeks ago and is being repaired. The danger of mines still exists, and one is posted missing somewhere in the bay.

When all the sunken ships have been removed—and political

considerations make it impossible to forecast the date of this—
there is still plenty of work to be done on the canal before normal
navigation can be resumed, even supposing the user nations can
agree with Egypt on the payment of dues and related questions
which went into abeyance when the canal was blocked.

The whole lighting system needs repair. The gas plant, which
was destroyed, is to be replaced by an electric one. Signal stations
and workshops must be rebuilt. And, finally, the canal must be
dredged to remove the accumulation of three months of inaction.
Dredging has begun, but most of the dredgers were sunk. Some
must be replaced, and others reconditioned.

At General Wheeler's headquarters all these problems are
faced with the breezy self-confidence which the general himself
exudes. Clearance is his job, says the general, and he is "not
getting political." But you don't need to get very political to fore-
see that a new crisis is approaching in the uneasy health chart of
the Suez Canal problem.

*This was a critical moment for the Arab leaders,
and when the heads of State of Egypt, Syria, Jordan
and Saudi Arabia met in Cairo at the end of the week,
they found themselves at a turning point in Arab
affairs. It was also a turning-point for American policy
in the Middle East, for the central issue was whether
or not the Arabs would accept the Eisenhower Doctrine
and tie themselves to American policy.*

CAIRO, FEBRUARY 24

King Saud and King Hussein arrived in Cairo this afternoon
for the conference of Arab heads of state. President Kuwatly arrived yesterday with his leading ministers and had a preliminary
meeting with President Nasser last night. A banquet was given by
President Nasser this evening in honour of his guests, and the talks
between the four leaders will begin to-morrow morning.

King Saud's leisurely return from Washington has caused
some speculation here, as well as the postponement of the present
meeting, which was originally announced as beginning on February 16. It was puzzling that he should have taken time to visit

Spain, Morocco, and Libya before discussing with his principal allies—Egypt, Syria, and Jordan—the upshot of his discussions in Washington. The delay seems to suggest that King Saud expects to hold the strongest hand at this week's talks in Cairo.

The talks are certain to produce a declaration of continuing Arab solidarity. What the Arabs need, however, is not a reiteration of brotherly feelings but the discovery of some common and constructive purpose and a means of achieving it. This discovery seems no nearer than before, and now, when the Eisenhower Doctrine at least gives the Arab world the chance of attacking its endemic problems of poverty and underdevelopment, the Arab states have so far been unable to agree on a common response.

The Syrian government has been uncompromisingly hostile; the Egyptian government has avoided committing itself, but has not restrained the hostile comments of a press for which "freedom" is a relative term. King Saud has let it be understood that Saudi Arabia (which in this context means King Saud) takes a favourable view of the plan, and poor little Jordan, like a more truculent Vicar of Bray, has sounded a vaguely defiant note but not loudly enough to annoy any interested party. The attitude which they will adopt towards the Eisenhower Doctrine is only one of the things on which the "Big Four" of the Arab world must agree or admit one more failure.

The next most pressing issue is the policy to adopt towards Israel if the latter persists in refusing to knuckle under to the United Nations and to allow Mr. Hammarskjold's men in blue to replace them in Gaza and Sharm el Sheikh. Voices have been raised in the Arab world, among them the supposedly responsible ones of both the Syrian and Jordanian premiers, in favour of driving the Jews out by force—that force being the combined armed might of the Arab states. Apart from the moral and political considerations involved, the presence of UNEF in Sinai would make this impossible, even if last November's campaign had not eliminated the Egyptian army and air force as morally or materially useful weapons for the time being. But the temptation to do something is obviously strong.

Egypt's only remaining weapon is the Suez Canal, whose

clearance is at present delayed by the refusal of the Egyptian authorities to allow work to begin on the most serious of the remaining obstacles, the tug "Edgar Bonnet." It will be a pity if King Saud cannot prevail on President Nasser to renounce the use of this weapon, which is unlikely to influence Israel but sure to lose Nasser friends elsewhere. Certainly King Saud is likely to use his best endeavours, since he loses some 30 per cent of his own oil revenues as long as the canal remains closed.

A further subject for discussion is the future of Jordan, on which no book-maker would give very generous odds. Execution of the agreement signed in Cairo, which provided for financial assistance to Jordan to replace the subsidies paid by Britain, will depend on Egypt, Syria, and Saudi Arabia finding a common attitude to the Eisenhower Doctrine and the future of the Suez Canal. For without the revenues, direct and indirect, which the canal brings to Egypt and Saudi Arabia, neither is in a position to give aid of any sort to anyone. Even with the canal in operation they will still be dependent on American goodwill for any advance in the living standards of their peoples, which are among the lowest in the world.

The key to these related problems seems obvious—to accept America's proffered aid. To do so will not be easy after all that has been said, but perhaps the best explanation of King Saud's slow journey from Washington is that he wanted to give President Eisenhower time to prove to the Arabs his good intentions over what will always be the exclusive point of interest for them— Israel. America's final stand over the question of an Israeli withdrawal from Gaza and the Straits of Tiran will have much more than an immediate bearing on future Arab policy towards the West.

Unfortunately, the only decisions on which the Arab heads of state could agree were those which they had no power to enforce. America's failure to bring the Israelis to heel meant a corresponding failure to win the Arabs, and the conference in Cairo proceeded in an atmosphere of growing futility.

CAIRO, FEBRUARY 26

The conference of Arab heads of state, which opened yesterday in the Koubbeh Palace, is hailed in the Egyptian press as "momentous and historic." The problems facing President Nasser, President Kuwatly, King Saud, and King Hussein are certainly vital ones, but there is a touch of unreality in the atmosphere just the same.

It is obvious to all that no decisions which the Arab rulers are in a position to take at the moment can affect the future of the Arab peoples as immediately as the decisions which must be taken —and taken soon—in Washington and in the corridors of the United Nations building in New York. In fact, what the kings and presidents decide in Cairo will stem directly from what is decided 5,000 miles away on the far side of the Atlantic.

Already the Cairo press is talking of an agreement reached by the Arab "Big Four" on a united Arab policy. What this means in practice is that they all want Israel out of Gaza and Sharm el Sheikh. But since this is a result which the Arabs themselves have no means of achieving—"Big Four" or no "Big Four"—it is exaggerating somewhat to call it a policy. And on anything more than this it is doubtful whether the Arab states can find a common stand at present.

On the question of Suez Canal clearance, for instance, they are divided, Saudi Arabia wanting clearance to continue, Syria critical of the fact that it was ever started before an Israeli withdrawal had been secured. At present Egypt seems to be leaning towards the Syrian point of view, and is still refusing permission for work to start on the critical obstacle, the sunken tug "Edgar Bonnet." If this refusal is prolonged the salvage vessels will have to be kept inactive at great expense to the United Nations, or released, which in turn would involve a considerable modification in clearance plans already endangered by delays.

But for Egypt to try to obtain an Israeli withdrawal by bringing pressure to bear on the maritime nations of the world seems unwise, since Israel is unlikely to be moved by their difficulties and the most probable result would be the loss to Egypt of some of the support she now enjoys in the outside world.

The question of adopting a common attitude to the Eisenhower Doctrine finds the Arabs similarly divided. If the Americans could bring about an Israeli withdrawal, President Eisenhower might win a vote of confidence from the "Big Four" here, but as long as Israel refuses to yield to American pressure the Arabs remain suspicious that that pressure is fictitious, and that while Mr. Eisenhower and Mr. Dulles shake reproving fingers at Mr. Ben-Gurion they are secretly encouraging his intransigence.

It is the fact that Israel is regarded throughout the Arab world as the spoilt child of the West (conceived by Britain but delivered under sinister circumstances by America) that prompts the Arabs to look the American gift horse so stonily in the mouth, rather than any fundamental misgivings about America's wish to dominate the Middle East.

Gaza and Sharm el Sheikh must be two of the most unattractive pieces of territory ever to excite the passions of warring nations. Of the two, it is the latter which has most real importance for the Arabs at the moment. Gaza is like a trophy which must return to Egypt's wall unless she is to admit defeat, but Sharm el Sheikh symbolises the larger issue on which Egypt is fearful of being outmanoeuvred by the Israelis. Ships navigating in the Gulf of Aqaba, which Sharm el Sheikh controls, must pass through what are admittedly Egyptian territorial waters, and Egypt has the right in time of war to control such navigation.

But by a ruling of the Security Council of September 1, 1951, while the armistice agreement between Egypt and Israel is in effective operation "neither party can reasonably assert that it actively is a belligerent or requires to exercise the right of visit, search, and seizure for any legitimate purpose of self-defence." Egypt fears that Israeli insistence on the present belligerent stand is designed to trap the Arabs into agreeing at least to a formal peace with Israel—by which they would lose the right they now claim to blockade her and impose all possible restrictions on her expansion and development.

Israel's port of Eilath at the head of the Gulf of Aqaba has a special importance in these plans, and one which threatens the Arabs at a sensitive point. The Israelis are now developing Eilath with a view to making it a transit port for goods which otherwise would have to pass through the Suez Canal. Roads and pipelines connecting Eilath with the Mediterranean, which are now under construction, would draw off some of the transit dues normally earned by the Arab states in the form of canal revenues and revenues from existing oil pipelines. They would also lessen the value of these Arab assets as counters for political bargaining with the West.

If Israel could win sufficient support among the United Nations for the enforcement of a peace settlement between herself and the Arabs, she would emerge from the present impasse with more solid gains than two barren strips of territory which she would then happily evacuate.

While the conference dragged on in Cairo, I paid a visit to the forward positions of the United Nations force in Sinai. It was an odd expedition, into an area still littered with the debris of the campaign in November.

EL ARISH, FEBRUARY 27

The advance headquarters of the United Nations Emergency Force has been situated here for a month, on the northern edge of the Sinai Desert, while the Israelis' refusal to withdraw from the Gaza strip has held up the final advance to the old Egyptian border.

At UNEF's base headquarters at El Ballah, thirty-five miles south of Port Said, on the west bank of the Suez Canal, General Burns's staff have their plans ready for an immediate advance into the Gaza strip, if word should come that the Israeli government is prepared at last to bow to the repeated United Nations injunctions to complete the withdrawal of its forces behind the armistice lines.

El Arish is thirty-five miles from the edge of the Gaza strip, and between the two UNEF has scattered in the desert advance outposts, whose task is to try to control movement in the border area and establish a buffer zone between the Egyptian and Israeli forces. The visitor who reaches one of these outposts after jolting for hours over camel tracks in a jeep gets the impression of something half-way between a Foreign Legion post and an improbably situated Boy Scouts' camp.

On the crest of a sand dune like thousands of others round about, two flags will be flying—one a blue United Nations flag and the other carrying the colours of Sweden, Denmark, or Yugoslavia. (These contingents occupy forward positions along the northern sector of the "front," while in the south there are Finns and Indonesians based respectively on El Tor and Shandura.) Below the flagpoles a dozen tents are pitched in a hollow depression. Most of the men one sees, apart from sentries on duty, wear no more than a pair of shorts and are peaceably and contentedly occupied in writing letters to Copenhagen or Split, in fetching or distributing rations, in studying the unexpected fauna and flora of the desert, or in warding off the friendly and unexpected visitations of the local Bedouins, to whom the arrival of UNEF in their untravelled world is a source of bewildered delight.

This holiday atmosphere, of course, would vanish overnight if the Israelis decided to let go their hold on Gaza and on Sharm el Sheikh in the south. As it is, it is restricted to these lonely outposts whose occupants genuinely enjoy their isolation. (After all, for young recruits from Scandinavia or the mountains and plains of Yugoslavia, the strangeness and sunshine of the desert in February are ample compensation for a little physical discomfort.)

For those at advance headquarters at El Arish—for the administrative and supply services, for the staff of the Norwegian field hospital, for those concerned with transport and vehicle maintenance—life is a more serious business. To give only one example of the problems confronting this multi-national force operating in an area unfamiliar to any of its components, water has to be carried daily by tankers to each outpost, which involves in some cases a return journey of six or seven hours from El Arish over desert tracks.

Where there were roads before, the Israelis destroyed them, bulldozing the tarmac off the sand and breaking it up into small pieces. One outpost manned by a Swedish platoon in the farthest north is not approachable by wheeled vehicles at all, and supplies, including water, are carried in daily on camels in the charge of their Bedouin owners but usually ridden by experimentally minded Swedes.

Supplies for the whole force have to come from the Canal Zone and, before that, from the rear base at Naples by air or through Port Said. From the Canal zone to El Arish it is a hundred miles across the desert, and the road is barely passable; improvised repairs consisted basically of sorting the remains of the old tarmac, putting them together like an endless jigsaw puzzle, and rolling the result into an approximately flat surface. But the railway from Kantara, which was also destroyed, has been rebuilt and is in spasmodic operation again. In addition UNEF has its own air fleet consisting of two Dakotas, six "Flying Box-cars," and four light passenger planes.

This supply problem might be greatly eased if UNEF headquarters could be moved to Gaza, since some supplies could be landed there direct, though only by lighters since there are no other unloading facilities anywhere in the Gaza strip. But though all is in readiness for such a move no one here is over-sanguine in expecting it immediately.

In view of their long resistance to the orders of the United Nations, from whom this international force takes its orders, the Israelis cannot expect much popularity here—especially since much of the damage they did to installations and communications in this area was done after they knew that UNEF and not Egyptian forces would follow on their heels when they withdrew. (For instance, after UNEF officers had reconnoitred El Arish during the Israeli occupation, and picked an old British rest camp as UNEF's future headquarters, every washbasin in the camp had the bottom knocked out of it by the Israelis before they withdrew).

UNEF has been held up for so long in this area by Israel's refusal to yield that few of its members seem overinterested in following any more the long haggle between New York and Jerusalem. If you ask them what they expect to happen next, the usual reply is: "They've gone this far, why would they give in now?" But mostly UNEF's members in this forward area are content to live from day to day in their strange and remote *Beau Geste* environment, leaving politics to those with a more humdrum window on the world.

The United Nations Emergency Force was the
only encouraging result to come out of the Suez dis-
pute, and apart from its immediate role in holding the
ring between the Arabs and Israel, it was a novel and
practical illustration of the possibility of an inter-
national police force.

EL ARISH, FEBRUARY 28

To-day the United Nations Emergency Force consists of some six thousand men from ten countries. It has had to wait since the middle of January for the final Israeli withdrawal from the Gaza strip and the Sharm el Sheikh area, and the breathing space has had its uses, giving this multi-national force a chance to shake down into a unified command.

The results are remarkable. That contingents from such diverse countries as Finland and Brazil, Denmark and Indonesia, should find themselves serving together, and in a terrain as un-familiar to any of them as the Sinai Desert, is unique to begin with. But more striking to the outsider are the strange juxtapo-sitions in which he finds their members: Indians taking orders from a Pakistani (Pakistan's contingent was refused by Egypt, but she contributed a single officer to General Burns's staff); a Nor-wegian doctor treating a Yugoslav in a field hospital; a public re-lations office manned by a Canadian, an Egyptian, and a Mexican; a Colombian playing darts with a Swede in the officers' mess.

Equally striking and, in the circumstances, one of its most valuable assets, is the fact that UNEF is a "small power" organisa-tion. In this it differs entirely from the United Nations force which fought in Korea, and which was in practice an American command with small attached contingents from the other par-ticipating countries. Not only is there no contingent from any country which could be thought to have a political interest in the Middle East, but the command is a genuinely unified one, under a Canadian commander whose chief of staff is a Norwegian and who is served by officers chosen from any of the national con-tingents according to their special aptitudes and capabilities.

Now it is UNEF's main responsibility to prevent the resump-tion of raids and counter-raids, especially in the area of the Gaza strip. Unless both sides show more willingness to co-operate than at present seems likely it is doubtful whether the UNEF at its present strength is large enough for this task.

The problems which have to be solved in the area remain, and until there is some more permanent agreement between the Arabs and Israelis than the old armistice agreement, it is difficult to see how the world could willingly allow UNEF to be withdrawn.

For it to stay, the permission of Egypt is necessary, and for the moment that permission is not likely to be refused. But later, as the pressure builds up again in the Arab world for a more "active" policy against Israel, it may be withdrawn. Then the world would be back where it was before the Israeli attack of October 29.

If we are to avoid that situation, one of two things must happen: there must be a political settlement between the Arabs and Israel (which for the moment the Arabs will not consider), or the United Nations must insist on the maintenance of its emergency force in the area.

Back in Cairo the "Big Four" conference had come to an end, and it was clear that the Arab leaders had failed to agree on a common approach to the main question confronting them.

CAIRO, MARCH 1

By its omissions the communiqué published in Cairo on Wednesday night announced the failure of the talks between the heads of the four Arab states.

Even an extra day's discussion had not proved sufficient to iron out the central disagreement, which concerned the attitude that the Arab world should adopt towards communism and the Eisenhower Doctrine. This failure, in the present excited atmosphere of the Middle East, is equivalent to the planting of a fresh minefield of dangers for this area and the world at large.

This latest series of talks between the "Big Four" came at a critical time for the Arab world. Israel's attack on Egypt not only saved Nasser, who was being suspected of using Arab nationalism for Egypt's own ends, but greatly strengthened him in the role of champion of the Arabs against Zionism and imperialism. Since then, however, his internal problems and the revival of feeling among his neighbours that Egypt's president is an uncomfortable bedfellow have exposed the weaknesses of his position.

The Eisenhower Doctrine offered a way of escape from the dilemma, but rather than accept it precipitately the Arabs deputed

ARAB NIGHTS ENTERTAINMENTS
World copyright by arrangement with the Manchester Guardian

King Saud to find out for them in Washington what the plan really amounted to. King Saud evidently liked what he found, as was shown by his renewal of the lease of the Dhahran air base to the Americans and the genial tone of the statements put out in Washington by both the Saudi Arabians and the Americans. Dur-

ing this visit King Hussein unexpectedly wrote a letter to the
Jordan premier drawing attention to the dangers of Communist
infiltration in Jordan, a step which clearly was aimed at reassuring
the Americans that Jordan, like Saudi Arabia, was anti-Com-
munist.

King Saud left Washington with the avowed purpose of explaining the Eisenhower Doctrine to his fellow Arabs, and in their
confident forecasts of the agenda of this week's conference Cairo
newspapers agreed in putting the Eisenhower Doctrine among the
foremost topics. But the Eisenhower plan is not even mentioned in Wednesday's communiqué; nor is the Arab attitude to
Communism, which King Saud would have liked to see defined
and which obviously has a close bearing on the Arabs' response to
the Eisenhower Doctrine.

Instead, the communiqué speaks of "working for the immediate and unconditional withdrawal of the Israelis behind the armistice demarcation line," of support for Egypt's stand over the Suez
Canal, of sympathy with the Yemenis in resistance to "aggression," and for the Algerians against imperialism.

Another paragraph, which contains the nearest thing to a
reference to the Eisenhower Doctrine, says: "The Arab States . . .
hereby reaffirm . . . their determination to protect . . . the Arab
world from the dangers of the cold war . . . and that they abide
by their policy of impartiality and positive neutrality, thus pre-
serving their real interests."

This paragraph was probably the one over which a subcom-
mittee was said to have worked word by word: what it probably
means in practice is that King Saud was unable to persuade President Nasser and President Kuwatly of Syria to agree to any
friendly mention of the Eisenhower Doctrine, but that no one
wanted to slam the door on it either.

Talking to prominent Egyptians yesterday I found them sensitive about the obvious gaps in the communiqué and its generally
inconclusive character. The official explanation of its silence about
the Eisenhower Doctrine is the fact that plans have not yet been
finally worked out nor has Congress approved it. This has not,
in the past six weeks, prevented the Egyptian press from commenting freely on it, nor the Syrian government from denouncing

it, nor the Jordan parliament from holding a formal debate about it.

And as long ago as January 19 at the conclusion of the last Arab heads of state meeting in Cairo, the Egyptian Information Department declared in a communiqué that these same Arab rulers (except that President Kuwatly was on tour in India and replaced by his premier) had met and discussed the Eisenhower Doctrine. The communiqué continued: "After each country had expressed its views on the project they all agreed on the rejection of the vacuum theory and decided that Arab nationalism was the sole basis on which Arab policy could be formulated."

The fact that this week's conference could not agree on what everyone took to be its principal topic of discussion and that it produced no practical plan of action for Arab nationalism is bound to add to the sense of frustration which now blankets the Arab world. Arab leaders have so long reiterated that the solution to Arab problems must come from the Arabs themselves, and they are so insistent in rejecting any lead from outside, that very soon they must find some positive line of action of their own or lose the confidence of their subjects, to whom jobs and bread and somewhere to sleep are of more pressing concern than windy pronouncements about "positive neutralism."

By Cairo's politicians and propagandists Wednesday's communiqué is interpreted as a counter to the present attempt by the West to win the Arab world away from Nasser. But the peoples of the Arab world are more likely to see it as one more promise of independence at the price of an empty belly.

The mistrust which the Arab leaders felt about the intentions of the West was rooted in the belief that the West—and for the moment this meant the American government—was in fact supporting Israel, whatever it might say in public about the necessity for an Israeli withdrawal. Mr. Dulles' public utterances only served, as they had done at so many junctures in the Suez crisis, to confuse both sides. At one moment he appeared to stand by the view taken by Mr. Hammarskjold, that the Israeli withdrawal must be uncon-

*ditional; while at the next he gave the impression that
certain definite undertakings had been given to the
Israeli government, to the effect that in return for their
compliance the American government (or the United
Nations) would see to it that they gained immunity
from provocative acts in the Gaza strip or the Gulf
of Aqaba.*

*When the Israeli government suddenly announced
their willingness to withdraw (on the evening of
March 1), the Egyptians were suspicious—and as
though anxious to confirm their suspicions, the Israelis
next day went back on their promise.*

CAIRO, MARCH 3

General Burns, commander-in-chief of UNEF, to-day can-
celled his projected visit to Lydda where he was to have discussed
with the Israeli chief of staff, General Dayan, arrangements for the
withdrawal of Israeli forces from Gaza and their replacement by
United Nations groups. This visit, which was originally arranged
for yesterday, when the Israelis announced their intention to withdraw, was first postponed until to-day, then "indefinitely" when
General Dayan stated to-day that he had no authority from his
government to make any immediate arrangements for withdrawal.

The scepticism with which the Egyptians greeted Friday
night's announcement that, after more than a month of obduracy,
Israel was finally prepared to accept the repeated order of the
United Nations to withdraw will thus be hardened. The Egyptians, for whom this withdrawal has become an urgent matter of
prestige, feel that they have an unassailable case and bitterly resent
what appear to them to be Mr. Dulles' many shifts of policy.
When the Israeli government said that it would recall its troops
from Gaza and Sharm el Sheikh "on the assumption" that UNEF
troops would retain control of those areas until a final settlement,
Egypt merely restated its view (which has the support of the
other Arab governments as well as Mr. Hammarskjold and, in
theory at least, Mr. Dulles) that any withdrawal must be unconditional.

Meanwhile the clearance of the Suez Canal, which is now

held up by only a single obstacle, the tug "Edgar Bonnet," will certainly not proceed until Israel's plans about withdrawal are made clear. The bucket dredger which has been raised from the bed of the canal near Suez was to be dumped to-day in the Great Bitter Lake. Work on removing the explosives which are said to be in the "Edgar Bonnet" has not begun, nor will it as long as the Israelis maintain their defiance of the United Nations.

The announcement on Friday night that Israel intended to give in seemed to promise the first easing of the immense log-jam of problems which still face the Middle East. Now that the Israel government (in response, from all accounts, to intense internal pressure) has apparently changed its mind again, the solution of those problems, of which canal clearance is the most urgent, is again postponed. And Arab mistrust of both Israeli and Western policy has been further strengthened.

Next day the tension eased again—but the harm had been done, and the Egyptian mood was one of extreme suspicion.

CAIRO, MARCH 4

The news that the Israeli government has decided after all to go ahead with its withdrawal, which was announced on Friday night to the General Assembly but later reconsidered, will relax the tension which has been mounting here after the ups and downs of the week-end. It will also release the Egyptian government from a dilemma.

The meeting here of Arab heads of state last week ended with a grandiloquent communiqué about "positive neutralism" which reaffirmed the strength and unity of the Arab world—but the presence of Israeli troops at Gaza and Sharm el Sheikh demanded something more practical of the Arab "Big Four." It is not at present within the power of the Arab states to drive Israel back behind the armistice lines, but voices were being raised with increasing insistence urging the Arab leaders to do just this if the United Nations would not or could not achieve it. Now the "Big Four" can virtuously relax and leave the job to Mr. Hammarskjold and General Burns.

Egyptian opinion, which was highly sceptical of Israel's sincerity even before the equivocations of the week-end, will now not count any chickens before they are hatched. Until UNEF can announce that its troops control every square yard of territory up to the armistice line, there is not likely to be any progress with the clearance of the Suez Canal, which would now be navigable for ships of 10,000 tons but for a single obstacle, the "Edgar Bonnet." It is now impossible for General Wheeler to keep to the schedule which promised March 10 for the achievement of this goal, but if Egyptian permission to start on the "Edgar Bonnet" is received within a week, another week could see it attained.

Meanwhile progress has been made with clearance tasks which belong properly to the later stage of General Wheeler's programme. In spite of the delay in reopening the canal to a limited category of ships, it should still be possible to have it in complete working order by the beginning of May.

I was glad to be in Cairo at this moment, for amongst the many loose ends which had been left over from the previous unhappy summer was the espionage case, in which four British subjects were involved, and which had been understandably shelved during the more pressing events of the autumn and winter. Now, to my surprise, I was able to visit two of the prisoners in gaol, and to attend the Cairo court in which they were formally arraigned.

CAIRO, MARCH 4

Four British subjects were in the court of accusations here to-day when the preliminary hearing was resumed of the espionage case which is now more than six months old. They were: James Swinburn, business manager of the Arab News Agency (which was recently dissolved by the Egyptian authorities); James Zarb, an independent businessman of Maltese extraction; Charles Pittuck, an official of the Marconi Company of Egypt; and John Stanley, manager of the Prudential Assurance Company's Cairo branch.

All four are accused, together with eleven Egyptians and a Yugoslav, of being members of an espionage network which collected information prejudicial to the security of Egypt and transmitted it to the British embassy here. The presiding magistrate referred the case to the Assize court, where it is likely to come up for trial in about a month's time.

Under one interpretation of Egyptian law, which rests on the assumption that Egypt remains technically at war (with Israel), Swinburn and Zarb face a possible death penalty. For Pittuck and Stanley the maximum penalty on conviction would be a term of imprisonment with hard labour. But the chief defence lawyer, Ahmed Rushdi, said at an earlier hearing that he would challenge this interpretation and was confident that it would not stand up to examination.

It was in August, when the Suez Canal crisis was a month old, that the first arrests, of Swinburn and Pittuck, startled Cairo, where both had lived for many years. Within two days the Egyptian authorities were claiming that both had confessed and that trial would start "within a week or two," as soon as the prosecution had had time to prepare its case against them. Weeks passed, during which a large number of other suspects were arrested, all but sixteen being later released; and the trial was regularly postponed until all thought of it was submerged in the political crisis and fighting of October and November.

Last month the prisoners were formally indicted, together with four other Englishmen who are to be tried in absentia, the Egyptian authorities asserting that they managed to leave Egypt before their complicity was discovered. The defence lawyers asked for time to study the dossier of accusations, which are said to run to 1,300 pages, and the hearing was adjourned until to-day, when the magistrate's decision transferred the case to the trial proper.

Yesterday I visited Mr. Swinburn and Mr. Stanley in prison and found both in good health and remarkably high spirited for men who had spent six months in solitary confinement. They confirmed what I had learned from the Swiss legation here— that they had been well treated, and allowed to increase their personal comfort by purchases from outside of food and clothing. They knew little of what was passing in the outside world, though they were allowed to communicate with their wives in England, but were not permitted to see newspapers. Inevitably their main desire was for the trial to start, putting an end to the unaccountably long period of suspense since their arrest—a period during which the sombre course of Anglo-Egyptian relations is bound to have lengthened the odds against them.

On March 6 the Israelis at last began their withdrawal from the Gaza strip, reminding us of the many other problems which remained in the offing.

CAIRO, MARCH 6

Egypt's reaction to any clashes between Gaza Arabs and Israeli troops is bound to be violent, and will strengthen her insistence on the return of the Egyptian administration to the Gaza strip—which the Israelis say would be unacceptable.

But with the Israelis apparently ready this time to carry through their evacuation of Gaza and the Gulf of Aqaba, attention here is turning again to the Suez Canal. The Egyptians have not yet given permission for work to start on the raising of the "Edgar Bonnet," which alone prevents the completion of the first stage of the clearance programme.

Reports from New York that Mr. Hammarskjold may visit Egypt next week are prompting speculation as to the reasons for his journey. He may wish to discuss problems connected with the civil administration in the Gaza strip after the Israeli withdrawal, but it also seems likely that he wants to find out exactly what President Nasser's stand will be on the freedom of navigation through the canal.

Mr. Krishna Menon, who passed through Cairo yesterday and had a four-hour meeting with President Nasser, said that he found him in conciliatory mood; but it is generally accepted here that Nasser will not allow any ships to use the canal unless they pay their dues in full to the Egyptian Canal Authority. He is reported to be adamant in refusing a suggestion that the World Bank should accept half the dues and hold them until full agreement is reached about arrangements for the future.

It is also possible that Nasser may demand the freeing of Egypt's blocked sterling balances or some form of compensation for damage done during November's fighting before he allows British and French ships to pass through. Finally there is the question of Israeli ships, on which Mr. Dulles seemed blithely and unjustifiably optimistic at his press conference yesterday when he "did not assume that Egypt would make trouble for Israeli ships."

> *Now that the log-jam was easing, the world found itself back again in front of the problems of the canal, problems over which negotiations during the summer had broken down, and which the Anglo-French "police action" had certainly done nothing to resolve.*

CAIRO, MARCH 7

It is expected here that the UNEF occupation of the Gaza strip and the Sharm el Sheikh area will be completed on Friday. When this is achieved the immediate crisis will have passed, and the Egyptian government, which has so far refused to make any overt move towards a settlement of the remaining problems, may decide to widen its angle of vision.

There is no word yet of any Egyptian intention to allow clearance of the Suez Canal to proceed, though the news that the Syrian government has promised to allow repair of the oil pipelines encourages the hope that Egypt may follow suit with the canal. When the Egyptians permitted work to start on the canal before obtaining assurances of an Israeli withdrawal they ran into severe criticism from the Syrians, who throughout have shown a more intransigent attitude. As a result the Egyptian government is now likely to require certain proof that the Israeli decision to retire is final before they sacrifice this last remaining bargaining counter.

An argument is developing about the future civil administration of Gaza, which Egyptians are adamant in insisting should return to Egyptian hands as soon as UNEF has completed the take-over from the Israelis. This is probably largely a matter of form, since administration of this heavily populated and unproductive area has always presented a headache for the Egyptians.

It is likely that some compromise which put the Egyptian authorities technically in charge but left the administration for practical purposes in the hands of the United Nations would satisfy the Egyptians—but only if the principle is unequivocally stated that Egypt has full rights in the area. Without this condition internal pressures could force Egypt to insist on the withdrawal of UNEF, with consequences fatal to all.

The Egyptians remain extremely suspicious of the technical hairsbreadth separating the generalised "assurances" (which apparently prompted Israel to withdraw) from the formal guarantees which the Americans say they have not given. On freedom of navigation in the Gulf of Aqaba, the Egyptians show no disposition to compromise, insisting that the Straits of Tiran, which separate the Gulf of Aqaba from the Red Sea and which are less than a mile wide, constitute Egyptian territorial waters, and that if Egypt considers herself at war with Israel she has the unquestionable right to close the Straits of Tiran to Israeli shipping.

It is likely that under pressure Egypt would accept the submission of this issue to the International Court, but this procedure, besides being slow, would impose no binding obligation on either side to put into effect the International Court's decision. In any case, some bilateral or international agreement would be required to provide an interim settlement of the dispute—and as long as Egypt claims belligerent status in relation to Israel a bilateral agreement is out of the question.

This problem, with that of the future administration of Gaza, will claim the attention of Mr. Hammarskjold if, as reported from New York, he visits Egypt next week. But the main purpose of his visit would be likely to be connected with the canal, whose opening should follow within about three weeks from the moment the Egyptians allow work to start on lifting the sunken tug "Edgar Bonnet."

Egypt at present refuses to consider the interim plan for payment of dues by which ships using the canal would pay half the charges to the Egyptian Canal Authority, the other half to be held by the World Bank. If this attitude is challenged, Egypt may demand payment of the dues withheld by British and French

ships, among others, between the nationalisation of the canal in
July and its closure in November.

Beyond this stretches a chain of claims and counter-claims
involving the blocked sterling balances, the property of British
and French subjects expelled from Egypt, damage caused by
the Anglo-French attacks, British stores taken by the Egyptians
from the Canal zone bases, and loss of revenues through blockage
of the canal.

*The immediate crisis seemed to be over, and on
the twelfth of March the Egyptians allowed work to
start on the raising of the "Edgar Bonnet." But at
once a new squabble developed over the administration
of the Gaza strip. General Burns, the commander of
the United Nations force, had set up his headquarters
in Gaza when the Israelis left, but now the Egyptians
asserted their claim to exercise authority in the newly
"liberated" area. (The Gaza strip was not technically
a part of Egypt, but had been under Egyptian control
since the armistice of 1949—until the Israelis occupied
it in November 1956.) It was a dispute in which
neither side showed much tact, and which would have
been unimportant but for the threat it posed for a day
or two of a breach between Egypt and the UNEF. In
their sensitive mood it seemed possible that the Egyptians might insist on the withdrawal of UNEF, in
which case the situation on the border with Israel
would have been dangerous in the extreme.*

CAIRO, MARCH 14

It is reported here that General Mohamed Hassan Abdel
Latif, who was appointed on Monday as administrative governor
of Gaza, arrived in Gaza to-day to take up his new post. General
Burns, commander of UNEF, also left Cairo this morning for
his headquarters at Gaza, accompanied by Dr. Bunche, the United
Nations under-secretary.

There appear to be two dangers—that if the Egyptian governor insists on asserting his authority immediately the position

of UNEF will be undermined and its troops unable to maintain order in the crowded strip, and that differing interpretations of UNEF's mandate will disrupt the force under General Burns's command. The Danes and Norwegians are annoyed at being told to go home by the Gaza Arabs as soon as they have helped to liberate the area from the Israelis. The Canadians are conscious of the suspicion which their government's stand on Gaza has aroused against them. The Yugoslavs alone enjoy the full confidence of the Arabs—a confidence they seem to have won by their individualistic interpretation of the orders given them by General Burns.

Soon after the departure of General Burns and Dr. Bunche a statement issued by the United Nations office in Cairo emphasised the "increasing normality" of life in Gaza, and a statement from the director of the Egyptian Information Service said that "the inhabitants of the Gaza sector look upon UNEF as friendly forces and co-operate with them for the sake of peace." These were outward signs of the *détente* which has followed the sharper exchanges, and patched up the quarrel which developed earlier this week over civil administration of the Gaza area.

Underneath the wounds are still open, with the Egyptians resentful and suspicious of the way the take-over of the Gaza strip was carried out (without reference to the Egyptian authorities), and the United Nations critical of the apparent irresponsibility with which the Egyptians complicated a very ticklish situation in Gaza. The situation there was reported quiet to-day, and yesterday's demonstration, though directed partly against certain United Nations contingents, was orderly and peaceable.

It now looks as though the Egyptians, having staked their claim to the right to resume civil administration of the Gaza strip, will let matters rest until Mr. Hammarskjold's arrival in Egypt, which is expected on Monday. The secretary-general's first concern now will be to negotiate an agreement on the future of Gaza, and the Suez Canal, which was expected to be his immediate preoccupation, will take second place. Work is continuing on raising the "Edgar Bonnet" from its resting place near Ismailia. It began on Tuesday when General Wheeler, director of the United Nations clearance operation, stated that his task would be completed by April 10.

> *Mr. Hammarskjold's visit was postponed for a few days, and in the interval another visitor arrived in the Middle East, whose aim it was to win the support of the Arabs (among other peoples) for the Eisenhower Doctrine. Mr. James Richards was the president's special envoy, and came to the Middle East to explain the famous Doctrine, which had just been embodied in a Congressional resolution. This declared: (1) that at the president's discretion the United States would "use armed forces" on behalf of any Middle Eastern state that asked for help against "armed aggression from any country controlled by international communism"; and (2) that in the four months until the end of June 1957, the president could use up to $200 millions for economic and military assistance in the Middle East.*
>
> *The $200 millions was money already appropriated by Congress for economic aid to foreign governments under the Mutual Security Program, and the new resolution merely made its distribution a little simpler, freeing it from certain restrictions which were applied under the Mutual Security Act. The first and most important part of the congressional resolution was, in effect, an attempt to plug a gap in America's system of defensive alliances against Russia, by forming an avowedly anti-Communist coalition of Arab states which would form a link between NATO (which reached as far east as Turkey) and SEATO (which reached as far west as Pakistan). The problem of the Richards mission, which now came to the Middle East, was to convince the Arabs that this arrangement had benefits for them and would serve their interests as well as those of American foreign policy—and the $200 millions was to be the bait.*

BEIRUT, MARCH 17

President Eisenhower's special envoy to the Middle East, Mr. James Richards, who is entrusted with the task of explaining the Eisenhower Doctrine to the Arab States, made a good beginning here in the talks which ended yesterday in Lebanese acceptance of the American initiative.

Mr. Richards has now gone on to Libya, where he can also expect a favourable reception after the Libyan premier's endorsement of the Doctrine at the conclusion of Vice-President Nixon's recent visit. Soon the going will become tougher for Mr. Richards, who is expected to visit some eighteen countries before he is finished. It has not yet been announced which Arab states are willing to receive him, and much will depend on the course of the forthcoming negotiations about problems outstanding between the Arabs and Israel as well as those which still divide the Arabs from Britain and France.

The Jordanian premier, Suleiman Nabulsi, speaking on Friday to a political rally celebrating the end of the Anglo-Jordan Treaty, referred very critically to the Doctrine which he said the Jordan parliament had rejected. Jordan's attitude will finally be decided by that of Syria and Egypt, both of whom are so far hostile, though the Egyptian government has avoided direct comment.

Iraq's support for the Doctrine can be counted on, and the ultimate balance may well lie with Saudi Arabia. King Saud made no secret of his approval in Washington in January, and his quarrel with the Syrian delegation at the recent four-power talks in Cairo almost disrupted the conference. However, a report from the Middle East News Agency in Jeddah yesterday implied that the Saudi government intends to take a strong line against the Israeli claim to enjoy freedom of access to the Gulf of Aqaba, which Egypt and Saudi Arabia claim as territorial waters. And if the United States supports the Israeli claim, as seems inevitable, King Saud's championship of the Eisenhower Doctrine may be an early casualty.

The Lebanese foreign minister, Dr. Charles Malik, at his first press conference since his return from New York, where he led the Lebanese delegation to the General Assembly, gave the

Arabs some good advice of the sort they seldom get and still more seldom take. He said, in particular, that the present American administration was the first to try to understand the real situation in the Arab states and to treat with justice their legal demands. This stand would not continue for ever, he said, and the Arabs should take advantage of it before it was too late.

Most Arab governments would like to do so and so would their long-suffering peoples. But until the Americans decide on a clear stand over the Arab-Israeli dispute it is difficult for Arab spokesmen to come out and say so.

> *While Mr. Richards went on his way, things were moving at last on the canal. The Egyptians had allowed clearance work to be resumed as soon as the Israeli withdrawal from Gaza was complete, and they had begun to allow small ships through the canal, all of which had paid their dues to the Egyptian Canal Authority. This was a shrewd move, for it meant that by the time the canal was ready for normal traffic the principle would have been established that the Egyptian Canal Authority was the proper recipient of dues, and would make it much harder for the old Suez Canal Company or a resurrected Users' Association to put in a rival claim.*

CAIRO, MARCH 19

The Suez Canal will be open to-morrow to ships of up to 1,000 tons. This was announced to-day by the Egyptian Canal Authority from Port Said. The United Nations clearance team expects to raise the sunken tug "Edgar Bonnet" on Sunday, after which the canal should be navigable for ships of up to 10,000 tons. Egypt has given permission for work to start on the final obstacle, the frigate "Abukir," on Friday.

Out of the Canal Company's dozen dredgers only three are now in operation. While the canal has been closed there has been little silting, but once ships start to pass through again it is doubtful whether these could keep the channel free. Tugs also present a problem, for eleven were sunk and only three are at present available for duty.

Much more important, of course, is the question of canal dues; to whom, by whom, and how they will be paid. The Canal Authority spokesman had no comment to-day on reports that the Egyptian government has circulated a memorandum to all countries, setting out the methods which the Egyptian government proposes to follow in the future operation of the canal. Another question pending is the cost of the clearance operation and how it is to be met. The cost is believed to be over $20 millions,* and suggestions as to how it is to be raised include a surcharge on ships using the canal, and a levy on United Nations members (opposed by Russia, who says that the "aggressors" should pay).

The canal is only one of the topics which are keeping the international band of trouble-shooters on the hop in and around Cairo to-day. The unsinkable Mr. Krishna Menon arrived this morning, to parry reporters' questions at the airport with his customary suavity before going on to a meeting with President Nasser which lasted an hour. Dr. Ralph Bunche, on his return from Gaza, called on the Egyptian foreign minister, Dr. Fawzi, who has also had a series of meetings with the American ambassador during the last two days. And Mr. Hammarskjold is at last on his way to Egypt after hearing the complaints of the Israeli foreign minister, Mrs. Meir, in New York.

Besides the canal, the principal problem awaiting the United Nations secretary-general is the future administration of Gaza, where the Egyptian civil governor is steadily taking over the offices as well as the functions previously earmarked for UNEF. Beyond that lies the dispute over the Straits of Tiran, commanding the entrance to the Gulf of Aqaba and the approaches to the Israeli port of Eilath. The Saudi Arabian government, which shares Egypt's claim to control both the straits and the gulf, has just taken up the running on this question from Egypt, thus complicating the American position, since America is at present relying on King Saud to champion the Eisenhower Doctrine in the Arab world and is thus reluctant to come out against him on an issue where it supports the Israeli case.

* The cost of clearing the canal was in the end much lower than had been expected, and amounted to $8.6 millions.

*Mr. Hammarskjold arrived in the small hours of
March 21, and characteristically gave himself only three
or four hours sleep after the flight from New York before he started his negotiations with President Nasser
and the Egyptian foreign minister, Dr. Fawzi. His task
was a threefold one.*

CAIRO, MARCH 21

Of the three problems now on the table the canal seems the
most immediately soluble, Gaza the most dangerously urgent,
and the Gulf of Aqaba ultimately the hardest to solve. The
canal, which is open to-day to ships of up to 1,000 tons, should
be ready for ships of 10,000 tons within a week. The 540 ton
Italian tanker "Christine," the first foreign ship to pass through
the canal since it was blocked, left Port Said for Italy to-day,
after making the passage in twelve hours and paying her tolls in
dollars to the Egyptian Canal Authority.

In Gaza, for the moment, the situation is quiet, with the
Egyptians in charge of civil administration and UNEF deployed
along the border of the strip. The danger is that threats or
frontier incidents might prompt the Egyptian government to
bring up troops or ask for the withdrawal of UNEF.

Navigation in the Gulf of Aqaba presents the thorniest
problem as it raises the fundamental question of belligerent
rights. If the Arabs renounce these they throw away their best
—almost their only—weapon against Israel: the right of blockade. (The other, as the Israelis know, is the threat of raiding
from the Gaza strip, which keeps the neighbouring Israeli settlements on permanent tenterhooks.) This they will never do if
they can avoid it, nor will they recognise the Israeli right to be
in the Gulf of Aqaba at all, since to do so means recognising
Israeli ownership of the Negev, which drives a wedge through
the Arab world.

*Again characteristically, Mr. Hammarskjold was
working for a limited objective—but even so, and
despite the official silence which surrounded his talks
with the Egyptian leaders, it was soon evident that he
was not making much headway.*

CAIRO, MARCH 24

After spending seven hours with President Nasser on Saturday, Mr. Hammarskjold to-day communed with himself all morning and then visited the Sphinx before taking on the foreign
minister, Dr. Fawzi, this evening. To-morrow morning he will
visit Ismailia to see the lifting by the United Nations salvage
team of the tug "Edgar Bonnet."

The fact that, after three days of discussions, no solutions are
in evidence for the problems of the Gaza strip, the Gulf of Aqaba,
or even for an interim settlement on the Suez Canal seems at
first sight discouraging. At the very least, it suggests hard bargaining. But to read into this picture the implication that Mr.
Hammarskjold's mission is a failure is to mistake his objective.

This is, at the behest of the General Assembly, to consult
with the parties in dispute and take steps for carrying out the
United Nations resolutions calling for the withdrawal of Israeli
forces behind the armistice demarcation line and for a strict
observance by both sides of the armistice agreement of 1949.

That agreement provides the only legal basis for positions
which either Egypt or Israel may adopt in areas over which they
find themselves in dispute, and it is clearly the secretary-general's
opinion that an essential preliminary to any settlement is recognition of its validity.

> While Mr. Hammarskjold was in Cairo, the new
> British prime minister, Mr. Harold Macmillan, had
> gone to Bermuda to meet President Eisenhower. It
> was in the nature of a formal reconciliation between
> the two governments after the breach caused by Britain's
> attack on Egypt and her failure to advise the American
> government of her intentions. The communiqué issued
> after the Bermuda talks had a significantly hostile re-
> ception in Cairo, where Mr. Hammarskjold still had
> very little to show for his days of discussion with Presi-
> dent Nasser and his advisers.

CAIRO, MARCH 25

Mr. Hammarskjold's mission is drawing to a close here with

the uncertain prospect of qualified success on only one of the three points of discussion.

The Middle East News Agency asserted yesterday that he and President Nasser had reached "understanding" over a statute for future navigation of the Suez Canal, and though a United Nations spokesman urged caution in accepting this news at face value, it does seem likely that Nasser has convinced the secretary-general that his proposals are basically consistent with the six points endorsed by the Security Council last October.

On the more intricate questions of the future of Gaza and navigation in the Gulf of Aqaba the impression here is that no advance has been made. Concerning Gaza, Mr. Hammarskjold's hope was to obtain an Egyptian undertaking that UNEF would be allowed to remain in the strip pending fuller settlement of border questions.

This undertaking the Egyptian government is unwilling to give without fulfilment by the Israelis of two conditions: full observance of the armistice agreement of 1949 (which would entail withdrawal of all but "defensive" Israeli armed forces from the Negev and of all Israeli forces from the supposedly demilitarised zone of El Auja) and acceptance by the Israelis of UNEF troops on their side of the armistice line.

That Mr. Hammarskjold has not gone to Jerusalem to ask the Israelis for assurances on these points can perhaps be explained by the thesis that he does not want to ask for something he knows he will not get. An Israeli refusal would merely harden the impasse.

The question of Aqaba involves the wider one of belligerent rights, which Egypt claims against Israel, among them the right to bar Israeli shipping from Egyptian territorial waters. Egypt will certainly not relinquish these rights without prior observance by Israel of her obligations under the armistice agreement—which the Israel government has called a dead letter.

Mr. Hammarskjold saw President Nasser to-night in what was expected to be their last meeting, but he has accepted an invitation to dine with the Foreign Minister, Dr. Fawzi, on Tuesday, so he will not be leaving Egypt before Wednesday and further discussions are possible to-morrow, if there is anything left to discuss.

The Egyptian press has given a very unfriendly reception to the Bermuda communiqué, which most commentators denounce for having misunderstood the problems of the Middle East and ignored the rights of the Arabs. Such comments should be seen as part of a wider process in which Egypt is drawing away from the West (including the United States) after the brief period following the Suez adventure during which America looked like winning and holding Arab confidence.

The communiqué from Bermuda had announced that the United States would join the military committee of the Bagdad Pact. This was a move so misguided (especially in its timing) as to recall the withdrawal of the West's offer of aid for the Egyptian High Dam. It did as much as anything to damn the Eisenhower Doctrine in Arab eyes—and this at the very moment when the president's emissary was trying to persuade the Arab governments to lend the doctrine their support. But in retrospect it is clear that the American decision to move closer to the Bagdad Pact (which was bound to antagonise Egypt, to whom the Bagdad Pact had always been anathema) was only part of yet another shift in the foreign policy of Mr. Dulles. The attempt to win Egypt had been abandoned, in favour of a policy which would isolate her (and Syria) from the rest of the Arab world. It was a fateful decision, one which may in the end even prove to have been fatal, though in the short run it promised certain easy advantages.

CAIRO, MARCH 26

Egyptian opinion is hardening against the Eisenhower Doctrine for the Middle East as the president's special envoy, Mr. James Richards, skirts the Arab world in his search for active supporters of the plan—now apparently rechristened the "American Doctrine."

Like a graceful figure skater Mr. Richards has so far swept

through the Lebanon, Libya, Turkey, and Persia, leaving behind him a trail of cheerful communiqués. His announced itinerary next includes Pakistan, Afghanistan, and Iraq, which confirms the impression that he is keeping for the time being to the edges of the lake, where, perhaps, the ice is thicker. In Ethiopia, Somaliland, and, perhaps, the Sudan, he can expect a continuing welcome.

But soon he will have to venture into the middle, where his reception is more doubtful. Jordan's minister of state for foreign affairs, Abdullah Rimawi, yesterday confirmed that Mr. Richards was expected to visit Jordan but said ominously that after his visit "we will in consultation with the free Arab states [meaning Egypt, Syria, and Saudi Arabia, as against Iraq] adopt a united attitude based on a policy of positive neutrality." The Syrian foreign minister, Salaheddin el Bitar, spoke in the same vein on Saturday, saying that Syria would listen to what Mr. Richards had to say and "acquaint him with Syria's viewpoint."

Here in Egypt three papers yesterday attacked American policy in general and the Eisenhower Doctrine in particular. Of these attacks, whose immediate cause was the American decision to join the military committee of the Bagdad Pact, the fiercest was in the Left-wing *El Masaa*, where Khalid Mohieddin wrote: "The Arab peoples and statesmen have already condemned the Bagdad Pact as an aggressive pact and a direct threat to the peace and independence of the Arab countries. Now it has been made abundantly clear that the Eisenhower Doctrine is but a supplement of the Bagdad Pact, the Arab peoples should muster their combined forces in combating the Bagdad Pact and the Eisenhower Doctrine most relentlessly."

Certainly American policy in the Middle East looks from here like an open attempt to isolate Egypt and Syria by promising military and economic aid to states more disposed to be co-operative. There have been four signs of this intention since the beginning of the year: first, the wooing of King Saud during his Washington visit in January; secondly, Vice-President Nixon's recent tour, in which he pointedly avoided Egypt while stressing American friendship for such lesser Middle Eastern lights as Tunisia and Ethiopia; thirdly, Mr. Richards' whirlwind trip, whose aim seems be to scatter largesse to those who will have it, leaving Egypt and her friends like paupers in the middle of a feast; and finally, America's closer alignment with the Bagdad Pact, to which the hostility of Egypt and Syria is relentless and irrevocable.

Logically this new American policy should be effective, since all Arab states want and need outside aid. Iraq—which is now celebrating "Development Week," demonstrating the benefits that can accrue from honest and intelligent use of oil revenues —should be a useful illustration of the advantages of collaboration with the West. But the Arab approach is seldom a logical one, and in this case there is too much at stake for promises of material advantage to have a compelling appeal. The stake is the leadership of Arab nationalism and the point at issue is the direction which that nationalism is to take.

Iraq may have the more promising future—but it is a future along lines which no longer have any appeal for other Arab peoples. For them, the vision of transforming their desert heritage into modern cities and fertile farmlands has its attraction certainly, as it must have for people anywhere who are plagued by poverty and disease and overpopulation.

But there is that other, less tangible, but emotionally infinitely more alluring vision, of a new and proud nationhood. This second vision may be only a mirage—but no approach to Arab affairs that discounts it has any hope of winning sincere support from inside the Arab world.

By the end of March the situation had eased a little. The Israelis had completed their withdrawal from Egyptian territory, and the Suez Canal was in partial operation again. But fundamentally there was little or no improvement. All the wranglings of the politicians, the intervention of the military men, the efforts of the internationalists, had only succeeded in restoring in the Middle East a state of confusion and suspicion like that which had preceded the attack on Egypt. The presence of UNEF in Sinai gave some slight reassurance that there would be no immediate outbreak of fighting, but otherwise we were back in the atmosphere of the previous August or September. The West was still reluctant to concede to Nasser unfettered control of the canal; a large part of the Arab world was behind Nasser in resisting what he represented as an attempt by the West to impose on it a new form of domination. And whatever might be the rights and wrongs of the points at issue, it seemed plain that the Americans, on whom now fell the responsibility for directing Western policy in the area, had found no better method of dealing with the Arabs than that which had brought the British to so conspicuous a failure.

CAIRO, APRIL 6

Six months ago, before the Israeli attack on Egypt and the intervention of Britain and France, it was being prophesied that economic pressure alone would be enough to bring Egypt into submission. After the fighting, with all that it entailed for Egypt of material loss and economic dislocation, the same cry was raised again, the "experts" asserting that within three to six weeks, Nasser would have to cry quits for lack of oil, wheat, spare parts, or foreign exchange. (There was variation in detail about the expert forecasts, though not about their ultimate conclusions.) To-day, Western policy towards Egypt—which means, effectively, American policy—is evidently based on the same prognostication, discredited though it must now be to anyone with an eye open to Middle Eastern realities.

Certainly the handicaps under which the Egyptian economy stumbles along are enormous: the country's large balances in Britain and the United States are blocked; most of her normal trade avenues are closed to her; the Suez Canal for four months has been a costly liability, producing no revenues from which even the staff's salaries could be met. Imports have been drastically cut back, with effects which extend far beyond immediate shortages, breeding unemployment, hoarding, a general rise in prices (principally, but not entirely, confined to imported, and so to luxury and semi-luxury goods), business dislocation, and a loss of confidence on the part of investors and of the public at large. Oil production has been seriously reduced by the destruction and dismantling carried out by the Israelis in Egypt's Red Sea oilfields. Many foreign businessmen, fearing the fate of others who were expelled, have left the country or are planning to leave, and some of them have found ways of exporting substantial amounts of currency in spite of the strictest currency control regulations.

The effects of conditions inside Egypt on the country's external trade position are equally serious. The Egyptian pound, which is nominally worth about nine Lebanese pounds, is now quoted at less than six on the Beirut market. In the present season, now about half-way through, less than half as much Egyptian cotton has been sold as in the same period last year. The stability of the Egyptian pound, already much damaged, has lately been further weakened by strong rumours that the note circulation has been arbitrarily increased during recent months and now greatly outruns the cover held by the National Bank of Egypt (whose statistics, by the way, are now treated with scepticism by Egyptian businessmen). A further cause of uncertainty has been the appearance of a very large number of extremely skilfully forged five-pound notes in circulation, and in Cairo shops to-day most cashiers have a list of numbers with which to compare any note presented.

The methods adopted by the Egyptian authorities to fight these evils have often been clumsy and ill-advised. A press censorship, which was abolished in theory months ago, fills the newspapers with unconvincing assurances that shortages (whose existence anyone can verify for himself) do not really exist at all. Meanwhile no mention is made of rumours, which circulate freely and gain credence just because they are suppressed, about disaffection in the army or the arrest of once prominent military or political figures.

What of the future then? Does the West's policy make sense, of squeezing Egypt until either her economy collapses or an internal revolution breaks Nasser's hold on the country? And if so, how long must we wait for one or other of these results—or both?

As to the possibility of an economic collapse, there are two facts to be borne in mind. The first is that beyond a certain point the Egyptian economy is virtually indestructible. The second is that whenever a particular shortage has become acute during the past six months the Russians have come to Egypt's assistance with supplies of oil or wheat (Egypt's two weakest points), or by buying Egyptian cotton, and they will almost certainly continue to do so as long as Nasser maintains his defiance of the West. With injections such as these the Egyptian economy can keep going indefinitely, since 75 to 80 per cent of the population are content to live, as they have always lived (and as President Nasser himself has remarked), just above the starvation level, producing nearly all that they and their town cousins need out of the unfailingly fertile Nile Valley.

There is one qualification to be made here. The fertility of the Nile Valley is not increasing; the population of Egypt is— by half a million a year. In other words, the ratio between agricultural production and population is changing all the time, to the country's disadvantage (hence the vital importance of the High Dam, or of some alternative large-scale irrigation project). In the opinion of some experts, the fertility of the delta, the richest part of Egypt, is even decreasing, for want of the application of proper drainage techniques. Whether this is a serious danger or not (and it is clearly not an immediate one), it remains true that Egypt's present independence of political action is being bought at the expense of future generations of Egyptians; conversely, it remains true that Egypt can, if she cares to mortgage her future in this way, maintain that independence of action for a long time before the bill has to be met.

As to the likelihood of an internal uprising which might unseat Nasser's regime, any forecast must be more cautious; autocracies commonly appear impregnable until they are destroyed. There appears to be no organised political opposition movement in being in Egypt at the moment, and the most serious danger to the regime probably comes from the Left-wing extremists, who call for a more aggressive Pan-Arab policy (relying on ultimate Russian support), and whose views find expression in Khalid

Mohieddin's newspaper *El Masaa*. The army remains a largely unknown quantity, but one over which Nasser's control seems to have been unaffected (or possibly re-established) since the Sinai campaign. Internal security remains firmly in the grip of the loyal and efficient minister of the interior, Zakariya Mohieddin (brother of the editor of *El Masaa*). In the streets of Cairo, from which traditionally any Egyptian politician has had most to fear, utter calm reigns.

In short, there seems little reason to expect that a new revolutionary movement will overthrow Nasser's regime, and still less to expect that economic paralysis will bring him to his knees. If these premises hold good, is it the best or the wisest policy to try to browbeat him—without, this time, envisaging the use of force even as a "last resort"? Are we not more likely, by so doing, to drive him ever farther into his nationalist corner, or into that open alliance with the Russians which he has so far managed to avoid?

If Britain and the United States are to devise a workable policy for the Middle East, we have to take the Middle East as it is, and not as we might like it to be. That means accepting Nasser as one element, and locally the most important element, in the pattern. It does not mean giving way to him—but it surely does mean abandoning a position which never looked tenable six months ago, and which the events of last November proved us unable to maintain. Over the canal Nasser's hand is, practically speaking, unchallengeable. Mr. Hammarskjold has said guardedly that the Egyptian proposals for a canal settlement do not conflict with the six points agreed to by the Security Council last October, and the Egyptians (who badly need the revenues of the canal, and the resulting foreign exchange) are ready to enter into binding commitments on the important practical points involved— the level of dues and the provision of a fund for improvement and maintenance.

The intelligent approach for us is to work for a settlement on these lines and then to back Mr. Hammarskjold's patient attempt to restore the efficacy of the armistice agreement (which means, among other things, obtaining the withdrawal of Israeli forces from the demilitarised zone of El Auja and the reduction of Israeli forces in the Negev to the agreed level). Until this is done it is useless to suppose that the Egyptians will abandon their claim to belligerent rights—a claim, however, which everyone agrees will lose any validity as soon as the armistice agreement becomes genuinely effective. Then, and only then, will it become possible to attack the real heart of the Middle Eastern problem—the questions of the refugees and of establishing permanent frontiers for the state of Israel.

PART 4   The Eisenhower Doctrine in Action

As a result of her stern opposition to Britain's Suez adventure, the United States had won from the Arabs an exceptional measure of confidence and respect. At the start of 1957 she had enjoyed advantages which no other Western power could claim in the Middle East. She was free from the taint of "imperialism," she commanded resources sufficient to launch a full-scale attack on the Middle East's development problems, and she was in a position to exert pressure on the Israeli government. Well used, these advantages could have enabled the United States to give the West a fresh start in the Arab world, by assuring the Arabs that if the vital interests of the West (oil and communications) were respected, the legitimate aspirations of the Arabs (for unity, independence, and an improved standard of living) would also receive sympathetic attention from the West.

Unhappily, within the first three months of the new year these advantages were dissipated one by one. During the long wrangle over the Israeli withdrawal from Gaza, Mr. Dulles' attempts to please everyone succeeded only in convincing the Arabs that the American government would always support Israel against them. The Eisenhower Doctrine, which at first had looked like a genuine attempt to bring security and prosperity to the Middle East, had turned out on closer inspection to be a very businesslike scheme to win Arab support for America's strategic interests. And now, only five months after Port Said, only five months after they had won Arab plaudits by dissociating themselves from the British "imperialists," the Americans, in

Arab eyes, were fatally tarred with the same brush.
The Arabs were perhaps hasty and oversuspicious
in condemning the Eisenhower Doctrine and the whole
new trend of American policy in the Middle East; but
there is no question that America, in her resentment at
these suspicions, reacted in the very ways that seemed
to justify them. From the beginning of April no oppor-
tunity was lost of demonstrating America's involvement
in the Middle East, of showing her concern for those
who sought shelter under the Eisenhower umbrella, or
of shaking a big stick at those who did not. Sometimes
these demonstrations were so ineptly mistimed as to
create the illusion that Mr. Dulles had somehow turned
the clock back and we were living in the heyday of gun-
boat diplomacy in the nineteenth century.

BEIRUT, APRIL 5

At the close of a two-day debate on general policy, premier
Sami el Solh will to-night ask the Lebanese parliament for a vote
of confidence in his five-month-old government. Most observers
expect him to get it with a comfortable majority.

Such a vote will be in particular a vindication of the government's foreign policy, which, under the direction of the foreign
minister, Dr. Charles Malik, has steered Lebanon firmly into
the Western camp. Three weeks ago Lebanon became the first
Middle Eastern state to sign a formal agreement with President
Eisenhower's special envoy, Mr. James Richards, an agreement by
which Lebanon indicated its full acceptance of the Eisenhower
Doctrine.

To-day by what is unlikely to be pure coincidence, as the
premier asks for parliament's endorsement of his policy, the
largest aircraft carrier in the world, U.S.S. "Forrestal," is steaming slowly outside Beirut harbour, with an attendant helicopter
playfully buzzing fishing boats and the carrier's own jet planes
whistling across the sunlit bay beyond. The Forrestal's sixty
thousand tons, scores of ultramodern planes, and 3,500 crew
members, are the plainest indications of what an American alliance is worth to Lebanon (and could be worth to her awkward

neighbours). Lest there should still be doubts, Washington last night announced the allocation of $10 millions in aid to Lebanon, which thus becomes the first country to benefit from the Eisenhower Doctrine.

The Richards mission, which to-day opened talks with the Pakistan government, has already won for the Eisenhower Doctrine the adherence of Libya, Turkey, Persia, Iraq, and Afghanistan. No date has yet been given for the mission's visits to Egypt, Syria, or Jordan, though each of these states has indicated in sulky terms that it will hear what Mr. Richards has to offer before refusing it.

The Lebanon was an easy catch, and in any case the Lebanon, with its large Christian element and with its business eye always open to the West, was not in the fullest sense a member of the Arab community. Egypt and Syria were the pacemakers of Arab nationalism, and their hostility to the American initiative was growing more open every day. Saudi Arabia was guardedly friendly, but King Saud was careful not to sever the links that bound him to the Egyptians and Syrians. Iraq, as a member of the Bagdad Pact (and so, in the eyes of the Arab nationalists, a lost sheep), could be relied on to stick with the West, at least for as long as Nuri el Said retained control. That left one Arab state still uncommitted—Jordan—and it was in Jordan that the next round was fought out.

The government of Suleiman Nabulsi, which had been in power in Jordan since the elections in October, "resigned" (in effect it was dismissed by King Hussein) on April 10. Three days earlier, acting on information which reached me through Bob Petty of the Arab News Agency, I had sent the following dispatch to the Manchester Guardian, with a message to the editor saying that he might think its contents alarmist, and I hoped they might prove to be so. The dispatch (by air mail) reached Manchester just after Nabulsi's resignation was announced from Amman.

Few competent observers give the kingdom of Jordan more than another year or two of independent existence—and the end might come next week. The tension which has long been evident between the twenty-one-year-old King Hussein and the coalition government led by Suleiman Nabulsi came dangerously near to the breaking point last week, with the cabinet's decision to establish diplomatic relations with the Soviet Union. King Hussein has not yet approved that decision, and if, as seems likely, he refuses to do so, his refusal would cause an open breach between himself and his government. If the struggle were not quickly resolved, it could mean a civil war in Jordan, or the country's partition amongst its neighbours.

The tension between king and cabinet springs from causes both general and particular. A general source of irritation is the young king's tendency to intervene personally in the field of domestic and international politics, as though harking back to the successful autocracy of his grandfather, King Abdullah. An example was the message the king sent to his prime minister in February, warning him of the dangers of Communist infiltration in Jordan. At that time the king won his point, and the government obediently adopted measures against the dissemination of Communist propaganda in Jordan. But their decision last week to recognise and establish diplomatic relations with the Soviet Union suggests that Nabulsi and his leftist colleagues in the government feel their position to have strengthened. By choosing to take issue with the king over the same question on which he asserted himself in February, they are making what looks like a direct challenge to his authority.

Another issue in dispute between them is the attitude which Jordan should adopt towards the Eisenhower Doctrine. King Hussein is known to be in favour of co-operation with the Americans, though at the meeting of Arab heads of state in Cairo six weeks ago he and King Saud were unable to persuade the presidents of Egypt and Syria to make any gesture of welcome to the American initiative. Nabulsi's government, which was elected in October last, with an express mandate to sever Jordan's long-standing connection with Britain, follows the line dictated by

Syria and Egypt over the Eisenhower Doctrine, as over other points at issue, and so far has not invited President Eisenhower's special envoy, Mr. James Richards, to visit Amman.

The immediate cause of the crisis which flared up in Amman on April first was the cabinet's resentment at the dispatch by King Hussein of a personal message to the Egyptian, Syrian and Saudi Arabian governments. This message, which was conveyed by one of the king's closest personal advisers, Mr. Bahgat el Talhouni, is believed to have been one of reassurance to King Saud and to President Nasser and President Kuwatly (who with King Hussein himself, make up the Arab "Big Four") that if the government in Jordan resigned or was dismissed, this would not mean any change in Jordan's attitude to the questions discussed at the "Big Four's" recent conference in Cairo. It is reported from well-informed sources in Amman that King Saud's reply indicated that he would support King Hussein, and—less confidently—that President Nasser's reply, too, was "satisfactory." There is no indication of the reply given by the Syrian president.

There are already both Syrian and Saudi Arabian troops inside Jordan, who were invited to enter the country last November in case the fighting between Egypt and Israel spread to the Jordan front. And since the termination of the treaty between Jordan and Great Britain, the British garrisons at Aqaba and Mafraq (which in the past were a principal guarantee of stability in Jordan) are to be evacuated within a few months. In the circumstances both Syria and Saudi Arabia are likely to try to establish a grip on parts of Jordan's territory, if only to prevent it from falling into the hands of their common enemy, Iraq.

In face of such possibilities, especially if their rulers appear to be at loggerheads with each other, the Jordanians cannot be expected to present a united front. Jordan is an artificial entity, a country carved out of the desert by British treaty-makers after the First World War, to which part of Palestine beyond the river Jordan was annexed after the Arab-Israeli war of 1948. The Palestinian Arabs look down on the less sophisticated Transjordanians, and neither feels any very deep loyalty to the Hashemite dynasty, which came to Amman less than forty years ago after being expelled from Arabia by King Ibn Saud, the father of the present king of Saudi Arabia. Many Jordanians think of themselves as "south Syrians," and one of the foremost schemes of the present Jordanian government under Suleiman Nabulsi has been for a federal union with Syria. (So far no more has been achieved than the abolition of passport regulations between the two countries and one or two "cultural" agreements about the harmonisation of education policies and the like.)

This is the situation at present—while King Hussein has yet to make up his mind whether to endorse the cabinet's decision to open diplomatic relations with Russia. If he refuses to do so, a trial of strength is likely to follow between king and government, in which the forces backing either side are difficult to assess. In the towns, where wages are low and unemployment runs at something near to 50 per cent, Nabulsi can reckon on strong support. Amongst the refugees, who make up about a third of Jordan's population of a million and a half, opinions are as shifting and uncertain as the lives led by these unfortunates in their camps and hovels. A quick oratorical campaign could swing them to one side or the other, especially if a strong appeal is made to their dreams of Arab unity, from which alone they expect an end to their tribulations. (It is significant that Nabulsi embarked on April 5 on a speaking tour, which was planned to take in Nablus, Ramallah, Hebron and Jerusalem by the end of this week—all four towns being situated in old Palestine.)

King Hussein is said to have the support of the Bedouin tribes, always the most conservative and loyalist element in the country (as was shown by the loyalty of the Bedouin units in the Arab Legion to General Glubb at the time of his dismissal a year ago). That leaves the army as the decisive factor, and one whose loyalties are divided and uncertain. The young commander-in-chief, General Ali Abu Nuwar, who owes his position to King Hussein's personal influence, is known to side with Nabulsi and the government, and his authority will count for a lot. But the king is said to have an influential supporter in his chief aide-de-camp, Brigadier Mohamed Maayta, formerly military attaché accredited to both Syria and the Lebanon.

In general, it looks as though the government now holds a stronger hand than the king. If this is so, he may decide not to

force the issue now, in which case it is likely to come to the fore
again within a month over the question of Jordan's attitude to the
Eisenhower Doctrine. When it does, and the gauntlet is thrown
down between king and government, the whole Middle Eastern
apple-cart is likely to be upset once again. For if neither side
can claim a quick victory, and Jordan becomes a prey, either to
internal strife or to a squabble for shares on the part of her Arab
neighbours, Israel may see a golden opportunity to settle her
eastern frontier problem once and for all, by a swift campaign
to absorb the rest of old Palestine up to the river Jordan.

> *There were a few anxious days of cabinet-making,
> during which the leftist elements held their fire, con-
> fident that no government could be formed without
> them and still survive. Then, on the night of April
> 13-14, the crisis came to a head in a shooting affray at
> Zerqa, a garrison town north east of Amman. The king
> gained the upper hand—but evidently his victory was
> not complete, for Suleiman Nabulsi found a place in
> the new government that was formed on the fifteenth.*

AMMAN, APRIL 15

After confused days of rumour and counter-rumour in Jordan
it was announced to-night that Dr. Hussein Khalidi is to be
premier in place of Suleiman Nabulsi, who was dismissed by
King Hussein on Wednesday. The new government, however, is
reported to include Nabulsi.

The dramatic events of the last forty-eight hours appear to
have won the king at least a temporary victory in the struggle
for power. On Saturday it looked as though Nabulsi and his
leftist colleagues would succeed with their challenge to the king's
authority, but after the skirmish on Saturday night between army
units at Zerka had raised the crucial question of the army's ultimate loyalty, the King apparently stepped in decisively.

Yesterday it was learned that a deputation of army officers
had been received by the king and had affirmed the army's allegiance to him. Censorship was imposed and, according to information here, some political leaders opposed to King Hussein were
either arrested or ordered to leave Jordan. General Ali Abu

Nuwar, who was chief of staff of the Jordanian army, is now in Damascus, and his functions have been taken over by General Ali Hiyari.

Meanwhile, though extreme tension prevails in Amman, there have been no demonstrations since those of Saturday in which demonstrators peaceably denounced the Eisenhower Doctrine and called for a "government of all the parties." The king's palace in Amman has been surrounded by a heavy guard, including armoured cars and artillery, and while the king's decisive actions of yesterday have evidently taken his political opponents by surprise, it remains highly problematical whether he can maintain his present advantage.

Demonstrations were reported this morning from Ramallah, on the west bank of the Jordan, where the Jordan radio transmitter ceased operation yesterday after repeated interruptions to the programme transmitting the text of the king's message to the nation. Reports say the station was sabotaged; certainly there was a struggle yesterday for control of it.

Of the dangers still surrounding the king, the most threatening is the likelihood that the defeated politicians will stir up feelings on the west bank among the Palestinians and the large refugee population. But the bulk of the Jordanian army is on the west bank, near the Israeli border, and if they stay loyal, as seems likely with the removal of General Nuwar, they could probably hold down the dissidents.

The story of events during Saturday night seems to be well established. Loyal Bedouin troops at Zerqa (the Third Regiment of the Jordanian army), learning of a plot against the king, planned to nip it in the bud and move on to Amman to protect the king. Fighting developed with the Fifth Regiment, during which it is estimated several were killed and twenty to forty wounded. King Hussein hurried out from Amman, appeared personally at the scene of the fighting, and was afterwards escorted back to the palace by two-hundred loyalist officers. With this party was Hiyari, one of the senior officers of the old Arab Legion whose nose was put out of joint by Nuwar's sudden rise to eminence after Glubb's departure.

Investigating reports that Syrian troops were entering Jordan from the north, I made an extensive tour of the northern area of they country yesterday, but found no supporting evidence whatever. At Mafraq, where the R.A.F. still maintains a base, a Syrian brigade has been stationed since November, but there was no sign yesterday that it had been reinforced.

There may be truth in reports that Syrians who were approaching the frontier were turned back by Jordanian troops. It is also reported that King Hussein has asked President Kuwatly of Syria to withdraw the brigade from Mafraq. Certainly the Syrian ambassador to Amman left for Damascus yesterday with a personal message from the king to Kuwatly.

For most of a week there was an uneasy calm in Amman, but each side was watching for the other's next move, and now that the king's party had seized the initiative, the danger of rioting by the leftists was increased. The new commander-in-chief of the Jordan army followed his predecessor into exile in Syria, where he put out a statement accusing the king, by implication, of encouraging a plot against his people by reactionary elements in league with "foreign non-Arab military attachés" (meaning the British and American).

In fact, the lines had been drawn in Jordan as they were being drawn all through the Middle East. Egypt and Syria were openly supporting the leftists against the king, Egypt by pouring out a stream of inflammatory propaganda from the "Voice of the Arabs" radio (the Egyptian press had been banned from Jordan early in the crisis), the Syrians by welcoming to Damascus the growing number of political refugees leaving Jordan, among them the two retiring commanders of the Jordan army. The king was believed to have had assurances of support from Iraq and Saudi Arabia, but for the moment he and his government held firm without calling for aid from outside. On the twenty-third the leftists called for a general strike next day (the appeal was

*broadcast by Cairo Radio), and the trial of strength was
imminent.*

*Next day the trouble started. I was up very early
to drive round the town and see what dispositions the
army had made. Then, after watching the first demonstrations, I caught a plane to Jerusalem and on to
Beirut, as I had obtained some relevant information
about the changes inside the army (on which the outcome of the crisis was likely to hinge), and I had no
hope of getting this past the censors in Jordan. The following dispatch was sent from Beirut that evening.*

AMMAN, APRIL 24

Demonstrators were out in the streets of Amman this morning shouting "Down with the Eisenhower Doctrine" and "Bring
back Ali Abu Nuwar." Bedouin troops, who had been brought
into the town in large numbers overnight, broke up the first
demonstrations by driving into the crowds in jeeps and lorries.
The demonstrators, who were mostly youths, dispersed to throw
stones from near-by cover.

The call had gone out yesterday (publicised mainly by the
Cairo Radio) for a general strike in support of the Left-wing
parties' petition to King Hussein. This called for an end to the
purge of the army which had been going on for ten days, the
resignation of Dr. Khalidi and the recall of the Nabulsi government, and the rejection of the Eisenhower Doctrine. The strike
was general this morning in the centre of Amman, but shops
were open in the side streets, where the attitude seemed to be
one of wait and see.

In Jerusalem a demonstration near the Damascus Gate of the
Old City was diverted by police and broke up quietly soon afterwards. Troops on all roads into the city prevented access from
outside, thus forestalling plans for refugees from near-by camps to
join the demonstrations. The air service between Jerusalem and
Amman, though much delayed by the difficulty of getting passengers out to either airport, was maintained, but road communications between the east and west banks of the Jordan were cut.

At dawn this morning Amman was ringed with troops, who set up roadblocks on the main roads out of the capital. No car was allowed past these barriers without special authorisation. The citadel, which commands Amman to-day as it did in Roman times (when the city's name was Philadelphia), was occupied, and the palace was still guarded by the Bedouin armoured-car regiment, which has been in position there since the king's successful coup on the night of April 13-14.

Detachments of Bedouin soldiers with blackened faces were on guard outside the British and American embassies. When the Bedouin blacks his face it is both practical and symbolic. Practically, it is a disguise to prevent his identification and to protect him against involvement in a blood feud with the relatives of those whom he may kill. Symbolically, it shows that he means business and has orders to shoot if necessary.

The events of the past few days have followed the classic pattern of Jordanian "political" life. First came the agitation in the west bank centres of Nablus, Ramallah and Jerusalem, culminating in the meeting on Monday of the Left-wing parties' Committee of National Guidance to formulate the opposition's demands. These were submitted to the King yesterday, facing him with a direct challenge to his own authority (though to avoid the appearance of this the emphasis was on the sins of "palace officials" and the American embassy), as well as to the authority of the Khalidi cabinet.

Meanwhile a propaganda barrage was opened up from abroad with pronouncements from Ali Abu Nuwar and Ali Hayari, the two former commanders of the Jordan army now in Damascus, accompanied by the urgings of the Cairo Radio. The latter has followed an inflammatory and irresponsible line, very similar to that of the Communists in leaflets distributed in Amman and Jerusalem, calling for a strike and mass meetings and falsely announcing last night the fall of the Khalidi government.

It looks as though the king means to face the challenge, and this morning's troop dispositions looked businesslike. If he does and can hold the line he may save the situation—but he runs the risk of violence in the streets and possible civil war. The choice is between taking this risk and capitulating to the Left wing.

The crucial factor is the army, whose reorganisation has been moving fast since the showdown of April 13. It is impossible to say yet whether the army will back the king unitedly or whether its morale has survived recent events, including the defection of two successive commanders. But its importance as a decisive factor is signalled alike by the king's swiftness in replacing doubtfully loyal officers and by the opposition's reiterated demand that the purge should be stopped.

The changes made in the army command since April 13 are far-reaching. In addition to General Nuwar and General Hayari, about eight senior officers have fled to Syria and a further dozen are in "detention" in Amman. Among those detained are the commanding officers of the artillery and engineers and the army's single tank regiment. All these are non-Bedouin units.

Of the five brigade commanders four have been changed, two reportedly having been removed by their own men. (Brigadier Maan Abu Nuwar, a cousin of the former commander-in-chief, who had command of the Bedouin infantry units, is variously reported as having been beaten to death and as being in hospital seriously injured.) In most cases the officers who have been removed have been replaced by Bedouin or Circassians, an exact reversal of the process after General Glubb's dismissal.

Apart from the question of key commands in the army, its disposition presents a difficult problem. In the circumstances the army has two tasks: to protect the frontiers and to put down any internal risings. For the second task only Bedouin units can be considered reliable, since for them the soldiers' loyalty is reinforced by the stronger traditions of tribal allegiance.

Bedouins comprise roughly half the army, being in general purely fighting soldiers as opposed to technical units. They form five and a half of the army's twelve infantry regiments and both its armoured car regiments. Of the latter, one is based on Zerqa, near Amman, and the other in the Aqaba area. Three Bedouin infantry regiments are on the west bank of the Jordan and another at Zerqa, together with a fifth regiment, which is only one-half Bedouin.

From these dispositions it appears that the government should be able to take care of the west bank provided that there is no immediate threat from across the Israeli border; but it might feel the need to withdraw some Bedouin units to hold Amman if trouble develops there. In Jerusalem yesterday I heard the gloomy view expressed that the government might feel impelled to leave the west bank to its fate (it is from there that the political troubles mainly originate), in which case the river Jordan would surely soon become once again the natural frontier which geographically it is.

A new, ultraconservative cabinet was formed late that night, and after its first meeting King Hussein imposed martial law throughout Jordan early on the twenty-fifth. The opposition collapsed—or went underground—and the internal victory rested with the king. But outside Jordan rival forces continued the fight. President Kuwatly of Syria flew to Cairo to confer with President Nasser, and the American Sixth Fleet sailed for the eastern Mediterranean. It was the first open trial of strength since Suez between the "positive neutralist" front, led by Egypt, and the West, for whom the United States now made the running.

It was King Saud who settled the issue, first by refusing to join President Nasser and President Kuwatly in bringing pressure to bear on King Hussein, and then by openly backing Hussein, who visited the Saudi Arabian capital on the twenty-eighth. This was an effective victory for the Eisenhower Doctrine, and Saud's support was seen by the Americans as the first fruit of his visit to Washington earlier in the year. But the victory was won at a price—the price of supporting a regime in Jordan which had now to rely on totalitarian methods to maintain order. This fact was to provide a rich mine of propaganda, which Cairo Radio was not slow to exploit.

The crisis in Jordan, which left King Hussein physically in control of a sullen and hostile country, involved both gains and losses for American policy in the Middle East. On the face of it, it was a victory, for despite a most vigorous propaganda campaign from Cairo and Damascus, Jordan had been torn out of the positive neutralist front. But this had only been achieved by the adoption of methods, both inside and outside Jordan, which were bound to have critical consequences. In Jordan order was only maintained by force, and by the abandonment of every principle of democratic existence—the suppression of political parties, the banning of public meetings, the suspension of parliament, the arrest of potentially "subversive" individuals. And America's close interest in the future of Jordan had also been demonstrated by a show of force, by the dramatic movement of the Sixth Fleet, which thus made its second irruption into the political arena in the Middle East. One day martial law would have to be lifted in Jordan, with consequences which seemed only too predictable; one day the Sixth Fleet might have to be used, with consequences which no one liked to predict. But for the moment it was young King Hussein's hour of triumph.

BEIRUT, MAY 2

King Hussein of the Hashemite kingdom of Jordan, who left Harrow at the age of seventeen to mount his throne five years ago, has just extricated himself and his little country from a crisis which promised to engulf them both. And in the process he has altered—for the moment at least—the whole balance of power in the Middle East.

During the three weeks of crisis which have just ended, the king enjoyed valuable support at the critical moments: from the older politicians who stood by him when he faced the leftists' challenge; from the bulk of his army when two ex-chiefs of the general staff withdrew to Syria and issued defiant pronouncements against him; from King Saud when the Syrian and Egyptian presidents tried to take the initiative away from Hussein; and from the American government, which finally put victory within his grasp by promising him $10 millions and sending the Sixth Fleet to show they meant it. But with all this, it was King

Hussein's own courage, both physical and moral, that gave him an initial advantage and enabled him to retain it to the end.

He showed his courage first by accepting the challenge of Suleiman Nabulsi and asking for his resignation as prime minister on April 10 rather than agree to open diplomatic relations with the Soviet Union. Nabulsi had chosen his ground carefully. The proposal in itself was not unreasonable, for after all there are Soviet ambassadors accredited to Washington and the Court of St. James. But it had a special significance, for two reasons. First, if it were put into effect it would indicate a closer adherence to the shadowy policy of "positive neutrality," which means in practice anti-Westernism and a disposition on the part of its authors to flirt with Russia to a point just short of actual seduction. Second, it would impose on the king an avowed abandonment of the firm position he had adopted in February, when he warned Nabulsi (and through him the people of Jordan) against the dangers of Communist infiltration, and forced the prime minister to make some show of suppressing the circulation of illegal Communist propaganda in Jordan.

In accepting this challenge King Hussein had to gamble (to outside observers, at any rate, it appeared to be a gamble) on retaining the loyalty of a sufficient section of the army. It was generally thought that the chief of the general staff, General Ali Abu Nuwar, would desert him (although it had been the King's personal favour that won Abu Nuwar his position), and no one knew how the army would choose, if a choice were forced upon it, between its king and its commander. At the first hint of dissension within the army, King Hussein showed his courage for the second time by driving out to Zerqa on the night of April 13-14 to make a personal appearance at the scene of a midnight affray (the circumstances are still not clear, but it seems certain that some units had mutinied and been engaged by a loyalist Bedouin regiment), later driving back to the palace with an escort of enthusiastic officers.

The Zerqa incident was a turning-point. Perhaps it was the dramatic appeal of the king's bravery, perhaps it was the more practical appeal of his success (which he used with moderation, resorting to no summary executions, and even forcing Abu Nuwar to accept the humiliation of exile instead of a martyr's crown), but after that not even the defection within a few days of Abu Nuwar's successor, General Ali Hiyari, shook the loyalty of the army—and it was on the army that the king now depended if he was to consolidate his position.

Zerqa had marked the end of the first round, which ended with a clear victory for the king. Hiyari's flight to Damascus a week later opened the second—and it was obviously designed to be the decisive round. It started with an intense propaganda barrage, from Hiyari himself (who alleged that there was a plot afoot between palace officials and "foreign military attachés in Amman"); from the Left-wing "national guidance committees" in towns like Nablus and Ramallah on the Palestine side of the river Jordan; from the Communists who distributed pamphlets in Jerusalem and Amman; and from the "Voice of the Arabs" radio, whose broadcasts, significantly, reminded listeners of the riots which followed General Templer's visit to Amman in 1955, and called for mass meetings and a general strike.

This campaign went on for three days, and culminated in the general strike and rioting of April 24. This was the climax of the crisis, and again the young king kept his nerve. A series of demands had been submitted to him on the twenty-third, calling for the resignation of the cabinet, the removal of certain palace officials, and the suspension of the courts of inquiry which were carrying out a purge of army officers. If the demands were refused, there was an implicit threat of rioting, and it was clear to everyone that the opposition intended to test the limits to which the king was prepared to go in facing this threat, and what strength he could command in the final emergency.

The answers were immediate and decisive. The citizens of Amman and Jerusalem awoke on the morning of April 24 to find both cities ringed with troops, who had set up roadblocks on all trunk roads—an important precaution in Jordan, since it prevents the refugees from near-by camps from joining in demonstrations in the cities. In the capital the British and American embassies were guarded by black-faced Bedouin troops, obviously ready for trouble, and in the streets were patrols armed with wicker shields to protect them against stones thrown by the rioters.

There was not, in fact, much violence on the twenty-fourth, but the situation was threatening enough to justify the king in taking the next step (one which had been foretold for a week) of declaring martial law. With a curfew enforced in all the main towns, security forces were able to round up most of the known agitators, and as an added precaution all forms of political activity were banned, parties dissolved, and the unfinished session of parliament indefinitely suspended.

King Hussein had been successful in asserting his authority inside Jordan: now he was faced with a challenge from outside. On the twenty-fifth President Kuwatly of Syria flew to Cairo to confer with President Nasser, and next day went on to Riyadh, taking an Egyptian delegation with him, to hold consultations with King Saud. The obvious intention was that three members of the Arab "Big Four" should bring pressure to bear on the fourth, and in fact it was stated in Cairo that a three-power mission would be visiting Amman to bring King Hussein "back to the Arab fold."

This visit never took place, and instead King Hussein, taking his courage in his hands once more, left his capital on the morning of the twenty-eighth accompanied by a small retinue which included Samir Rifai, and flew to Riyadh, where he talked things over with King Saud, returning to Amman very early the next morning. Having scattered his enemies at home and avoided the ministrations of his Syrian and Egyptian "brothers," Hussein had only one more worry. He had depended on Egypt and Syria, as well as on King Saud, to fill the gap left in his budget by the ending of the British subsidies last month. But on the afternoon of April 29 he left it to the American ambassador to fill in the last piece in the jigsaw puzzle with the announcement that the American government would advance Jordan an extra $10 millions of economic aid.

And so the crisis has ended—for the moment—revealing King Hussein not only as a brave young man but also as an extremely skilful strategist. But no final solutions have been reached, and the same problems which caused the crisis will remain to be solved when martial law is lifted and conditions in Jordan return to normal. Ten million dollars (the equivalent of about three months' allowance of the old British subsidy) will not cure Jordan's economic weakness: a purge of Left-wing leaders will not remove the grievances on which they have played among the unemployed and among Jordan's 500,000 Palestine refugees.

His own problems will remain, but young King Hussein, if he can hold the line, will have done several things for the Arab world. He will have shown that in order to overturn a government it is not necessarily sufficient to send two or three hundred demonstrators out into the streets. He will have proved that even one of the "liberated Arab states" (Iraq is excluded from this fraternity by her membership in the Bagdad Pact) can defy Egyptian propaganda without being struck down by a thunderbolt. Most important of all, he will have so weakened the "positive neutrality" front among the Arab states as to drive Egypt to concentrate either on the more logical scheme of the unity of the Nile Valley, or—best of all for Egypt herself—on her own pressing internal problems. Either way he will have done the Middle East a service.

Early in May I returned to Cairo, where the espionage trial in which four British subjects were involved (and four others in absentia) was at last to begin. The first arrests had been made in Cairo eight and a half months earlier, within a few weeks of the nationalisation of the Suez Canal. In our minds it had always been linked to the Suez crisis, and the fate of the prisoners had seemed to depend in large part on the course of events on the wider stage. It was a relief, after attending the court for a few days, to find the atmosphere orderly and unemotional.

CAIRO, MAY 13

The conduct of the trial so far seems scrupulously correct, with Judge Abdel Latif unquestionably the dominant figure in his own courtroom. If the first impression of that courtroom is an untidy one, with rough benches crowded, and street cries and the clank of the water-sellers' brass mugs drifting in through the open windows, it is apparent at the first hint either of impropriety or imprecision that Judge Abdel Latif (he is the chief of the three judges in the case) has things in hand. Up to now his interventions have more often been to the advantage of the defence than of their opponents.

From the arguments advanced in these first three days of the trial it is clear that the fate of the defendants will rest on the court's decisions over two principal points. The first is the question of whether Egypt at the time of the alleged offences was in a state of war (the only ground on which the death sentence could be passed on any of the accused). The second is the question of whether the information which the defendants are alleged to have gathered had a specifically secret or military character.

Regarding the first of these points, the defendants were arrested in August and September when the only possible and technical enemy Egypt could claim was Israel. At that time Britain was technically the ally of Egypt, since the abrogation of the Anglo-Egyptian agreement of 1954 did not come until after Britain's armed intervention in Egypt in November. Regarding the second point, the prosecution devoted most of yesterday's session to an attempt to establish the secret nature of the information which it alleges was gathered by the defendants; and the defence, when its time comes, is likely to concentrate largely on trying to refute this contention.

Swiss and British legal observers were in court again to-day at the instance of the Foreign Office and are pursuing their attempts to gain permission to visit the prisoners, which so far have been unsuccessful. Three British correspondents were also present and were allowed to exchange brief greetings with the prisoners through the grille which separates them from the body of the court. All four British prisoners appeared well and in good spirits, though puzzled by the fact that they have had scarcely any contact with their lawyers.*

The Egyptians were in conciliatory mood altogether, and there was a keen desire to return to normal

* The trial lasted until the end of May, and the panel of judges gave their verdicts three weeks later. Zarb and Swinburn were found guilty, and sentenced to ten years and five years hard labour respectively. Stanley and Pittuck were acquitted, and left Egypt after nearly ten months in prison.

relations (at least commercially) with Britain. They took encouragement from the prime minister's announcement on May 13 that British ships would in future use the canal once more (paying dues to the Egyptian Canal Authority).

CAIRO, MAY 14

The first British ships to be rerouted through the Suez Canal since Mr. Macmillan's announcement yesterday are expected at Suez within three days. They are likely to be tankers homeward bound from the Persian Gulf.

Cairo has taken quietly the news of Britain's intention to return to the canal, and there is much less emphasis here on the British "surrender" than on hopes that the dam of ill will and misunderstanding may at last be cracking for good. This is understandable, since it is certainly for Egypt's good that commercial relations at least should be reopened with Britain, and that sterling, which for so long was the traditional medium for Egyptian trade, should once again be available to finance much-needed imports.

All the same, it shows unusual restraint (almost certainly imposed from on high) that only one of Cairo's four Arabic morning papers chose to treat the canal story from the angle of an Egyptian triumph. This was the extremist *El Shaab* which, under the headline "The Price of Victory," extolled Egypt's stand against intimidation and armed intervention, reminding its readers of the sacrifices that this involved "in financial and manpower resources."

A note more representative of the attitude of the rest of the press was struck by the English-language *Egyptian Gazette*, which looked ahead to the prospect of talks on Anglo-Egyptian financial arrangements "relating to transactions unconnected with the Suez Canal" (Mr. Macmillan's words). The *Gazette* expressed the hope that Britain's leaders in future dealings with this part of the world would show sincerity and straight-forwardness, "which, after all, are not un-British traits"—an unsolicited tribute which leaves one blinking these days.

But such gentle words, however stumblingly they may come

to the pens of Egyptian editors, undoubtedly express the conviction of the majority of Egyptians, who, in spite of the recent efforts of propagandists, still regard the British as their most natural allies outside the Arab world. This fact emerges again and again from conversations with business men, lawyers, taxicab drivers, and civil servants, who half understood our attack in October—though they thought it wrong—were puzzled by our decision to call the attack off—though they thought it right—and have spent the last six months wondering why we ever got into this tangle and looking forward to the day when the English would return and all this foolishness be forgotten.

Two days later Egyptian optimism seemed to be justified, when it was announced that trade talks were to be held with the British later in the month. It was an odd commentary on the aftermath of the Suez crisis that at this moment of reconciliation with Britain, who had attacked Egypt, the Egyptians remained deeply suspicious of the Americans, who had taken her part.

CAIRO, MAY 16

A delegation headed by the Egyptian under-secretary for economic affairs, Mr. Lutfi el Banna, left Egypt to-day for Rome, where it will hold talks later this month with a British delegation on the question of reopening commercial relations between the two countries.

The delegation included representatives of the National Bank of Egypt, the foreign ministry, and the currency controller's office. Before meeting the British delegation, probably on May 23, it will negotiate a new payments agreement with the Italian government.

Since Mr. Macmillan's announcement that British ships would again use the Suez Canal, Cairo has been buzzing with reports of a speedy resumption of trade relations between Britain and Egypt. Such a development would be warmly welcomed by all sections of Egyptian society, from large importers of cotton-ginning machinery and aircraft spares to the humblest retailer of razor blades—not to mention the donkey-boys and guides, who acknowledge sadly that their donkeys have grown thinner and their basic English has rusted during the last six painful months. While Egyptian hearts are warming again to the absent British, America is fast losing her fleeting popularity by her support for the Israeli threat to send a test ship to Suez; by the fact that unlike Britain she has made no move to unfreeze Egyptian credits; and most of all by her successful wooing of King Saud, which knocked a hole in the façade of positive neutralism big enough for King Hussein of Jordan to drive a horse and cart through. All these have revealed America to Egyptian eyes as the real villain of the piece.

The number of ships using the Suez Canal is rising steadily. Yesterday twenty-seven passed through, including one British and one America. The Canal Authority to-day announced that there would be three convoys daily from Saturday, when the first British tankers to be rerouted through the canal are expected at Suez from the Persian Gulf.

Only France, who raised the question again at the Security Council, still challenged Egypt's de facto victory over the Suez Canal. The Egyptians found plenty to console them for the disfavour of the French.

CAIRO, MAY 21

With between twenty and thirty ships using the Suez Canal daily, as against ten or twelve a month ago, Egypt can afford to take a caustic view of France's rearguard action in the Security Council.

The Egyptian press, which is concentrating much of its attention on the election campaign which has just opened (and which as a topic of discussion has at least the merit of being totally novel in post-revolutionary Egypt), finds space for full reports of the proceedings in the Security Council. But these have, for the Egyptians, an agreeably academic character alongside the news that four British ships went through the canal yesterday, among them the first British tankers from the Persian Gulf; that seven are expected to-day; that passengers from the British liner "Caledonia" went ashore in the good old tourist style; and that the remaining members of the Egyptian delegation to the trade talks with Britain leave for Rome to-morrow. All these items are good news to the Egyptians, not because they underline Egypt's triumph, but because they hold the promise of renewed trade with the West and of the resumption of normal relations with the world outside the iron curtain and with Britain in particular. In short, Egypt, especially now that her mastery of the Arab world has just been successfully challenged in Jordan, feels more than ever her isolation from the Western world with which for the past century and a half she has had close cultural, economic, and technological links, and looks forward to getting out of coventry again.

> *Jordan had been a setback for Egypt, but the canal was a victory, and for the time being it seemed that the Egyptian government had wisely decided to lie low while both were digested. The first general election in post-revolutionary Egypt was due early in July, and this provided a convenient distraction for the Egyptian press and public opinion.*

CAIRO, MAY 19

The election campaign is already under way, with banners and posters urging the claims of candidates in Cairo streets and suburbs. Sixteen members of the present cabinet have come forward as candidates, eleven of them for Cairo constituencies and five in other parts of Egypt. Other candidates include army officers (who must resign their commissions if elected), lawyers, financiers, a few women, and at least one actor.

This is the First Egyptian election in which women have been candidates, and it was only last year that they gained the right to vote at a plebiscite. That was the one which approved the new constitution and elected Gamal Abdul Nasser president of Egypt.

After the elections the national Assembly will hold its first meeting on July 22, on the eve of the fifth anniversary of the Egyptian revolution. Political parties are banned in Egypt, and in the existing circumstances it would be absurd to expect any opposition movement to spring into life overnight with the creation of an assembly from which the principal sources of opposition had been carefully excluded. But it would be equally rash to write off Egypt's projected essay in graded democracy as a sham.

In the first place, it is a stage in the redemption of the revolutionaries' promise to restore parliamentary forms as soon as practicable (and not before). In the second place, no one who knows anything of Egyptians can imagine 350 of them being shut up in one room and failing to disagree, and presently to voice their disagreement, about most things under the sun.

At its worst the national assembly will provide a platform from which sections of society totally excluded from public life during the past five years (like businessmen and lawyers), will be able to express points of view perhaps sectarian but still relevant to the general interest. At its best it will have an opportunity to broaden the basis of Egyptian policy-making by keeping Egypt's leaders in closer touch with elements of society at present unrepresented in the nation's councils, and to remind the leaders that Egypt's long-term interests may not always be best served by scoring immediate points off political opponents abroad. Lastly, this potentially important development in Egyptian political life should serve to concentrate the country's attention inwards onto Egypt's own domestic problems, which at the moment would be a service alike to Egypt, to the troubled Middle East, and to the world at large.

The candidates who offered themselves were carefully screened, and about half of them were ruled out before the election by a government selection committee. Even so, the decision to hold an election at all at this juncture showed a confident attitude on the part of the Egyptian leaders, for Egypt's situation was as difficult as it had been at any moment since the start of the Suez crisis nearly a year before.

CAIRO, MAY 25

King Hussein's open defiance of Cairo's claim to speak for the "liberated Arab world" advertised the weakening of Egypt's grip on the loyalties of neighbouring Arab governments. But the root of that weakness lay in the defection of King Saud—partial and inexplicit though it was—after his visit to Washington early in the year. It was King Saud's support which enabled Jordan to assert its independence, and it was the *rapprochement* between Saudi Arabia and its old enemy, Iraq, which exposed the growing isolation of Egypt in the Arab world.

A year ago, when Cairo called the tune, Arabs danced from the borders of Turkey to the southern fringes of the Arabian peninsula. To-day Egyptian newspapers are banned even in the easy-going Lebanon, the "Voice of the Arabs" radio is jammed in Jordan (and intermittently in Iraq), and there have been complaints about the subversive activities of Egyptian propagandists or official representatives, not only in these three "sister Arab states," but also in Libya, Ethiopia, and the Sudan.

Egypt's reply to her critics is that whatever enemies her policy may make for her among the Arab governments, she retains the loyalty of the bulk of the Arab peoples, of whose interests and aspirations she claims to be the champion. Nobody knows with any precision what Arab aspirations are, and as for Arab interests, Egypt could hardly claim to have furthered them by her policies during the past year. But that she does retain the loyalty of the masses of the Arab peoples is indisputable, and certainly the rulers of Jordan or Iraq or Saudi Arabia are in no position to dispute it, since none of them can claim for his authority the sanction of public opinion.

But for all that, the argument is largely an academic one, and must remain so until public opinion counts for more than personalities in the Arab world. That day may not be far distant, but until it comes the Egyptians know as well as anyone else that they must have the support of governments as well as peoples, if they are to retain their leadership in the Middle East.

With the tide of opinion in the Arab world running strongly towards a resumption of normal relations with the West, Egyptian propaganda has almost ceased its attacks against Western policy—except, of course, against the French, whose obstinate perseverance in the mood of Suez, coupled with their involvement in Algeria, earn them the unanimous recriminations of the Arab world.

In the past the government in Cairo cannot claim to have

taken much more account of public opinion than do the governments it criticises in Bagdad or Amman. The business classes in
Egypt, by and large, are frankly hostile to a foreign policy which
has cut Egypt off from its traditional trade partners and reduced
the value of the Egyptian pound by a third on the international
market. The man in the street and the peasants up and down
the Nile Valley know and care nothing of the march of events
beyond their narrow horizon; for them, Arab aspirations are much
less meaningful than the price of beans and the fact that the
government has guaranteed the price of cotton for the coming
season.

Until last month President Nasser's government was prepared to impose—and the Egyptian people to accept—an austerity
regime, rather than yield to Western pressures. But Egypt's
waning popularity in the Arab world, as demonstrated by events
in Jordan, called for a more flexible approach to the outside
world, and President Nasser's victory over the issue of the Suez
Canal gave him the opportunity to bargain from a position of
apparent strength. The outcome was the meeting in Rome between British and Egyptian trade delegations.

Inside Egypt the prospect of resumed trade relations with
Britain is viewed with an enthusiasm born of more than commercial self-interest. It is natural to find the large retailers in
downtown Cairo rubbing their hands at the prospect of renewing
their stocks of English cloth, English shoes, English books—but
less natural, if one cast one's mind back a mere six months, to find
that most Egyptians look forward to the day when the English
themselves will return, and to be treated with genuine friendliness
as the forerunner of a new and peaceable and mutually profitable
invasion.

Egyptian optimism at the thought that the private iron curtain behind which they have lived for six months will shortly be
lifted may be premature. But public opinion in Egypt has in this
respect run ahead of the government, and the government, mind-
ful of the criticisms it has encountered within the Arab world, is
showing a new moderation and a willingness to let bygones be
bygones. The way in which the controlled Egyptian press treated
the British decision to use the Suez Canal again was an indication

of this; with rare exceptions, the note of triumph was carefully muted, and the emphasis thrown much more on the possibility of a gradual return to normal relations between the two countries.

All these factors have their importance on the eve of Egypt's general election. In one sense, they give the government in Cairo a sound reason for turning its attention, and that of the Egyptian people, inwards onto an important domestic issue at a time when Egyptian foreign policy seems to have run into the doldrums. In another, the election comes at a moment when Egyptians have been reminded of the need to have at least a working relationship with the West, of the dangers of a propaganda machine which is strong in attack but has shown no capacity for suggesting constructive approaches to the problems facing Egypt or the Arab world.

At the same time elections were in prospect in the Lebanon, at the other end of the Arab political scale. Polling was to start on June 9, and on May 30 there was rioting in Beirut, where an opposition meeting was held in defiance of a government ban, and was broken up by the police. Seven people were killed, and the army had to be brought in to keep order in the capital. It was unfortunate that in the Lebanon and Jordan, the two Arab states which had frankly accepted American support, the governments had to rely on tanks against their own subjects. The Lebanese opposition, of course, made capital out of this, as did Cairo Radio. Resenting the way in which the Lebanese government headed by Sami el Solh and his strongly pro-American foreign minister, Charles Malik, had (as they said) tied the Lebanon to America's apron-strings, and cut her off from the stream of Arab nationalism, they tried to make foreign policy an issue at the election.

In fact, the election was fought out along traditional lines, in which the dominant factor was not foreign policy but the unvarying Lebanese preoccupation with material interests.

BEIRUT, JUNE 10

The government of Sami el Solh gained a substantial advantage yesterday in the first stage of the Lebanese general election, winning fifteen of the twenty-two seats contested in Beirut and south Lebanon.

The pro-Western policy of the present government, which was the first in the Middle East to subscribe without reservation to the Eisenhower Doctrine, was one factor in securing for it this electoral advantage over the mixed "National Front" of opposition parties.

Other factors were the lack of a sincere or coherent policy on the part of the National Front, which had hoped to make do with slogans about pan-Arabism on Egyptian lines; some public revulsion against the tactics of violence employed by the opposition which spilled over into rioting and bloodshed on May 30; and not least in importance, the government's superior "organisation" during yesterdays voting, when Beirut taxi drivers had a field day, ferrying more or less willing voters to the polling stations at the behest of the party leaders.

The comments in to-day's Beirut papers on the relative fairness of yesterday's voting are illuminating. And most illuminating of all perhaps is the summing-up by one voter: "We've never had such free elections," he said. "No pressure at all. There's money for anyone who wants to sell his vote, and anyone who wants to follow his conscience can do that, too." The prices of votes were being freely quoted during election day and seem to have varied between about five and eight dollars, the latter figure being attained late in the afternoon by those canny enough to wait.

The army capably held the ring outside the polling stations, and its intervention otherwise proved unnecessary. The only serious incident reported was from the Armenian district of Beirut, where one man was killed and three wounded in a shooting affray which developed out of a political argument. This did not prevent commentators from describing these as the "calmest elections Beirut has ever known."

The full results of this general election will not be known

until the end of the month, since other areas of the Lebanon have still to vote. They will do so on the remaining three Sundays of June, but the voting elsewhere is likely to follow the general pattern set yesterday, and the Government's eventual victory seems assured.

In the succeeding stages of the election, govern-ment candidates maintained this early advantage, but the actual results of the election were almost forgotten in the battle of words in which each side accused the other of corruption, falsification and incitement to vio-lence. On June 23 twenty-three people were killed in and around a church at Miziara, in north Lebanon, and altogether some fifty people were killed during the month the elections lasted. The Lebanese government protested to the Soviet Union about attempts to inter-fere in the internal affairs of the Lebanon, and pro-gov-ernment papers accused Egyptian and Syrian agents of bribing voters in the Lebanon. Opposition leaders claimed that the election of foreign minister Charles Malik had been "managed" by American intervention, and neutral observers noted that the first shipment of American arms to reach the Lebanon under the Eisen-hower Doctrine arrived in Beirut on one of the four polling days.

It was interesting to compare these elections in the "democratic" Lebanon with those which soon followed in Nasser's Egypt.

BEIRUT, JULY 3

Egyptians went to the polls to-day in the first general election since the revolution of 1952. Of some 2,500 candidates who offered themselves for election, about half had been eliminated by a committee of three (all close associates of President Nasser) acting in the name of the National Union, which in theory is a nation-wide political party, and the only one entitled to put forward candidates. The remaining 1,300 candidates are contesting 350 seats, from the low-lying delta towns on the Mediterranean coast to the remotest settlements on the Upper Nile near the

Sudanese border—an area, incidentally, which will be completely inundated if the High Aswan Dam is ever built.

At first sight, with the elimination of so many candidates and with no rival parties, this was an unconvincing essay in democracy. But before dismissing it with a sniff as unsatisfactory by Western standards, it is worth considering it as it should be considered, in its own Middle Eastern context, and instructive to compare it with similar exercises in neighbouring countries, in particular with those whose governments support Western policies in the area.

Take the Lebanon, for instance, nominally the most advanced Arab state, which has just emerged with a sigh of relief from a month of elections during which one person was killed for every two deputies elected. Government candidates finally gained a majority of about four to one—by methods certainly questionable and which, according to one of the opposition leaders who is also an ex-premier, included the falsification of returns, threats, the exertion of strong pressure on officials, the buying of votes, and the intimidation of voters.

A neutral observer, after making allowances for the bitterness of defeat, can only confirm that some of these accusations are well founded. The trade in votes was open from start to finish; prices were discussed in the newspapers and on street corners. Without it, not even the 50 to 60 per cent of the electorate who turned out would have done so, either through fear of becoming involved in faction fights or because of threats of the consequences if they voted the wrong way.

The election of the Lebanese Foreign Minister, Charles Malik, was only assured when his chief opponent was "induced" to withdraw at the last moment after an interview lasting most of the day at the president's palace. In short, this election gave about as accurate an indication of Lebanese opinion as a British election in the time of Lord North, and it was conducted along very similar lines. President Nasser's methods are at least more open and involve less bloodshed.

Or take Iraq, whose parliament was prorogued last week with the disarming comment that "there is nothing abnormal in this measure." There have been no free elections in Iraq yet, nor are any in prospect. Even if a "free" election were held, most observers agree that two-thirds of the present deputies would be returned, because their position depends not only on the support of Nuri el Said's electoral machine and the the Iraqi army, but on the feudal tribal authority which rules undisturbed outside Iraq's few cities. This is the class of wealthy conservative landowners whose power was broken in Egypt at the time of the revolution, but which in Iraq is too influential to be sacrificed by the government in the name of social progress.

Then there is Jordan, where political life is outlawed as it is in Iraq. Jordan had one experience of free elections when Suleiman Nabulsi was returned to power last October (to be astutely bundled out again six months later by King Hussein and the American Sixth Fleet). The experience is not likely to be repeated in the near future, so that—pace Mr. Dulles—the pro-Eisenhower Arabs do not compare very favourably with the Nasserites.

Regrettably, it is in Syria that the least unpromising shoots of independent political thinking appear—and Syria stands uncompromisingly on the wrong side of the line from the orthodox Western standpoint.

From this tangled pattern emerge two uncomfortable morals. First, in their present stage of development none of the Arab states is ready for fully representational government, and, that being so, they are much better off without the elaborate pretence of liberty where no liberty exists (and where few people would know how to employ it if it did exist).

Second, while the Arab governments which show most partiality towards the West are in general hanging on to outdated positions with, at the best, unwilling support from their peoples, those which oppose us have at least a rallying cry, distorted and imprecise for the moment, but none the less effective. It is Arab nationalism which the West must learn to live with and, if possible, to lead, if it is ever to come to terms with the Arabs.

Since America had taken over the direction of Western policy in the Middle East, the divisions between the Arab states had grown deeper—and this was

*no coincidence. The American policy-makers insisted
on judging the Arabs on the basis of their attitude towards communism. They used hostility to communism
as a kind of yardstick by which to separate Arab sheep
from Arab goats, and this forced unwelcome decisions
on the Arab leaders, to whom communism, if it mat-
tered at all, was not relevant to their own ambitions
and preoccupations. None of the Arab states were pro-
Communist, or had within them Communist parties of
any significance, though Jordan in particular was threatened by the possibility that communism might appeal
to the desperate and abandoned refugees from Palestine.
In Egypt, against whom the charge of fellow-travelling
was most often laid, the Communist party was illegal,
and such Communists as raised their heads from time
to time were promptly clapped in gaol.*

*But the Soviet Union had an obvious interest in
complicating the West's relations with the Arabs, and
starting with the arms deal with Egypt in 1955, it had
been doing this with success ever since. As the Americans set out, with the Eisenhower Doctrine, to win the
allegiance of the Arab states, so the Russians entered
into open competition with them, offering exactly what
the Arabs wanted, in the shape of arms and economic
assistance, but without insisting that in return the Arabs
should bind themselves to a particular policy or a particular ideology, as did the Americans. Inevitably the
Russians were much more successful, especially in winning popular support as opposed to the lip-service of
governments. After the fate of Jordan had been decided—for the time being—it was on Syria that both
the Americans and the Russians concentrated their attention, with the Russians in a much more promising
position from the start.*

DAMASCUS, JUNE

Talking to Syrian officials these days you are liable to be
asked at the start—with a disarming smile—what it feels like to

step behind the iron curtain. And once you have exchanged the preliminary courtesies and sipped your first cup of sweet coffee (and in Damascus both coffee and courtesies retain the smooth richness that characterises social intercourse in the Arab world), you will almost certainly find yourself discussing in turn the three questions which to-day dominate the Syrian political horizon: communism, the Eisenhower Doctrine and the recent events in Jordan.

Damascus is only a couple of hours' drive from Beirut; but the frontier post on the eastward slope of the Lebanon mountains marks a dividing line which has more reality to-day than at any time since the artificial borders between the several Arab states were drawn after the First World War. The Lebanon, facing the Mediterranean and the trade route to Europe, has thrown in its lot with the West; Syria, whose deserts and wide plains are shut off from the sea, is Egypt's only firm ally in the drive for an Arab federation free from all outside "entanglements" and treading the uncertain path of "positive neutralism" between the world's opposing camps. So effectively has this division rent the fabric of Arab unity that Lebanese newspapers are banned in Damascus to-day, just as Egyptian newspapers are banned in Beirut.

But the traveller crossing this frontier need expect no more bitterness or hostility on the eastern than on the western side of it. "*Ahlan wa sahlan*," smile the Syrian frontier guards: "Welcome"—and if they charge you two pounds more than you expect for a visa, in return for a piece of paper which you imagine to be some necessary permit but which later turns out to be a ticket for a football match you know nothing about and could not possibly attend, why, this should only be taken as an instance of the Syrian's traditional eye for business. And as you drive into Damascus refreshed by the sight of the tumbling waters of Abana and Pharphar, and admire the spacious boulevards and trim gardens of the modern section of the city (laid out after the French left Syria); or later, when you walk through the shadowy canyons of the ancient *suq*, or rest in the shade of the graceful cloister which faces the Mosque of Sultan Selim, it is not any signs of political animosity you are likely to be confronted with, but, instead, a student whose English studies have been interrupted by the closing of the British Council, and who wonders whether you can help him to get to England.

This is a typical paradox in the Middle East of the mid-twentieth century—the Arab who voices his nostalgia for Western ways, while over his shoulder an ugly poster calls for the rejection of the West and all its works. Politically the West has lost its grip on the Arab world; but culturally, as well as technologically, its imprint is ingrained and inescapable. To take only two of the most obvious instances, the streets of Damascus are full of shops exhibiting tape recorders, machine tools, agricultural equipment (much of it, at this moment, made in Germany, but much, as in the past, from Britain or France or America); and the Syrian minister who answers your questions will do so in suave French, and in a context of political thought which can be traced back to Montesquieu and Rousseau and Hume.

How, then, have we come to such a pitch of estrangement from these people, who have borrowed so freely from us in the past, who still treat us, on the personal level, with their own inborn civility and humour—but in whom our every move in the political sphere prompts a reaction of edgy and unvarying suspicion? With the second cup of coffee, and the third, you begin to approach this mystery. You hear the oft-repeated story of Britain's (and France's) past sins against the "Arab nation"; of the Balfour Declaration; the failure to redeem in full our promises to the leaders of the revolt in the desert; our favouring of the Jews in Palestine; our opposition to the dream of Arab unity (but no mention of how little the Arabs themselves have done to realise it); and the final, fundamental sin of allowing the creation of Israel, and then, in unholy alliance with the Americans, of supporting it and encouraging its fierce design for the eventual subjugation of the Arab peoples. All this is part of the very fabric of the Arab mind, and must be accepted by the Westerner searching after truth in an Arab environment as his daily fare, something as familiar as the pattern on the wallpaper of the room in which he wakes each morning—to be reminded only of its ugliness.

But at least this far the pattern is clear, and to all but the few Westerners who would reject entirely the premises, the conclusions have logic of a sort. It is when you come to the present—to say nothing of the future—that the Arabs' conception of their destiny seems to dissolve into a world of cotton wool, where slogans flash and flutter like badly installed neon signs, and where rather than take an idea and shape it and mould it into something positive or constructive, even the bolder Arab spirits seem so often to trail off into self-pity and recriminations against those who could have built a better future for them and didn't.

It is not that there is any unwillingness to talk—in Syria at least. (In Egypt the official mind is much more wary of exposure to the journalist's tiresome probing.) It is, rather, that beyond a certain point, after which the Arab case (if one is to be made) must develop into something more than a recital of grievances, you run always into a set of rigid assumptions, facile and tedious to the Western mind, but to the Arab an infinitely dangerous substitute for objective argument, since they excuse—indeed they prevent—him from thinking things out for himself. Communism? It is incompatible with the precepts of Islam, and so no danger to an Arab society. The Eisenhower Doctrine? A self-evident attempt to impose a new domination on the Arab world, an intolerable affront to Arab "sovereignty" (the most tiresomely ubiquitous word in the Arab "newspeak"). The crisis in Jordan? Obviously the outcome of a reactionary-imperialist (or imperialist-opportunist, or even, in extreme cases, imperialist-reactionary-Zionist) plot, against which the "Arab nation" stands united in condemnation.

What makes these assumptions the more dangerous, of course, is the fact that they all contain some truth. Communism has certainly very little appeal for the Arab mind, and the evidence of its growth in the Arab countries (especially Syria) has been greatly exaggerated. But it is impossible to get an Arab to see that he might one day find himself ruled by a Communist government without having asked for it, or even wanted it. The Eisenhower Doctrine was clumsily presented, and the recent use of the Sixth Fleet, while it helped to secure an immediate objective in Jordan, gave a fatally useful handle to America's enemies in the Middle East. But Arab leaders know in their hearts, and will admit in private, that America's aim is not to "dominate" the Middle East, but to see that it does not fall under Soviet control and to protect the indispensable oil supplies of the West. As to Jordan, to maintain, as do the Syrians and Egyptians, that the whole crisis was engineered by the Americans with the collaboration of reactionary forces inside Jordan, puts them in an impossible quandary; for it involves acknowledging the fact that King Saud—whose support of King Hussein was so vital a factor—interprets the role of a leader of Arab nationalism quite differently than do President Nasser and President Kuwatly.

For the moment it is difficult to see how the West can break through these barriers of apparently wilful misunderstanding to arrive at any more fruitful relationship with the Arab world. Arab leaders, as so often in the past, are to-day the prisoners of a mythology they have themselves created. What they have told their peoples about the outside world, those peoples now believe in large part (shuttered as they are against outside influences)— even though the leaders never seriously believed themselves, but used words rather in the way the Americans used the Sixth Fleet, to gain immediate ends, without considering too closely how the weapon might one day become an embarrassment to them.

The only hopeful sign lies in the fact that the last six months (during which to a large extent Western diplomatists and businessmen and purveyors of culture have been absent from the Arab lands) have reminded Arabs of the advantages as well as the trials of their long association with the West, and that to-day the time seems ripe for a resumption of at least the less formal of the links that used to unite us. In Syria the Iraq Petroleum Company has been quietly back at work for two months; permission has been granted for the return of BOAC; there is talk of the British Council reopening before long. For the moment there is certainly more to be hoped for from contacts of this kind than from the formalities of diplomatic intercourse, since they are contacts which depend on mutual needs and promise mutual advantages. Well handled, in the freshening breeze of welcome which seems to blow in Damascus to-day, they may even help to build truer foundations for the formal relationship between ourselves and the Syrians, when the time comes for its resumption.

But the battle for Syria was almost lost. The Syrians, proudest and most intractable of the Arabs, resented what seemed to them an attempt by the Americans to dictate to them the course they should follow. Their suspicions of the West, more deeply ingrained than ever since the Suez affair, were in their own eyes justified by the events in Jordan, and by America's continuing support for Israel. In any case, they were assured of Russian assistance on terms much more attractive to them than anything the Americans were prepared to offer. (Further Soviet military aid, and a huge development loan to Syria, were announced after a Syrian delegation had visited Moscow in August.)

Meanwhile there was one Arab state on whose allegiance the West could count, for at least as long as the ruling group remained in power—Iraq. Iraq yielded place to none of the other Arab states in its nationalism —expressed principally in implacable enmity towards Israel—but it was bound to the West by two links; its membership in the Bagdad Pact and its dependence on oil revenues for a large part of its national income. The first made it suspect in the eyes of the "neutralist" Arabs; the second gave Iraq its best hope of one day wresting the leadership of the Arab world from Egypt.

BAGDAD, JUNE

The Arabs have their own private iron curtain, their own cold war. While the alliances on either side shiver and shift, in response to pressures domestic or dynastic or international, the anchor-state at each end of this local tug-of-war remains so far constant. At one end stands Egypt, champion of the "free Arabs" (as opposed to the "kept Arabs"); at the other, again as the champion of the "free Arabs" (but this time in contrast to the "fellow-travelling Arabs"), is Iraq.

Pictured from Cairo or Damascus, Bagdad rises in the mind as a latter-day Sodom, or as a Babylon modernised only in the infamous techniques of despotism and servitude. According to the gospel of Cairo Radio, Iraq is an unwilling outcast from the Arab family, its people straining vainly towards the embrace of their brothers in Egypt, their natural inclinations thwarted and frustrated by rulers who cling to the shabby coat-tails of their imperialist masters in the West. It is a gospel the bitterness of which perhaps gains emphasis from the fact that Iraq is at present in the grip of a development boom, based on its oil revenues of about £70 millions a year, while Egypt, with little oil and a rapidly growing population, is in the trough of economic depression.

Six months ago Iraq was indeed an outcast, and the personal ascendancy of Nuri el Said was never more clearly illustrated than when he showed himself able to survive the storm which Suez raised about his ears. Here was an Arab leader whose policy was based first and foremost (as that of any Arab leader must be) on hostility to Israel, but finding himself compromised by his alliance with Britain, whose armies appeared to be supporting the Israelis in an attack on another Arab state. Since the beginning of this year the tide has turned, and Nuri Pasha (the use of the grandiloquent but out-of-date title is symbolic) has had only to hold to his course to see the position of Iraq strengthened, as the fortunes of Egypt steadily declined.

Nuri el Said's resignation from the premiership on June 8 was a mark not of any growing opposition to his leadership, but, on the contrary, of his self-assurance. It was an indication that through the hot summer months at least, the Pasha could trust another hand to hold the reins, while he took a well-deserved rest in the gentler climate of Europe. And if his successor should essay a few tentative steps in the direction of a more liberal regime at home, why, Nuri Pasha on his return could either endorse them, if they had proved successful, or go back on them and restore the benevolent autocracy which he prefers (as he did on his last return to power in 1954).

For Nuri Pasha remains, beyond any peradventure, the

dominant figure on the Iraqi scene, whether he be technically in office as premier or not. Basically this is explained by his long record of successful statesmanship; his freedom from the taint of corruption (a rare distinction in Iraq, even among those whose opportunities have been infinitely fewer than the Pasha's); and his association from the start with the movement for Arab liberation. (Nuri el Said first appears on the international scene as an ex-officer of the Turkish army, who joined the Emir Hussein's revolt in the desert in 1916.) But more important than all is the fact that Nuri Pasha knows what he wants for his country, and has a clear idea of how to achieve it. Democratic freedoms play an inconspicuous part in the programme he has mapped out for Iraq—but until his critics can show that an advance in this direction would positively benefit the country (instead of merely making it easier to counter criticism from outside), the Pasha is not likely to pay much attention to them. Nor is he likely to interest himself in schemes for economic or political union between Iraq and one or the other of her Arab neighbours (even though he was an original protagonist of the plan for a Greater Syria), until those neighbours prove themselves to be more stable allies than would appear at present, and until Iraq's young development programme has given the country a firmer economic groundwork.

This development programme is the basis of Iraq's hopes for the future—indeed, it is difficult to avoid the conclusion in Bagdad that it is the cause of a widespread complacency which the facts do not yet justify. The intensive construction of new bridges, dams, and housing projects is admirable in itself; it provides employment, improves the economy of the country, raises living standards. (In the last five years the income per capita in Iraq is reckoned, on the basis of some not particularly reliable statistics, to have risen from £30 to £53 a year.) But it does nothing to cure the restlessness of a new class of educated young Iraqis, who see no political future for themselves or for the brand of London School of Economics democracy which they have imperfectly absorbed. Nor does it do anything to undermine the dominant position, in either the social or the political structure of Iraq, of the traditional tribal landlord class.

To stress these criticisms, which one hears voiced in loosely organised "opposition" circles in Bagdad (there are of course no officially constituted opposition parties), is to lay oneself open to the retort that everything cannot happen at once in a country so bare as Iraq of all the modern essentials of social, political, or economic organisation. This is true, but the comment still seems justified that there is very little emphasis on education—or, indeed, on general sociological factors—in the development programme, and it is difficult to escape the conclusion that this neglect is deliberate on the part of leaders who are staking everything on carrying through an economic programme swift and striking enough to stifle the demand for a parallel social advance. It would be absurd to suggest that revolution was round the corner in Iraq, but it is a possibility which few would discount altogether.

Why should it be a possibility at all, in a state where one quarter of the national income is dropped in the government's lap by an oil company (the Iraq Petroleum Company's contribution to the Iraqi economy has jumped from less than £2 millions in 1946 to £69 millions last year), and where the government is devoting every penny of this unearned income to the national welfare? The question brings us back to the tug-of-war in the Arab world. If Arab unity should ever move from the field of polemics to that of practical politics, it must surely be centred (at least for several generations to come) on either Cairo or Bagdad. During the first six months of 1957 Bagdad has notably advanced its claim to eventual leadership; but while Cairo has temporarily lost the initiative, it still has much to offer that Bagdad cannot rival, and indeed that has a strong appeal even for Iraqis whose spirits chafe against the bonds of a restrictive political system. Whatever one's judgment may be of the domestic success or unsuccess of the Egyptian revolution, President Nasser has overturned an outdated social and political framework; he has broken the power of corrupt and irresponsible elements in Egyptian society; he has put through a programme of agrarian reform.

Given ten years of peace in which to build up her own economic strength, it may be that Iraq could oust her rival (for reconciliation with Egypt seems as distant a prospect as ever). In the long run she has much more to offer to the other Arab states than Egypt, and in particular a generous use of her oil revenues to solve the development problems of her neighbours as well as her own could enable Iraq to give a practical basis to the slow dream of Arab unity. For the moment one finds little disposition to share the new wealth which a freak of geographical fortune has given to Iraq and denied to Jordan, though Iraq has recently made some investment in the scheme for developing Jordan's potash industry. Iraqis claim that there is so much to do in Iraq itself ("it would take us ten years even to catch up with Syria") that they cannot afford to help their neighbours as well. The answer surely is that they cannot afford not to, unless the aim is to build an oasis of prosperity in the midst of a hostile and envious Arab world.

> *In tracing the course of events in the Middle East during the "Suez year," I have made only passing reference to a problem that, in one way or another, has a bearing on everything that happens in the area. This is the problem of the Arab refugees from Palestine, and it is the one problem which can bring the Arabs to forget their own discords and speak with a common voice. It is never far below the surface of the Arab mind, and during June it was the subject of much comment and speculation.*

BEIRUT, JUNE 27

Preoccupied to some extent by its own internal feuds, the Arab world has reacted less violently than might have been expected to rumours of discussions going on with a view to the settlement of the Arab refugee problem. In spite of Mr. Dulles' denials, it is clear there have been exploratory talks on American initiative, and there seem to be three reasons for raising the matter at this particular time.

First, Mr. Henry Labouisse, director of UNRWA is touring America and Western Europe to explain that unless more funds are forthcoming UNRWA cannot continue its work for refugees beyond the end of this year—and governments which contribute to the agency would probably prefer to devote money to solving the refugee problem instead of to perpetuating it.

Secondly, the American government, which is seeking urgently to find a basis for a general Middle Eastern settlement, finds itself always coming up against this intractable problem of a million Arab refugees, for whom the Arab governments, demand the full letter of the United Nations resolution of 1948 (calling for their repatriation or compensation by the Israeli government), failing which they prefer to keep the refugees as a bargaining counter.

Thirdly, the present moment, when the collapse of Egypt's "positive neutralist" front has shown Arab unity to be as much of a mockery as ever, perhaps seems to the Americans to be an appropriate one at which to try to impose a solution in the matter of refugees. This would be fallacious reasoning, for the only thing that could lead the Arabs to shelve their internal disputes would be the need to draw together against any outside intervention on behalf of Israel.

Nor should it be imagined that the Arab states which are friendly to the West would respond any differently from the others to attempts to solve the refugee problem on lines which ignore the general Arab claims for the refugees. Just because they are more or less well disposed to the West, Saudi Arabia and Iraq feel they need to be particularly uncompromising in their stand against Israel. Saudi Arabia has, in any case, an immediate quarrel with Israel over the Gulf of Aqaba, while Iraq is the only Arab state which has not signed even an armistice agreement with Israel.

Certainly until some solution to the refugee problem can be found, stability in the Middle East is unthinkable. But whatever realistic thoughts they may have in private, the present leaders of the Arab world could not afford to sponsor an attempt to resettle the refugees outside Palestine. If Egypt and Syria denounce, as they have done, this latest initiative, Iraq and Saudi Arabia can do no less, and Jordan, if she supported it from the desire to rid herself of her own huge refugee population (whose presence constitutes a constant threat to organised government), would earn redoubled insults from her enemies and lose all hope of financial help from her friends.

The only hope of finding a solution which the Arabs would or could accept must start from a genuine concession by the Israelis. It is no use appealing to the Arabs to be "realistic" and accept a *fait accompli*, as long as the records of the General Assembly and the Security Council both contain rulings endorsing the Arab case over Palestine—which have never been fulfilled. In demanding their complete fulfilment the Arabs know (though they must not admit it) that they are crying for the moon. But to ask them to forget the whole subject and agree to a new and unpalatable—and unjust—solution is to be no more realistic than they themselves and with less excuse.

And for Israel to carry on relentlessly with her policy of "ingathering" the remainder of the scattered Jewish people to settle them on lands which the United Nations has told the Arab refugees are rightfully theirs (while they must huddle in sub-human squalor just across the border), is to add needless fuel to the bonfires of hatred that line Israel's borders.

> *From the facts and figures it is easy enough to grasp the refugee problem—in the abstract. To understand it, you need to visit the refugee camps in the Arab lands bordering on Israel. The dispatch that follows is one that I wrote to the* Manchester Guardian *after my first experience of the refugee camps in Jordan, the Lebanon, and the Gaza strip, soon after I arrived in the Middle East in the spring of 1956. Since then the facts have not changed—except that the problem is nearly two years older, and the refugees are more numerous and more desperate than ever.*

BEIRUT, APRIL

Amid all the questions in dispute between Arabs and Israelis, there is one issue on which the United Nations declared its firm verdict more than seven years ago; a verdict which no amount of legal quibbling can disguise as anything but a simple statement of elementary human rights. This is the issue of the

Arab refugees, some eight hundred thousand of whom left their homes during the fighting in Palestine in 1948 (their numbers have since swollen to almost a million) to take temporary refuge in the neighbouring Arab states, and who have been existing on the charity of United Nations agencies ever since. Yet within a few months of their original exile the General Assembly had resolved, on December 11, 1948, that "the refugees wishing to return to their homes and live at peace with their neighbours should be permitted to do so at the earliest practicable date, and that compensation should be paid for the property of those choosing not to return, and for the loss of or damage to property."

There are two things that we should remember about the problem which this resolution was supposed to solve: first, that nearly a million people, most of them simple farmers and peasants who understood nothing of the currents raging about them, lost in this miserable exodus their homes, their lands, their chance of earning a livelihood, and—it gradually came to appear—all hope of ever again leading a life that was anything but a precarious subsistence, in areas so inhospitable that they had remained unoccupied even by nomads and beggars; second, that this fate overtook people who until a few months before had been the wards of the British government, from whom the United Nations had supposedly taken over the responsibility for their safety and welfare. And this is to say nothing of the fact that they and their ancestors had lived in Palestine for more than a thousand years, before the British government introduced into their homeland the people who were finally to dispossess them.

UNRWA—the United Nations Relief and Works Agency for Palestine Refugees in the Middle East—was created in 1949 to provide relief for the refugees and to attempt to resettle them. It was conceived as a temporary agency which would deal with a gradually diminishing problem, after which it would be disbanded; instead the problem has grown larger, and the life of the agency, already six years old, has been prolonged for four years to come. Of its budget of almost $30 millions, $23 millions is spent on direct relief. The agency supplies rations (amounting to 1,550 calories a day) to over eight hundred thousand refugees;

it provides medical services which have so far been astonishingly successful in maintaining the general health of the refugees; and it is now able to give primary education to all children of school age and secondary education to a steadily increasing proportion. (Almost half of the refugees now are children.)

But where resettlement is concerned the agency's hands are tied by political considerations. The Arab states which have given reluctant hospitality to the refugees are unwilling to do anything which may saddle them with permanent responsibility. Certainly they cannot escape the charge of using the refugees as a political counter—but it should not be forgotten that these are poor countries, which have enough to do to see that their own peoples have work and shelter and something to eat. Nor should it be forgotten that the United Nations has ruled that the refugees should be allowed to return to their homes across the border. In any case, with the utmost co-operation from the Arab countries and the fullest use of existing or potential facilities (such as those that could be provided by irrigation schemes in the Jordan valley and the Sinai peninsula), it is unlikely that even a third of the refugees could be resettled quickly within the Arab countries. (Development schemes in Syria and Iraq could absorb a large number in the remoter future.)

What this boils down to is that no real solution of the problem is possible without a realistic gesture by Israel. It is very hard to establish how many of the refugees would wish to return to their "homeland" if this meant in effect immigration into Israel. Probably not many. Thus acceptance by Israel of a limited number might be invaluable as a gesture. And, before the armistice lines have hardened into frontiers, Israel could still do an incalculable amount for her own eventual benefit and for the world by yielding some of the border territory she seized outside the United Nations partition line. She could thereby make possible a return to normal life in numerous border villages. It is true that the Arabs have to recognise that Israel is there to stay, something they were unwilling to do before the Bandung Conference; and they have to recognise it as a permanency. It is no less true that Israel has to recognise that the

Arabs are there as her neighbours—and neighbours who may be right in thinking that time is on their side.

From every point of view the problem is one which cries out for a new and urgent approach. In itself it is a monstrous injustice; but beyond that it lies at the root of the poisoned relations between the West and the Arab peoples, and it is a standing challenge to the reality and worth of the United Nations as an arbiter in world affairs. For Britain and for Israel it is something more. Those refugees, on their stony hillsides and in desolate valleys, on the sandy wastes about Gaza and in hovels on the fringe of glittering Beirut, are a million witnesses to the fact that Britain failed in something to which she had set her hand, and to the further fact that as a result of that failure the state of Israel came into being.

PART 5   The Balance Sheet

It is appropriate that my story should end on the note of Palestine—for the Palestine question is the fundamental cause of the misunderstandings between the Arabs and the West. The support given by the United States to Israel makes it impossible for the Arabs to believe in the sincerity of American aims in the Middle East, or for them to give unqualified support to American policies. The attempt to hustle the Arabs into joining defence pacts, and the ostentatious supply of arms to those who do so, only make matters worse, by deepening inter-Arab divisions and breeding fresh mistrust. If the Eisenhower Doctrine had produced a really ambitious design for the security and development of the Middle East as a whole, promising the Arabs protection against the only enemy they really fear—Israel—it might have had more success. By its insistence on political commitments which had no interest for most of the Arabs, and by giving them no guarantee against further Israeli expansion, the Doctrine failed and a great opportunity was lost—as another opportunity had been lost when the offer of aid for the Egyptian High Dam was withdrawn, touching off the whole sorry train of events which forms the theme of this book.

But in truth the Suez crisis did not begin with the nationalisation of the Suez Canal, any more than it ended when the canal was reopened. What we call the Suez crisis was simply a stage in the larger crisis in our relations with the Arab world. The purpose of this book has been to follow that crisis through an arbitrary period of a year—the year that followed Egypt's nationalisation of the canal—in the hope that by examining

*events as they unfolded (and as they appeared to one
observer in their midst), the reader might see more
clearly the successes and failures of Western policy in
its dealings with the Middle East. My own conclusions
appear in the two articles which follow, and which were
written to mark the first anniversary of the nationalisation of the canal.*

I

BEIRUT, JULY

A year ago, on a steamy night in Alexandria, President
Nasser announced to an excited crowd the nationalisation of
the Suez Canal. Since July 26, 1956, nothing has been quite
the same in the Middle East—and yet the Egyptian government's action did nothing to change the basic facts of life in
the area. Rather is it true to say that nationalisation (and the
reaction to it abroad) heightened existing tensions, and gave a
tremendous acceleration to processes which were already under
way in the Middle East.

The year that has passed falls naturally into two parts, with
the actual "police action" as the watershed. (It is interesting to
compare the terminology used in different places about the
November campaign. We in Britain seem to have settled down
to "the Suez adventure"; to the Egyptians it is simply "the war";
to the Lebanese, who have to hedge their bets carefully, it is
"les evènements.") For three months after July 26 each side
watched and waited, trying the while to spy out the weaknesses
of the other's position. Politically, the position was unchanged
when the attack finally came—but when it came, and quickly
spent itself, the political developments which had been implicit
in the Middle Eastern situation since July, and before, began
swiftly to take effect. Now that most of the dust has settled it
is possible to examine them, and to see whether the chances of
a stable settlement in the Middle East have been helped or
hindered by the hurly-burly of the past twelve months.

Three major trends are clear. First, there is the irrevocable✗
involvement of the United States in the Middle East, marked
by the principal milestones of the Eisenhower Doctrine, the

intervention in Jordan in April (with the use of the Sixth Fleet setting an awkward precedent), America's closer association with the Bagdad Pact, her wooing of King Saud, and her close interest in the Lebanese elections. Second, there is the virtual elimination of British "influence," in the old-fashioned sense, from the Middle Eastern scene, with the exception of Iraq and the Persian Gulf. (It is interesting to reflect that it is only just over a year since there were British garrisons not only in three bases in Jordan but also in the Suez Canal zone.) And the third major trend is the disintegration of the Arab "neutralist" front, with King Saud pulling cautiously away from his close association with Egypt, and King Hussein's government in Jordan frankly hostile. This is at first sight the most surprising result of the Suez crisis and its aftermath, but it, too, has its roots in the pre-Suez past; King Saud, the conservative autocrat, and President Nasser, the revolutionary leader, were patently improbable bedfellows, even before Nasser's policy over the canal caused a serious decline in Saud's oil revenues.

In brief, since the Suez crisis America has replaced Britain as the principal Western influence in the Middle East (as she was bound to do one day), and has embarked on a vigorous policy aimed at winning away from Nasser what might be called the reclaimable Arabs—or rather (and the distinction should be made) the reclaimable Arab governments. A corollary of this has been an increase in Soviet penetration of the Middle East, as American actions aroused fears and resentments among the more extreme elements of Arab nationalism—but this is still a potential more than an actual result. Apart from the grip she has established on the economy of Egypt and Syria through trade concessions, and an apparent increase in the numbers of Soviet "technicians" who have accompanied Russian arms shipments, the Soviet government has few practical gains to show for its hypocritical support of the Arab cause.

The State Department shows a surprising complacency about the recent march of events in the Middle East. King Saud, the Americans seem to feel, has been won over to respectability by the courteous reception given to him when he visited Washington in January (even if he still tends to speak out of turn about the Gulf of Aqaba); King Hussein in Jordan is pictured as the gallant defender of his country's independence, whereas, for all his courage and the astuteness of his advisers, he remains in fact the precarious ruler of a hostile kingdom— and, what is worse in Arab eyes, an American pensioner to boot. A complacent view is taken of Nasser's economic difficulties, which are indeed acute, but which will never alone bring him to heel. Even the Lebanese elections, which in fact were a characteristically Middle Eastern scramble for office, were mis- represented abroad as an expression of popular feeling against Egypt and in favour of the Eisenhower Doctrine.

All this is dangerous nonsense, not only because Nasser won a clear and popular victory over the Suez Canal, not only be- cause he was able to turn Israel's military victory into a diplo- matic defeat which has embarrassed Ben-Gurion on the internal front, not only because the Suez episode raised Nasser's standing to a point where the secretary-general of the United Nations had to visit him and return empty-handed after a week of negotiation. These are details beside the central fact that, whatever the atti- tude towards him of the other Arab governments (of which only the Lebanese looks as secure as his own), Nasser still and more than ever has a hold on the minds of the Arab peoples, many of whom feel a stronger loyalty to him as the leader of Arab nationalism than they do to their own governments.

With every demonstration of American power, and as it becomes clearer that this power is directed towards the undoing of Nasser, Nasser's popularity increases among the Arab masses. The central error of American policy in the Middle East is that it is based exclusively on governments and takes no account of popular feelings (ignoring the fact that in the Middle East cur- rents of thought commonly endure much longer than govern- ments). It is the mistake we made so conspicuously in the past, with a little more excuse, since a generation ago there was so little in the way of public opinion to take into account. But the story of the Wafd in Egypt should surely be a lesson—the Wafd, whose leaders we opposed, exiled, and imprisoned, until in the end we had to come to terms with them, and indeed to depend on them during the Second World War, because with all their faults they were the nearest thing to a progressive force in Egypt and represented the hopes and the ambitions of the majority of Egyptians. Exactly the same is true of Nasser, and unless the Americans are prepared in the last resort to send the Sixth Fleet to carry him off to whatever is the American equivalent of Malta or the Seychelles they (and we, too) would do better to learn to live with him. For the moment, America provides Nasser with a perfect scapegoat, the more so because of her involvement with Zionism. If he were no longer able to blame all the misfortunes of the Arabs on American interference (as he used to blame them on British interference), Nasser would be forced to do something positive for the Arabs who have claimed him as their leader. As it is, he can play the easier game of passive resistance, with the powerful propaganda weapons at his command.

Whatever the current line of Egyptian propaganda—and recently its heavy guns have been swung away from Britain and on to the newer targets of America and its "satellite" Jordan— its voice is heard and for the most part believed in Damascus, Bagdad, Amman (though in Jordan every attempt is being made to keep out the Egyptian press and jam the "Voice of the Arabs" radio), along the Persian Gulf, in Saudi Arabia, in Aden, and, of course, westward along the coast of North Africa as far as Algeria and Morocco. It tells the Arabs what they want to hear—that from Morocco to Bagdad all are Arabs, that one day they will be united, and that unity will free them from the threat of outside domination. America—and, of course, Israel— are represented as the principal obstacles to the achievement of these goals.

II

BEIRUT, JULY

The Suez crisis last year marked the end of the long phase in which Britain had been the dominant power in the Middle East. Most of our effective influence had already been lost when the withdrawal of British forces from Egypt removed the linch-pin of the system. If the attempt to reach an understanding with Egypt after our forces were withdrawn had succeeded, it might have been possible to retain some of that influence, on a quite new footing. As it was, the failure of the attempt (which was never pursued with much conviction) created a climate in which a crisis sooner or later was inevitable; and the formation of the Bagdad Pact drew the lines between those who were with us and those who were against us in the Middle East too clearly for compromise to be possible. The expulsion of Glubb Pasha from Jordan early in 1956 was a prelude to the real trial of strength between Britain and the new leaders of Arab nationalism.

When our positions crumbled after the dusty adventure at Port Said, the Americans stepped in to take over our role in the Middle East. They started from a position of great strength, not only because of their standing as the leading exponents of Western social and technical advance, but in particular because of the clear stand they had taken against our action over Suez. Yet within six months they had made themselves as unpopular as the British had ever been, and they lacked the reserve of experience and sympathy which had often saved us from disaster before. In Cairo last November I remember an American who pasted the Stars and Stripes on to the windshield of his car. To someone who joked with him about it he said: "I just didn't want it to come out at the inquest that I wasn't an Englishman." To-day it is not fanciful to picture a situation where the loan of a Union Jack might get him out of trouble.

Why should this be so? In the first place, because Britain has shot its bolt and lost the power to harm the Arabs. In the second place, because the Americans find themselves supporting conservative and illiberal regimes which appear to the Arabs to stand in the way of the achievement of their most cherished ambitions. And more than this, because the manner of America's involvement in the Middle East has been even more clumsy than Britain's was, at a stage in history when far greater care needs to be taken than ever before not to offend national susceptibilities. British gunboat diplomacy always had its drawbacks, but at least a gunboat was just a discreet reminder of what lay beyond the horizon. What can the Arabs, in their present mood of nationalistic fervour, be expected to think of the appearance off Beirut (at the time of the crisis in Jordan in

April) of a dozen ships of the Sixth Fleet, with jet planes and guided missiles with atomic warheads, the whole armada headed by an aircraft carrier the size of St. Paul's Cathedral?

Nor need power be demonstrated quite so blatantly as this to arouse enmity. A principal factor in the growth of Arab nationalism has been the desire of the Arabs to end a state of affairs where the backstairs diplomacy of a foreign embassy could make or break an Arab government. Is it then surprising that voices should be raised in protest when a shipment of American arms arrives in Beirut as the Lebanese go to the polls in a general election? Or when the Sixth Fleet, whose movements presumably involve some fairly detailed planning, anchors off Beirut on a day when the pro-American Lebanese government happens to be asking parliament for a vote of confidence? The Americans have adopted the Lebanese government, and the State Department wants to make it known that those who shelter under the American umbrella will not be the poorer for doing so. (American aid to the Lebanon this year works out at fourteen dollars for each man, woman, and child in the country.) Surely the point need not be driven home with such sledgehammer emphasis, or America's enemies in the Middle East be given quite so many opportunities to claim that the only friends America can make in the area are those she can buy.

This, briefly, is the situation to-day. The Arabs, divided among themselves, emotionally upset by the contrast between their dreams of greatness and their present inability to achieve (or even to decide on) the most limited common objectives, are intensely suspicious of the West and see America's initiatives as only the old paternalistic, imperialistic policies writ large. Nervously in some cases, defiantly in others, some Arab leaders have veered towards Soviet Russia, not from any ideological fellow-feeling but in the delusion that Russian help is given "without strings," and that the Russians are sincere in their affectation of sympathy for "Arab aspirations." While, in Arab eyes, the West (and that means for the moment America) appears to be supporting certain Arab governments—all of them unpopular—the Russians have achieved the reputation of being on the side of Arab nationalism. Therein lies their strength, and our corresponding weakness.

To escape from this impasse the West has to find a policy which can win the sympathies of the Arabs, and this involves first arriving at an understanding of what the Arabs themselves hope for. Amid much that is insincere, there are four ambitions which are common to almost all the Arab peoples, and to which no one can raise any reasonable objections. The Arabs hope to achieve genuine independence, a greater degree of union among themselves, an improvement in their pathetically low living standards, and security against further Israeli expansion. If we can show that we understand and sympathise with these ambitions, we shall have a basis on which to build a policy for the Middle East—and for the moment Britain is in a better position than any other Western country to make the attempt.

The first essential is to reach a modus vivendi with Nasser. We have tried, and failed, to upset him (and the Americans are still trying) and have succeeded in making his position technically and materially much more difficult. Morally—in the eyes of the Arabs—it remains almost impregnable. If we continue to oppose him we may in the end bring him down, to be replaced almost certainly by something worse, from the point of view of ourselves as well as the Egyptians. If we decide to deal with him, the opportunity is to hand in the negotiations over the resumption of relations between our two countries (in which Britain holds the stronger hand). In return for a relaxation of our economic blockade of Egypt, we should demand a more reliable agreement over the future of the canal and a suspension of the irresponsible propaganda broadcast by the "Voice of the Arabs" radio.

Next, we should make contact with forces and groups other than those on whom we have traditionally relied in framing our Middle Eastern policies. Instead of princes and sheikhs whose wealth and rigid conservatism set them apart from their peoples, we should be in touch with the rising middle classes, the Socialists, the intelligentsia, the radical would-be politicians, the Western-trained economists and technicians, who tend to become, for lack of opportunities in the economic or political life of their own countries, either cynical business men or else the angry young men of the Arab world. This could best be done not on the official level but by the provision of facilities for

✗ further education and the exchange of views and information, building perhaps on the groundwork already well laid by the British Council in the Arab countries. Money devoted to such ends would be better spent than much that is at present wasted (whether in dollars or pounds) on the provision, for instance, of jet planes—which are useless to most Arab countries for lack of the corresponding technical staffs and equipment on the ground.

Third, we should use our influence, where we still have it (and for Britain that means in Iraq and along the Persian Gulf), to encourage social progress and not to prevent it. Feudalism is doomed in the Middle East, as it is in any rapidly developing society, and we should do well to urge those rulers who will still listen to us to recognise this, instead of supporting them in their hostility to progress. With the oil-rich states, in particular, we should encourage the wider distribution of the new wealth, and its use without a strict regard for frontiers which are in any case artificial. Iraq and Kuwait have a tremendous opportunity to lay the foundations of a wider Arab community, which would include some of their less fortunate, and inevitably envious, neighbours.

For the West to propose terms for a settlement between the Arabs and Israel is profitless until the West can overcome the suspicions of the Arabs and make some progress towards winning their confidence. The most the West can aim at for the moment is the maintenance of peace on the borders, and to this end we should work through the United Nations for an enlargement of the United Nations Emergency Force and its deployment along all the armistice lines between Israel and the Arab States. Every frontier incident postpones the eventual settlement, and only by sealing the borders can the opportunity be given for tempers to cool. The creation of UNEF is so far the only tangible benefit to emerge from the Suez crisis and its aftermath; but if the West (and Britain in particular), by a dispassionate appraisal of the developments of the last twelve months, can adjust its policies accordingly, it should still be possible for us to find a more solid basis for our relationship with the Arab world.

Postscript

Between refugee camps and frontier incidents, wrecked pipelines and rigged elections, with the echoes of the Suez dispute reverberating about him and the din of Cairo Radio in his ears—the horizon of the correspondent in the Middle East looks a desolate and discouraging one. And yet within that horizon are also the fountains of Damascus, the minarets of Cairo, the honey-coloured walls of old Jerusalem, and the whole dusty, distinctive panorama of Arab life. Behind the editorials and the public speeches, behind the frosty diplomatic notes with their monotonous insincerity, are the Arabs: men and women not so different from ourselves in their ambitions, anxieties, prejudices—yet tantalisingly hidden from our understanding by the veils of their separate history and environment; passionate and ineffectual, dreamers of great dreams which they have seldom the patience or the practical ability to carry into effect; individualists all, and yet so easily the dupes of an idea, the slaves of a cheap slogan.

Their faults are easy to see and hard to forgive—their selfishness, their inability to translate thought into action, their incapacity to solve their own problems and their resentment at anyone else's attempt to solve them for them, their pride which yet cannot save them from lapsing into self-pity, their laziness, their cynical acceptance of corruption and insincerity as inherent in human relations. What is harder to remember is the extent to which these faults have been ingrained in them by forces over which they have had no control— by the accidents of climate and geographical situation, by foreign domination, by the whim of a providence which for centuries spared them hardly any of the

219

*natural resources on which civilisations are built, and
then at a stroke revealed their homeland as one of the
richest oil-producing areas in the world, making it a
target for envy and intrigue from all sides.*

*Against this background, the development of the
Arab states during the past forty years has been astonishing. In each decade they have been forced to grow
up through a century, and if political maturity still
eludes them, surely the wonder is that they should have
advanced so far in so short a time, rather than that they
should find themselves still short of their goal.*

*For the progress they have made the West can
claim much of the credit, and it cannot escape a share
of the blame for their failures. It is natural, but futile,
for the West to complain of Arab ingratitude for benefits received, or to be surprised when Arab nationalism,
in whose formation Britain especially played so large a
part, turns its new weapons against its old masters. The
pattern is a familiar and inevitable one—but it need
not end in estrangement, as the story of India shows. It
will do so, however, unless each side makes a genuine
effort to understand the aims and the interests of the
other; and it is up to the West, with its greater strength
and authority and political maturity, to make the first
move.*

Index

Abdul Illah, crown prince of Iraq: 105

Abdullah, late king of Jordan: 114, 167

Abu Suweir: 86

Aden Colony and Protectorate: 112

Akhbar el Yom, Cairo newspaper: 56

El Akhbar, Cairo newspaper: 25, 122

Alexandria: raids on, 84; mentioned, 2, 5, 75, 82

Allen, George, State Department envoy: 3

El Amal, Beirut newspaper: 105

Amer, General Hakim, Egyptian minister of war: 28, 45

American National Broadcasting Company: 12

American embassy at Cairo: evacuation of, 82; mentioned, 5, 76, 79

Amman: 64, 70-71, 105-106, 115, 166, 168

Anglo-Egyptian relations: 75, 182

Anglo-Franco-Israeli conspiracy: 86, 89, 109

Anglo-French forces: 80-81, 83, 86, 89, 109, 145

Anglo-Jordan treaty: 103-104, 106

Arab "Big Four": 168, 180

Arab League: 15, 16, 18, 49, 56, 63

Arab Legion: 109, 169

Arab News Agency: in Beirut, 41; in Cairo, 42, 62, 166

Arab refugees: from Palestine, 184, 207

Arabs: ambitions of, 217; federation of, 196; and nationalization, 18, 21, 22, 93, 106, 138, 158, 194, 216; and series of meetings, 70, 71; and "Solidarity Pact," 102, 104-106; unity of, 3, 6, 9, 15, 18, 65-68, 78, 105-106, 203

El Arish: 45, 132, 133, 134

el Assali, Sabu, Syrian prime minister: 100

Aswan. *See* High Dam

Atiyah, Edward: 107 fn

El Auja: 155

El Azhar University: 32

Bagdad Pact: 104, 156-159, 166, 181, 200, 212

Banias: 97, 101

Bandung Conference: 208

el Banna, Lufti, Egyptian under-secretary, 184

Bedouins: 134, 169, 173, 176, 179

Beirut: 24, 92, 190, 196. *See also* Lebanon

Ben-Gurion: 131, 213

Bermuda Conference: 153, 156

el Bitar, Salaheddin, Syrian foreign minister: 157

Bitter Lakes: 52, 59, 63, 125

Brioni Conference: 3

British: bases in Jordan, 104; bombers in Cairo, 91; correspondents in Cairo, 84; discredit of diplomacy of, 32; evacuation of canal base, 75; government, 1, 7, 26, 83, 107; gunboat diplomacy, 215; journalists, expulsion of, 32; Middle East policy, 105; position crumbled, 215; spy ring, 32, 41, 42; subjects imprisoned, 30-31; Treasury, 26, 28, 40; mentioned, 7, 20, 25, 74, 80-84, 88, 90, 101, 106, 168

British embassy at Cairo: evacuation of, 84; mentioned, 5, 38, 40, 57, 80, 82, 120

Bunche, Dr. Ralph, United Nations under-secretary: 147, 148, 152

Burns, General, commander of UNEF: 140, 141

Byroade, Henry, ex-ambassador to Cairo: 43, 49

Cairo: "Big Three" conference in, 100; evacuation of, 84, 88-91; gen-